TONGUES OF FALLEN ANGELS

"Whosoever has built a new Heaven has found the strength for it only in his own Hell." —Nietzsche

Selden Rodman

TONGUES OF FALLEN ANGELS

Conversations with Jorge Luis Borges, Robert Frost, Ernest Hemingway, Pablo Neruda, Stanley Kunitz, Gabriel García Márquez, Octavio Paz, Norman Mailer, Allen Ginsberg, Vinícius de Moraes, João Cabral de Melo Neto, Derek Walcott

A NEW DIRECTIONS BOOK

ACKNOWLEDGMENTS

Grateful acknowledgment is made to the editors and publishers of maga-
zines where some of the material in this book first appeared: *American
Poetry Review, The American Way, Modern Poetry Studies, Review 72,
Saturday Review-World.* The chapter "Gabriel García Márquez" was originally published in *Antaeus.*

Previously unpublished material by Ernest Hemingway, Copyright © 1974
by Mary Hemingway

Extracts from Pablo Neruda's "Lazybones," from *We Are Many* (Copyright
© 1967/1970 by Cape Goliard Press Ltd., distributed in the United States
of America by Grossman Publishers, New York), reprinted by permission
of Jonathan Cape, Ltd. (London).

Manufactured in the United States of America
First published clothbound (ISBN: 0–8112–0528–2) and as New Directions
Paperbook 373 (ISBN: 0–8112–0529–0) in 1974
Published simultaneously in Canada by McClelland & Stewart, Ltd.

New Directions Books are published for James Laughlin
by New Directions Publishing Corporation,
333 Sixth Avenue, New York 10014

CONTENTS

To Andrew Glaze
poet, critic, friend

PROLOGUE

Asked by her philosophy teacher whether she considered her-self fallen angel or risen ape, my older daughter, Oriana (more poet than humanist), replied "fallen angel." I doubt that she was rejecting Darwin or testifying to any crushing burden of sin. Rather she was affirming, as all artists do, that innocence of vision must be recaptured on the poet's tongue—no matter how crippling or bestial life's experience.

So much for my title; but if the book itself requires ex-egesis it will have missed the mark. It is not intended to "prove" anything about writers or the art of writing. Nor have its twelve subjects been chosen as "representative" or because they exemplify anything, except perhaps genius in the broadest sense. Naturally I exercised choice in selecting those whose works measured up best to my notions of significance and excellence. But if any other principle was involved it was the pleasure principle. I loved the different ways these men wrote, and found their personalities sympathetic. I took plea-sure in talking with them, drawing them out on matters of mutual interest, photographing them. It delighted me to re-discover in my journals what they had said, and under what circumstances. Other writers of as much genius whom I knew at one time or another—Thomas Mann, James Agee, Ezra Pound, Dylan Thomas, William Carlos Williams, W. H. Auden—may have had as much or more to say, but didn't say it to me. Except for Agee and Williams, I didn't feel at ease with them.

Opportunity played a part in my selection. Latin America, for the past sixteen years, has been my "beat." In the course of writing books and articles on the countries stretching from Mexico and Trinidad to Chile and Brazil, I had the chance to make friends with the seven authors who are not my com-patriots—none of whom at the time were well known in the United States. As for the other five, Frost and Hemingway were youthful idols whom I came to know in their last years; Mailer, Ginsberg, and Kunitz were old friends.

One's choice of friends is determined, of course, by one's personality; and what one talks about depends on one's preoccupations. As an extroverted introvert I enjoyed being with writers who did something besides write. Experiences and influences can be profitably discussed, but craftsmanship resists analysis, and when analyzed produces only boredom. Technique, often as not, is a mystery to the artist himself since it consists so frequently of instinctual responses beyond his control.

Sixteen years ago when I brought out the prototype of this book, *Conversations with Artists* (New York, Putnam), there was no precedent. Nor had creative people often been treated as human beings, at least in their own lifetimes. Boswell's Johnson and Vasari's Michelangelo were exceptional "interviews." We know a great deal about what writers like Donne, Blake, and Keats thought, but almost nothing about what they said—or what they were doing while they said it. Among artists, no one seems to have bothered to talk to Rembrandt or Goya, Aleijadinho or Orozco.

My approach was controversial, arousing bitter debate. Then as now, I didn't ask prepared questions or use a tape recorder. Informality, unrehearsed give-and-take seemed more important than being "covered" against demurers. Yet only one of the thirty-four artists interviewed claimed in print that I had misquoted him, and several of the abstract expressionist painters whose very aesthetic I questioned wrote me that they welcomed the infighting and felt that they had been treated fairly.

Conversations with Artists was a by-product of *The Eye of Man* (Old Greenwich, Conn.; Devin-Adair, 1955), a highly opinionated re-evaluation of Western art, and was treated as either scripture or blasphemy. That polemical note is not sounded in the present more extended conversations. Nevertheless my philosophy of art has not changed. I believe that an artist's work is a product of his life and times and is more meaningful for his acknowledgment of the relationships. The minor poet is primarily concerned with form or innovation; the major one uses these tools almost unconsciously to say something he feels he has to say—and which the world will be better for hearing.

Art may not change the world, but it is made by those who would like to change it. This moral fervor, when combined with the capacity to make sounds or images expressive enough to convey its meaning, is what enables the major creator to communicate with an audience in excess of other artists and intellectuals, and to reach beyond the limitations of place, language, and time.

Oakland, New Jersey   S. R.

Upper left: Jorge Luis Borges in the Argentine National Library, Buenos Aires, 1969. Upper right: With Norman Thomas di Giovanni, Buenos Aires, 1972. "Borges seized him by the elbow . . . 'Norman! . . . Avoid veracity!'" Lower left: Borges's mother at ninety-five, Buenos Aires, 1972. Except for a two-year marriage hiatus in 1969, the poet has always lived with his mother. Lower right: Borges in 1972. "No wonder he looks just a little mad! The pupil of the right eye is so enlarged it almost fills the iris. The pupil of the left eye is very small and a little off center."

Chapter One

JORGE LUIS BORGES

*"I was quite old when it occurred to me that poetry could be
written in a language other than English."*

1

The first time I saw Borges he was seated at a large conference
table in Buenos Aires's National Library staring into space. He
looks at first more like a harassed, tired executive than Argentina's great poet who, in middle age, had received world-wide
renown for his "metaphysical" fables of circular time, and now
almost blind in his seventies was beginning to write poems
again. It was only when he got up to lean on his cane, grasped
me just above the elbow, and started to pour over me (at very
close range) his passion for literature and his distaste for most
things contemporary, that I caught a gleam in those piercing
blue eyes under their drooping lids, and a sense of the dedicated, almost Gothic bony structure of that long, slightly
pouchy aristocratic face under sparse gray hairs and unruly eyebrows. He talks fluently in English but with an accent, almost
a Scottish burr. And it's not easy to stop him once he starts,
because he has a disconcerting way of looking you straight in
the eye, holding you close to him, and occasionally laughing at
his own sallies with a flash of white teeth; you can never rid
yourself of the notion that he really sees you.

When he heard that I'd been with Pablo Neruda recently, he
started to say something about his great Chilean antagonist,
but then broke off to approach the subject more indirectly.

"You've come from Chile by way of Brazil," he said. "What
difference strikes you most entering Argentina?"

"Not seeing a single black on the streets of Buenos Aires,"
I said. "I can't get used to it. Weren't there any slaves here?
Didn't they have children?"

5

"I can't explain it either," he said. "In my childhood one saw them everywhere. All our servants and laborers were Negroes. Maybe this was one reason we began to think of ourselves as close to you. This was white man's country, not a country of Indians and half-breeds like Peru or Bolivia—or Brazil, which is just an extension of Africa, no?"

"Hardly," I said, "though the blacks provide the most vital element in that unique culture. You know their literature, I suppose."

"They have a literature?"

"A rich one, classics included. You must have read Machado de Assis."

"No."

"Euclides da Cunha?"

"Yes. His book is a kind of sociological curiosity, isn't it? I was impressed until I read Cunningham-Graham's version of the same episode and saw how a real writer could handle it."

He hadn't heard of the distinguished modern poets like Cabral de Melo or Vinícius either but had been "once familiar" with some poems of Carlos Drummond de Andrade. I mentioned that Drummond, at least during the Thirties when he was a member of the Communist party, had been quite close to Neruda. "But Neruda," I added, "when I expressed admiration for your writing, made a remark that I know won't surprise you. 'Literature,' he said, 'is like a good beefsteak and can't be put together out of other literatures.' "

He smiled. "There are several answers to that remark." He paused.

"While you're selecting the best one," I said, "tell me what that ancient tome lying in front of you is."

"It's Dr. Johnson's *Dictionary*," he said. "The preface—made up of many literatures—is a great piece of prose. This copy was sent to me by a man from Sing Sing."

"The prison?"

"No. The town."

"But there is no town by that name any more. They renamed it Ossining. It must have been a prisoner who sent it to you, Borges!"

He liked the idea. "Yes. A prisoner of the eighteenth century. What a good place to be imprisoned. With all those Latinisms!"

"Can I ask you a Johnsonian question?"

"Like: What would I do if locked up in a tower with a baby?"

"Exactly. I'm writing a travel book, you know. What does Argentina need most?"

He pondered. "More curious minds, perhaps—like yours. You saw that girl at the desk when you came in? Can you believe it? Her mother burned her books one day. She said to her: 'We're simple folk. We don't need books.' That's what we're up against."

"You were saying about Neruda—?"

"He's a fine poet, of course. Some of his early poems are very good. But then he wrote a book denouncing the South American dictators—and left out Juan Perón."

"Why?"

"Perón was then in power. It seems that Neruda had a lawsuit pending with his publisher in Buenos Aires. That publisher, as you probably know, has always been his principal source of income."

I questioned the accuracy of this observation, its implications at any rate; perhaps only outsiders can have ambivalent feelings about the aging dictator who had so radically undercut the old landed oligarchy at the behest of his militant mistress, the late Evita Duarte. And I thought, too, of Borges's little essay about the mourning general who set up a tiny shrine in the Chaco one day in 1952 and accepted contributions, candles, and flowers from the poor who came to worship the blond doll inside:

What kind of a man, I ask myself, conceived and executed that funeral farce? a fanatic, a pitiful wretch, or an imposter and cynic? Did he believe he was Perón as he played his suffering role as the macabre widower? The story is incredible but it happened, and perhaps not once but many times, with different actors in different locales. It contains the perfect cipher of an unreal epoch, it is like the reflection of a dream or like that drama-within-drama we see in *Hamlet*. The mourner was not

Perón and the blond doll was not the woman Eva Duarte, but neither was Perón, Perón, nor was Eva, Eva. They were, rather, unknown individuals—or anonymous ones whose secret names and true faces we do not know—who acted out, for the credulous love of the lower middle classes, a crass mythology.[1]

I asked Borges if the tale was true. He said it was; he had had it from two men in the Chaco who didn't know each other. He gave me a long account he had had from a friend of torture by electric wires in one of Perón's prisons. He described the various parts of the body shocked, almost clinically. He told with relish several stories making fun of Evita Perón as an ex-prostitute who had put on airs. He spoke lightly of the constitutional presidents who had bumbled in the wake of Perón, but with respect of the current military strong man, General Onganía. "He is a gentleman. He does not raise his voice or strike poses . . ."

Borges's conservatism is moral. He is offended by Perón's morality—his lack of morals. There are overtones of snobbism in the description of the religious Peronista—the use of the words "the woman" and "credulous." He is not interested in the social welfare, labor benefits, and public works of the first Perón period. He is concerned only about the means—which is a tenable philosophical position, of course.

We went to pay a call on Borges's mother who lives nearby and who is astonishingly alert at ninety-three. She moves, in fact, more nimbly than her son. Borges's sister Norah, who paints, was leaving as we entered the eighth-floor apartment. Señora Borges told us that she was reading English again—"lest I forget." ("Mother often calls me a quadroon," Borges confided behind his hand, "for being a fourth part English.") He had always lived with his mother, until two years ago his marriage to a widowed boyhood sweetheart in her fifties surprised his friends.

---

[1] Jorge Luis Borges, "The Sham," in *Dreamtigers*, translated by Mildred Boyer. Austin, University of Texas Press, 1968; available also as a paperbook, New York, Dutton, 1970.

I asked Borges on the way down in the crowded elevator if my favorite among his stories, "El Sur" ("The South"), was autobiographical. Did it reflect a physical accident that had turned him from poetry to prose? "Yes, yes! of course, and it is one of my favorites too, because it is on so many levels— the autobiographical, the man who kills the thing he loves, the—"

The elevator came to a jerking stop, and we were spilled out into the lobby without my finding out what the other levels were.

2

Fame came to Borges as a young poet in Argentina. Years later it was his "metaphysical" tales that aroused awe and admiration throughout the world. Today the *avant-garde,* paradoxically, is making a culture hero of the archconservative. But there is another Borges who deserves to be at least as well known: Borges, the wit; Borges, the nonconformist who delights in poking fun at Latin America's fetishes; Borges, conversationalist extraordinary.

My talks with Borges were spread out over three week-long visits to Buenos Aires in 1969, 1970, and 1972. No doubt they would read well enough as unadorned dialogue. But to present them that way, divorced from the Victorian *décor* and courtly ballet that make Borges, Borges, and without introducing Norman Thomas di Giovanni who made the encounters possible and at whose home Borges sometimes held forth while I was guest, would be awkward and ungracious.

Though my first visit to Buenos Aires was to "research" a travel book, on which I was then working with Bill Negron as illustrator, my goal from the start had been to meet the poet-fabulist and try to convey Argentina's essence through his eyes. I had loved the stories for years. But behind the intricacy of their plots, behind their philosophical implications—that time is circular, that everything that happens has happened before and will happen again—I sensed a human warmth transcending Borges's passion for literature, an affection for Argentina transcending (if indeed it wasn't dictated by) the writer's despair over his country's tawdry politics and its capital's decay.

Though we bore no introductions, Negron and I had taken a taxi directly to the National Library. There we were informed that Borges was "being taped" by some French T.V. crew but that his aide would speak to us. A stocky young man with thick black hair and eyebrows and burning eyes came out, and when I had introduced myself he said: "You wouldn't remember it, but I visited your house in New Jersey ten years ago with Mark Strand and Rico Lebrun. But long before that your *100 Modern Poems* [2] changed my life. I doubt whether I'd be here in Argentina were it not for that anthology. Borges will be happy to see you, I know; but while he's tied up in there let's go out and have a drink."

Over *chopps* the story of Norman Thomas di Giovanni began to unfold. It threw a good deal of light on Borges's personality and on Argentina. In New Hampshire where he had been working on a novel, Norman had heard that Borges was lecturing at Harvard and had gone to see him. Soon after Borges left he decided to chuck everything and fly to Buenos Aires. He had majored in Spanish at school, he loved Borges's work, and he saw no reason why the poems, on which Borges's early fame in Argentina rested, shouldn't receive as much recognition in the English-speaking world as the stories. He would try to convince Borges of this, and then he would organize poet-translators from all over the world to prepare a book, under his and Borges's supervision.

He succeeded beyond his wildest expectations. Borges was delighted with the idea. So delighted, in fact, that he soon began concentrating on writing poems again. The result was Borges's first new book in nine years, *In Praise of Darkness*. Translators began sending in their versions which Borges and Norman would scrutinize, mailing them back for im-

2 New York, Pelligrini & Cudahy, 1949.

provement whenever necessary. Happily for both men, the younger quickly became indispensable to the older, as go-between with the increasingly unwieldy flow of visitors, promoters, lecture-agents, and publishers; and as friend, for the Argentine writer has always felt closer in spirit to the Anglo-American literary world than to the French-oriented one traditional in Argentina.

But Norman's sudden eminence baffled the intellectual community of Buenos Aires. Who was this upstart—from North America of all places—attached to their great man? It made them feel better about it to invent all kinds of academic credentials for Norman. He began to be referred to in the press as "Dr. di Giovanni" or as "the well-known scholar from Harvard." And Norman, with a typically American contempt for titles, would have none of it, though Borges said, "Can't you see it makes them happy to call you Doctor, Norman? Go along with them. Play their little game." One day when they were sitting next to each other at a T.V. panel interview, Norman had lunged forward to protest his Harvard identification; Borges seized him by the elbow and whispered in his ear: "Norman! . . . Avoid veracity!"

A friend in Chile, Nena Ossa, had already told me something about Borges's humility. She had met him in Santiago and taken him to a television studio where he was to be interviewed. "I was trying to guide him across the streets, but he insisted on guiding me. I was with him when the girl was putting pancake make-up on his face. "I'll never forget the way he apologized to her for 'this indignity—having to touch this old and ugly visage.' The girl, thrilled by the privilege of so intimate a contact with such a great man, was speechless."

Norman confirmed the genuineness of Borges's reaction by telling us of the time he had accompanied Borges and his wife on a speaking engagement to a town in the south of Argentina that involved an exhausting six-hour journey by rail. They arrived only to discover that a mistake had been made in the invitation: the lecture was to have taken

11

place the day before. The college officials were furious. "We'll get to the bottom of this unforgivable insult, Dr. Borges. The secretary responsible for the error will be fired!" Borges turned to them open-mouthed. "But why?" he said. "Can't you understand that I'm delighted? I won't have to lecture now!" But their outrage—and Señora Borges's—persisted. "At least the offender must be exposed—" "Please, no, no," Borges insisted. "Can't you see that I'm grateful to her? She's my benefactor. If you punish her, I'll never come back."

3

Walking to the Library, we re-entered the gloomy structure that was once the National Lottery, its brass balustrades on the grand staircase having as their motif the spherical baskets in which the tickets are shuffled. The Director's office, with twenty-foot ceilings and ornately carved wainscoting, has a curved desk designed for Paul Groussac, Borges's predecessor, who was also blind. (Was there something symbolic, I wondered, about these blind librarians in a Latin American institution devoted more to reverence than to use?)

The restaurant to which Borges invited us to dine with him is a homely establishment called the Caserio. On the way to it, he never stopped talking. Bill and Norman would get a block ahead of us and then stop to let us catch up. Borges tugged at my elbow so hard it was difficult to avoid lampposts and keep out of the gutter. (Norman told me that he had a sore arm for a week after arriving in Buenos Aires and that he still walks like a crab.) Once we were agreeing that Goethe was overrated as a poet, and I delighted him by quoting the passage from *Faust*, Part II, beginning *Wenn im unendlichen dasselbe* to prove that Goethe was best in philosophical nuggets like that, he pulled me off the curb and with taxis barreling by intoned a dozen lines from *Beowulf* to indicate the bridge between the Teuton and English tongues. At an intersection he stopped me in the middle of the street to quote José Hernández—the idea being that *Martin Fierro* was somewhat cheapened by its propaganda content—"The poem was written, you know, to stop the killing of the Indians by the Gauchos. Hernández's Gaucho complains too much. Real Gauchos are not so self-pitying."

"Is the Gaucho in *The Purple Land* more real?" I asked.

"No. Less so. Hudson was a first-rate naturalist but not a first-rate novelist. His memory of the Banda Oriental played him tricks. I could give you a dozen instances of inaccuracy. He romanticized the Uruguayan back country hopelessly, all those silly loves, and so on."

By the time we were seated for dinner we were quoting and counterquoting. He'd quote Tennyson; I'd quote "a better poet of the same time, Hopkins." He'd quote a war poem by Browning; I'd quote "a better poet, Owen." He'd cite Kipling or Chesterton or Stevenson; I'd cite Stephen Crane. I asked him whether he admired César Vallejo's poetry. "Vallejo? Never heard of him." I couldn't believe my ears. "García Márquez's fiction?" I ventured. "Never heard of him either." I retreated to safer ground. "Leopoldo Lugones?"

"Of course. Lugones was our greatest poet. But very limited, very Paris-oriented, by way of Rubén Darío who worked for years in Buenos Aires as a journalist. Lugones showed his basic insecurity by frequently prefacing a sententious remark with 'As Rubén Darío, my master and friend, and I agree. . . .' Ah, he was a very distasteful person, Lugones, very negative. His mouth seemed shaped by nature to pronounce the word 'No.' Later on he would invent reasons to justify this word that his soul and facial muscles so automatically shaped."

Borges had to admit that he had read some Cortazar but he didn't like the expatriate Argentine novelist. "He is trying so hard on every page to be original that it becomes a tiresome battle of wits, no?"

When discussing English or American literature, Borges's

whole personality changes. He beams, he expands, he glows. "You know I was brought up on English in my father's library. I was quite old when it occurred to me that poetry could be written in a language other than English."

He ordered a plate of rice, butter, and cheese, while our mouths watered at the thought of the Argentine steaks we'd soon be served. "I hate steaks," Borges said. "They are so common in this country. I can't eat more than one or two a year."

Norman said: "Borges, I heard you mention Eliot a while back—"

"Eliot is a little dry, don't you think?" Borges said. "I prefer Frost. You like Frost, Rodman?" He was glad that I preferred Frost to Eliot. He asked me how Frost looked and talked. Did I think that Frost's reserved Americanism had any kinship with Whitman's boisterous brand?

"I think Frost was a direct descendant of Emerson," I said.

"And Whitman was influenced by Emerson more than by anyone! That essay about the ideal American democrat, pioneer, truthteller, yea-sayer—with a bit of Asiatic-Indian philosophy thrown in—"

" 'I greet you at the beginning of a great career,' " I quoted.

"—And how distressed Emerson was that Whitman made big publicity out of that letter!" Borges said. "Yet why not? If Emerson didn't expect it, why did he write it? Whitman was right . . . but don't you think Whitman *tries* too hard, that he's really a quite unspontaneous writer?"

"Not in 'Song of Myself,' " I said. "That's the most spontaneous poem in the language. Even some of the lines in the later poems are pure magic, impossible to will."

"For instance?"

" 'I repose by the sills of the exquisite flexible doors.' "

Borges said it over several times. "I don't get it. What's so wonderful about it?"

"You've revealed to me at last that English is only your adopted language," I said.

He laughed. "They didn't find me out at Harvard, or at

Texas either." The lectures he had delivered at Austin had been a great experience, he added. "Every South American should visit the United States to see how perverted by lying Communist propaganda the local image of America is. The students, compared with ours, are so alert. I'll not forget the one who pointed out in class that my story 'The Golem' was a reworking of 'The Circular Ruins.' I was amazed! 'My God,' I said, 'you're right! I've never thought of it, but it's true. Well, I only wrote it—once. You've probably read both stories many times.' "

He leaned toward Bill to answer a question, and Norman said to me: "He says things like that all the time. He really means them. He thinks his present fame is a matter of luck, not necessarily deserved, and that any day the bubble may pop and he'll be forgotten, or relegated to a very minor role. Of course he's enjoying it while it lasts, rather astonished by the adulation, the translators all over the world haggling over the meaning of this or that arcane phrase—but not at all taken in by it, or spoiled, as you can see."

"Here," said Borges turning back to me, "examinations are like lottery tickets. In Texas a student wanted me to give a course all over again, unsure that he'd profited by it thoroughly, unconcerned about quick credits . . . That could never happen here."

4

We had been to Borges's apartment on Belgrano several times, but one day the maid, who always rushed to the door and then looked as though she'd been interrupted at an embalming, said that only Señora Borges was in. Never having met her, we said we'd be pleased to have that privilege. She could not be disturbed but we could wait in the parlor. Bill escaped and I settled down, making a *catalogue raisonné* of the premises to pass the time: two potted rubber palms, two green-cushioned Morris chairs, a spindly dining room set, two glass-enclosed bookcases, two etchings in the style of Whistler, two eighteenth-century engravings (Arch of Titus, Pyramid of Caius Cestius), a Dürer etching, a painting of angels by Borges's sister, a student exercise by Silvana Ocampo of a woman's back from the waist up, a cabinet containing Borges's medals and other literary awards, a wall rack with brandy decanters and glasses of red glass in brass holders, a Harvard shield, a glass coffee table containing an ash tray, Joyce's *Ulysses* (Borges thinks Joyce should have filled it with character studies rather than catalogues), Apollinaire in Spanish (*El Heresiarca y Cia*), and the complete works of Dürer in folio.

Presently Borges came in and I made a date to meet him here at four in the afternoon and then go to the Library for drawings and photos. I told him I'd like to meet his wife. He went through one of the closed doors and came back, closing it after him.

"She excuses herself. She just had a bath."

"I'm beginning to think you don't have a wife, Borges."

He smiled wryly. "Maybe it's better if we keep up the mystery."

He took me to the elevator and I had trouble closing the accordion gate which has to be shut before any Argentine elevator will start. "Is this some diabolical Argentine invention?" I said.

"Heavens no," he said, as my head began to disappear below floor level," the Argentines could never invent something as complicated as an elevator—or for that matter anything at all."

At four o'clock I picked up Bill and drove back to Belgrano. This time La Señora emerged and greeted us. She is a buxom, rather handsome woman in her fifties. She surrendered her husband to his guests unceremoniously. To get Borges across the street to a taxi was, as always, a tug of war. This time he was talking about his story "Funes the Memorious" and about what a terrible thing it was to have insomnia.

At the Library we rang the bell but no one answered. Borges had no key. Finally a man came up to us from across the street, concerned to see the old man with a cane standing hatless under the fierce sun, and asked us if we'd like to have a whisky or a Coke. Borges said we'd like to have a Coke but that was the last we saw of our presumptive benefactor. Borges, by now engaged in quoting Longfellow's translation of an Old English poem, "The Grave," showed very little interest when the watchman, who should have been on duty, finally arrived with the key. To get the natural light for photography and drawing, we took three chairs out on to the narrow balcony that runs around the top of the huge, glass-domed main reading room.

I asked Borges how important in shaping Argentina's history was the fact that the Argentine was a dependency of Peru from 1563 to 1776.

"Not at all," he said. "Communications were much too difficult in those days to give Argentina much sense of inferiority. We were pretty much on our own, with Spain giving us most of the trouble. In the War of the Pacific in 1879, everybody here sided with Peru against Chile. But the city of Buenos Aires has always been democratic compared with aristocratic Lima . . . Argentina has always been far too large, I've always thought. Our northwestern provinces, with their surviving Indians, would be better off as parts of Indian Paraguay or Bolivia."

I asked him whether he thought the nineteenth-century domination of Argentina, by the British economically and the French culturally, had had a schizophrenic effect on his country.

"I don't think so," he said. "Both influences were accepted quite naturally, in my family at least. But we were not devoted to Spain. We thought of Spaniards as servants. I recall someone coming back from meeting the Infanta and reporting scornfully 'She talks like a *gallego*'—the equivalent of saying that a British princess talks like a limey."

He went on to say that Paris had had a bad influence on

intellectuals and poets—"Like your Ezra Pound, for instance, who adopted his ridiculous pose there. Or was it in London that he first affected cowboy dress and talk? . . . Even Victor Hugo felt he had to strike an attitude, though he was a serious poet and a great one."

I reminded him of André Gide's famous remark—"Victor Hugo, alas"—when asked who he thought was France's greatest poet. "Do you think Baudelaire and Rimbaud were better poets?" I asked.

"Of course not," he said. "Baudelaire is overrated, and Rimbaud was a mere freak . . . Do you know Hugo's splendid poem 'Boaz Endormi'?" I didn't and he quoted it all, with its ending:

> . . . L'herbe était noire;
> C'était l'heure tranquille quand les lions vont boire . . .

I told Borges that I was haunted by his story "El Aleph," especially by the passage describing the magical appearance on the cellar step of the small iridescent sphere "whose center is everywhere and its circumference nowhere." I asked him about the connection between the first part of the story and the last. "It's not clear to me." And I explained why.

"Now that you mention it, it's not clear to me either," he said. "I think I'll change it and put in a much clearer relation between the buyer of the house and the seller, a hint at the very beginning that someone is going to buy the house. And I will put your name in it too, if you have no objection, as a tribute to you for improving it."

I laughed. Was he pulling my leg, mildly making fun of me—which he had every right to do? He told me about a reporter in Madrid who had come to him and asked him seriously whether the Aleph existed in fact. "Later on I wished I had encouraged him in this tomfoolery, but at the time I said, 'Of course not,' and he left quite crestfallen, and even disgusted with me for making such a deception! Tomfoolery should always be encouraged, don't you agree? But I let the poor man down and he felt disconsolate." He added that the poet satirized at the beginning of the story was drawn from life and that his mother had begged him not to make it so obvious. "But I said to her: 'He'll never recognize himself'—and he didn't!" I asked him where he found the title. "I took it from Bertrand Russell's Introduction to his *Philosophy of Mathematics,* where it is used as the symbol for transfinite numbers."

"Why is the house in which the Aleph appears destroyed in the end?" I asked.

"It had to be destroyed," he said, "because you can't leave things like an Aleph lying around in this day and age, the way Aladdin left his lamp lying around. Not any more. The premises have to be tidied up, the supernatural suitably disposed of, the reader's mind set at rest."

Which, of course, is exactly what Borges doesn't do. For part of his genius is to leave the mysteries suspended, very disquietingly suspended, in these "real" settings which make the metaphysical content so alarmingly believable. Untypical in this respect is "La Intrusa," which I'd just read after being told that Borges regarded it as his best story. I told him that I liked it less than the earlier stories, and he asked me why.

"The woman's reactions to what the two brothers are doing to her are never hinted at," I said, "with the result that I can't feel any involvement in her fate. I'm stunned by the conclusion, but emotionally indifferent to what happens to the woman. Why would it detract from the story if you presented her as a human being rather than as the animal they feel she is?"

"The more we are made to think of the woman as a kind of thing," Borges replied, "the easier it is for the reader to feel about her as the brothers did—and to understand that the essential subject of this story is friendship, not brutality. I wonder if you noticed, by the way, that the older brother is the only one whose words we are allowed to hear? It is he who dominates the story, finds the woman, invents the scheme of sharing her with his brother, sells her to the brothel, buys her back, and in the end knifes or strangles her."

While he was saying this, I had a close look at Borges's eyes.

No wonder he looks just a little mad! The pupil of the right eye is so enlarged it almost fills the iris. The pupil of the left eye is very small and a little off center.

5

Borges asked me where I'd been the past week when I came to his apartment to say good-by. I'd been to Bariloche in the Andes and to Montevideo.

"What has Bariloche to do with Argentina?" he said. "In my childhood it didn't even exist. It is an invention of the Swiss and is populated with tourists and those who live off them. Of course it has mountains. But I spent the most impressionable years of my boyhood in Geneva where there are mountains just as good and a civilized society as well.

"Uruguay is something else again," he continued. "It is a very small and poor country, so things like poetry and football are taken overseriously. They say—as they never would here, or with you—'I want you to meet my friend the poet so-and-so.' You can't joke about the Gauchos or their national heroes, either. But it's like that all over South America, isn't it? In Peru they asked me seriously: 'Are you on the side of Pizarro or Atahualpa?' We don't think of such ethnic absurdities here. My best friend, the poet Carlos Mastronardi, comes of Italian stock on both sides. I'm all mixed up racially myself. It doesn't matter. We're all Argentinians. So we never think of it. In Berlin Miguel Angel Asturias made a speech beginning, 'I want to tell you I'm an Indian.' He'd be laughed off the stage if he said that here. I'd say to him: 'Then why do you speak Spanish and wear Western clothes? Why do you publish books and not *quipos*?' In Colombia, though there's an enormous gap between the rich and the poor—and that terrible *violéncia*—they're more sensible. They say: 'The only hope for us is the American Marines.' " He smiled mischievously. "—And the only hope for South America as a whole is that you can conquer it. Nowadays you fight only small wars which you're not very good at, and which you wage halfheartedly, with a sense of guilt—like the British in South Africa when they almost lost to the Boers. You both win the big wars, of course; and if you were to conquer South America in the same spirit, without any misgivings, you'd be universally admired for it, you can be sure!"

"You've got to be kidding, Borges," I said.

"Not so much as you might think," he said with a smile.

I showed him a copy of a book by Fernando Guiberts called *Compadrito*, which I'd picked up in San Carlos de Bariloche, asking him whether the following description of the hoodlum of the Buenos Aires outskirts was accurate:

> . . . his betrayal and oblivion of the pampas, where this without-a-horse man was born . . . this dismounted peasant no longer riding his destiny . . . his mother out for hire by day, dragging her tasks along; the father only a forsaken portrait in the bureau drawer . . . his passion servile and sticky, a craving to be the man he will never become . . . attending to the drama of his own vital impotence . . .

I had seen enough of the deracinated slum-dweller in Lima, Mexico City, and Santiago to be sure that there was some truth in this description, but I knew Borges well enough by this time to know that he wouldn't recognize it as his truth. He said he had lived in those neighborhoods "in the time the writer pretends to describe," and that it was not like that. He had me read another bit, about knife fights. He went out and came back with two wicked-looking silver-handled poniards. He demonstrated that instead of holding the point down as Guiberts indicates, it should be held up—"to get up under the shield of the poncho wrapped around the left forearm. Of course there are instances of all these attitudes he describes, but to harp on them only produces caricature."

The knives reminded me anew of the fatal encounter at the end of his story "El Sur."

"What were the other levels," I asked Borges, "on which that story was written—the levels you were starting to tell me about the other day?"

"Well," he said, "one is that it was all perhaps a dream. You remember there's a circumstance hinted at in the beginning —that the protagonist may have died under the surgeon's knife. Then, at the inn, the protagonist has the *Arabian Nights* with him again, and the storekeeper is like the intern at the hospital, and the store reminds him of an engraving. So couldn't it all be a dream at the moment of dying? . . . The autobiographical level is in the thinking of the violent death of his grandfather—as I did so often of mine. A student once asked me in Texas: 'When did the protagonist die?' I answered: 'You pays your money and you takes your choice! . . .' Still another level is the protagonist's love for the South—and its symbolic knife. He loves it, and it kills him."

I thought of the exaltation of courage in Borges's poems, not the physical courage he may have lacked, or thought he lacked as a young man—as some have conjectured—but courage as a spiritual legacy, as in the poem about his great-grandfather, who turned the tide during the Battle of Junín:

. . . His great-grandson is writing these lines,
and a silent voice comes to him out of the past,
out of the blood:

"What does my battle at Junín matter if it is only
a glorious memory, or a date learned by rote
for an examination, or a place in the atlas?
The battle is everlasting and can do without
the pomp of actual armies and of trumpets.
Junín is two civilians cursing a tyrant
on a street corner,
or an unknown man somewhere dying in prison." [3]

Or the poem about the dying thoughts of Doctor Francisco Laprida, set upon and killed September 22, 1829, by a band of Gaucho militia, which Norman had translated from the same book:

[3] Jorge Luis Borges, "A Page to Commemorate Colonel Suárez, Victor at Junín," in *Selected Poems 1923–1967*, edited by Norman Thomas di Giovanni, translated by Alastair Reid, New York, Delacorte, 1970.

> . . . I who longed to be someone else, to weigh
> judgments, to read books, to hand down the law,
> will lie in the open out in these swamps;
> I see at last that I am face to face
> with my South American destiny.
> I was carried to this ruinous hour
> by the intricate labyrinth of steps
> woven by my days from a day that goes
> back to my birth . . .

We told him we must leave, but he wanted us to stay and have tea. We declined, thinking we'd stayed too long already and were tiring him. As we edged our way toward the elevator, I asked him whether he'd like to have a copy of the biography of Byron's sister which I had ordered for Neruda.

"Some poets, like Byron," he said, "are so much more interesting than their poetry, aren't they?"

"Hemingway, for instance," I said.

"Yes," he said. "A very uninteresting writer, really."

"It was a great pleasure meeting you, Borges," I said lamely as we stepped into the cage and pulled the accordion doors shut.

"It was a pleasure and great honor meeting you," he replied graciously.

"We'll always remember it," said Bill in a louder voice as we started down.

"If you do forget," we heard his laughing voice say as we plunged out of sight, "write it down and remember the spelling—B-O-R-G-E-S—Borges!"

On the plane to Lima, quite possibly directly over Junín, I translated the last four lines from one of his poems:

> I seem to hear a stirring in the dawn
> of multitudes departing; I perceive
> the loves and memories that now are gone;
> space, time, and Borges take their leave.

When I returned to Buenos Aires two years later, Borges hadn't changed but the circumstances of his life had. He was back with his mother, and he was not contesting his wife's demands for exorbitant alimony. I asked di Giovanni why.

"He's been living in constant fear that he *won't* have to pay alimony! He feels guilty as hell. He thinks he alone is responsible for the failure of the marriage and should pay for it. Also, don't forget that while Borges is kind, generous, humble, imaginative, and noble, courage isn't part of his character. When his wife cursed him loudly at the airport once, with people all about listening in, he just stood there next to me with head bowed taking it without a word of rejoinder. He'll do anything to avoid facing up to a situation and asserting himself."

"Does his religion have anything to do with this self-abnegation?" I asked.

"Not really," Norman replied. "But his religion is one of the things that makes Borges so different from other Latin American intellectuals. Though his mother is a devout Catholic and his father was an atheist, Borges is a Protestant at heart. 'What Protestant church do you think I should join?' he once asked me only half jokingly. Ethics and belief in the value of *work* are central with Borges. When we were working on the autobiography last year, I wrote the phrase 'Amateur Protestant that I am . . . ,' and he exclaimed with delight: 'That's it! That's exactly it!' "

The moment Borges arrived for dinner, we started arguing. I'd just come back from Mar del Plata with Norman and his wife, Heather, and remarked about Buenos Aires's clammy heat.

"In my childhood we were not aware of such changes in the weather," Borges said. "At least it was not the custom to mention them. My father wore a thick coat with a high collar and a neckerchief at all times. Maybe it was cooler that way."

"Take your coat off and relax, Borges," I said, mopping my forehead.

"I'll take my coat off, but not my tie," he said. "Don't move me ahead too fast! Where have you been besides Mar del Plata? And what's new in poetry?"

I read him a poem by Stanley Kunitz, "After Pastor Bonhoeffer," and I told him I'd had a talk with García Márquez. "I know you won't read *Cien Años de Soledad*," I said, "in view of what Bioy Cáseres has told you about it—a bad novel, incompetently written—but he's wrong. It's a great novel, comparable to *Don Quixote*. García Márquez, by the way, is a great admirer of yours."

He looked pleased. "How can we judge the work of others when we can't even judge our own? Cervantes thought that his only good book was a dull, obscure work entitled *Trabajos de Persiles y Sigismunda: un novela septentrionál*. I've been rereading Sinclair Lewis recently. Did you ever know him?"

I told him about the time I was an undergraduate at Yale and accompanied Lewis to the library to present (unsuccessfully) his Nobel medal.

"He's not a great writer," Borges said, "but he's a good one. The best thing about him is that he makes you sympathize with even the characters he ridicules, like Babbitt. He must have been a kind man."

"When he wasn't drunk," Norman said.

"Do you know why I don't drink?" Borges said. "Because when I was a young man I used to drink a lot of whisky Saturday nights, and one day I heard myself referred to as 'that drunkard, Borges.' Naturally I didn't want to go through life being considered a drunkard, so I stopped drinking."

"Lewis wasn't a drunkard but he certainly was drunk that day at Yale. But now let me ask you one. Did you ever meet Stevenson? And how can you consider him a major writer? For me he's minor—compared to you, for instance!"

"Thank you very much," he said, with a courtly smile in my direction. "I'm grateful, and sorry for you at the same time!— As I was when you referred to Neruda as a major poet. I think Neruda was a poet of some talent, derivative of Whitman, who gave up writing poems for political tracts. To me a 'major' poem is any very good poem, so a man who writes even one good poem, like George Meredith, for example, may be classified major. No?"

"Emphatically no," I said. "The distinction has to do with the whole body of a poet's work. If it changes poetry, the times, the race, it's major. Whitman and Neruda are major, no matter how many bad poems they wrote—and they wrote a lot, though Neruda has written some of his best in this decade, unlike Whitman who wrote very few after 'Song of Myself.' Poe, on the other hand, is minor—except perhaps to the French."

"Yes, I agree with that. Only his stories survive," Borges said.

"And a very few poems, like 'Sonnet to Science,' with magical lines—"

"Like that one of Whitman I didn't get? How did it go?"

" 'I repose by the sills of the exquisite flexible doors.' " Norman said. "Not bad as an epitaph for an elevator operator!"

"The line the French consider their greatest—'*La fille de Minos et de Pasiphaë*'—doesn't even sound like a good epitaph for Racine's heroine," I said. "But would any French poet be stunned by Milton's 'Smoothing the raven down of darkness till it smiled'?"

"I am," Borges said, "that's major!"

"Thanks for putting that word back in circulation, Borges," I said. "You consider *Don Segundo Sombra* a major novel?"

"Certainly not," Borges said, "though a quite interesting one. But it came out of *Kim,* a better book, just as *Kim* came out of *Huckleberry Finn,* a still better one. It was based on an actual character, you know. Don Segundo Ramírez Sombra actually existed. Maybe that is why the character is not larger than life. The book is an elegy for a vanished time. Daydreaming, wishful thinking by a conservative about the *criollo* past. Güiraldes died in 1927 of cancer, the year after this best of his books came out here."

"You knew him?"

"He came to our house in Montevideo once on his way to

Europe. He was very sad to be leaving and asked if he could leave his guitar on our sofa as a kind of symbolic pledge that he would return. He was a gentleman, never saying an unkind word about anyone."

"Speaking of gentlemen," I said, "I remember that that was the word you used to describe Juan Onganía two years ago. You regard the present strong man as highly?"

"I had an audience with President Levingston some weeks ago," Borges replied, "hoping to get him to raise the salaries of the Library employees who get an average $65 a month. You know what came of it? He raised *my* salary of $200 a month, which was perfectly adequate, and none of the others . . . No, it's a big step backward. They don't have any ideas for spending that make any sense. Like this repaving of Calle Florida, which only causes confusion. My chain of command used to go from me to the Minister of Education and then to the President. Now it's an organigram. There are seven links —seven dead bodies I must step over, and all receiving big salaries for doing nothing."

"Well," I said, "Chile has finally gotten Allende. Argentina's turn may be next."

"They've gotten what they wanted by way of free elections," Borges said, "—the fetish that brought us Perón, twice! We'll go to the dogs, if we go, via free elections. . . . But my philosophy is that some day we will deserve *not* to have governments."

7

"You really turn him on," Norman said, after we'd taken Borges back to his mother's apartment. "I haven't seen him so animated in months. Here they fawn on him and bore the hell out of him. He loves being told he's all wet once in a while, being introduced to new things. I wish I could accompany you to the Library to say good-by to him."

Borges was standing up, talking to Bioy Cáseres on the phone, when I entered his office. When he'd finished he apologized and sat down with me at the long table. "How did you come up?" he asked.

"On foot," I said, "the elevator wasn't working."

He chuckled. "Why don't you say 'lift'? It's so much shorter. But Americans, though always in a hurry, use the four-syllable 'elevator.' You use 'garbage can' too, though there's a shorter word for that. But maybe you don't use it at all, it's such a disagreeable word!"

I assured him we had plenty of short words—"like 'can' for *escusado,* 'balls' for *cojones,* 'lab' for 'labóratory,' and so on. But we have lots of words that are much too long, I agree; like 'explicate' for what a professor does to a poem he can't get through his senses—"

" 'Explicate'?" he said, "not just 'explain'? That's fantastic!"

"What are you working on now, Borges?"

"An article on Keats."

"Saying—?"

"I don't know. I'll find out when I start writing it."

"I'm relieved to hear you say what I've said so often. To publishers especially."

"They think a book starts with an outline."

"Instead of a feeling."

"You like Keats?" Borges asked.

"Tremendously. The letters, which reveal the man, are the best in the language. The longer poems, well—"

"They're not very good, are they? Not many long poems are—"

"But the shorter ones, beginning with 'Chapman's Homer'—"

"Even that one is a little dated, isn't it? 'Much have I travelled in the realms of gold' has an artificial ring, hasn't it?"

"Perhaps deliberately," I said, "but the sestet is superb, with one unforgettable line—"

" 'Looked at each other with a wild surmise'?"

"Yes. The syllables trip over each other to convey the excitement. Just as the line from Blake I quoted to you last week—'The lost traveller's dream under the hill'—has the opposite effect, interminably stretched out to suggest death. I'm more moved by Blake at this point in my life."

"He got all that from Swedenborg, didn't he?" Borges said.

"Only what he found usable, what echoed his own philosophy. Swedenborg didn't see those 'dark Satanic mills' as the obverse side of the 'garden of love' . . . By the way, I've never heard you mention Emily Dickinson."

"I like her, of course," Borges said, "but not as much as Emerson, a happier spirit."

"Were you pulling my leg two years ago when you said you'd never heard of Vallejo?"

"No!" he looked deliberately startled. "Not at all. Who is he?"

"Come on, Borges, you must have at least *heard* of the most famous South American poet after Neruda."

He laughed. "What the hell do I have to do with South America?"

"But he is a great poet, Borges, and not at all a public, declamatory one like Neruda. You might even like him!"

"Great poets are overrated. Whom would you consider the great Spanish poets?"

"Quevedo? Góngora?—"

"Very overrated, both. Góngora is famous for his influence on the Elizabethan poets of England. Quevedo is not interesting. I much prefer Fray Luis de León—"

"*Who?*"

"You see! Never heard of him?"

"Never. What is his poetry like?"

"Full of serenity. Unobtrusive rhymes . . . Beauty is very common actually. In the future maybe everyone will be a poet . . . But to come back to Keats, do you know Kipling's story 'Wireless'? It's about Keats and Fanny Brawne. You must read it. Come. I'll show you."

We went into a dark corridor and I guided him through two closed doors to a book-lined chamber. He went to a shelf containing a thirty-volume set of Kipling in red. "Which volume, Borges?"

29

"No idea. Let's start with the first."

"I'll miss my plane to Rio!" I read him the table of contents of the first three volumes while he stopped to give me the plots of several favorites. Fortunately 'Wireless' was in the fourth volume. I skimmed through it. We walked down into the lobby and he accompanied me to the revolving door.

"I hate to put you in this," I said.

"It's like a whirlpool. I may be scrambled."

"You may come out changed."

"I hope so."

8

The talks I had with Borges during my third and last visit to Buenos Aires, in 1972, revolved about the book of new stories he'd just published,[4] and an anthology of English poets I was then working on and which he asked me to read him.

When I arrived at the Library about nine in the evening he'd just finished a session with Maria Kodama with whom he was studying Norse and Old English. We took a taxi to a restaurant. The street was torn up, and as we stumbled over potholes to the entrance he said: "This country is going to the dogs, isn't it? First we gave up being Spanish. Then we became amateur Frenchmen. Then came the English stage, followed by the Hollywood one. Now—mere ignorance! . . . Of course," he added, as we selected a table, "no one admires commercial empires, and that's the only side of the United States most Argentines ever see. Besides, you're a Protestant country. Catholics don't think in terms of right and wrong."

As he settled down to his frugal repast of honeydew melon draped with thin slices of ham, I asked him for his version of Neruda's Paris-bound transit of Buenos Aires some months ago. "Ask him," Norman had said, after telling me with considerable outrage of Borges's failure to respond to the generous telegram the Nobel laureate had dispatched from

4 *Doctor Brodie's Report* by Jorge Luis Borges, translated by Norman Thomas di Giovanni in collaboration with the author, New York, Dutton, 1972.

Santiago requesting an audience with "Argentina's greatest poet."

"Of course I couldn't see the ambassador of a Communist government," Borges said; and then, perhaps recalling my friendship with Neruda, he added: "To be sure, he's a fine writer. We did meet forty years ago. At that time we were both influenced by Whitman and I said, jokingly in part, 'I don't think anything can be done in Spanish, do you?' Neruda agreed, but we decided it was too late for us to write our verse in English. We'd have to make the best of a second-rate literature."

"It's that poor, Spanish?" I said.

"Of course. For one thing, the words are too long. English has the short Saxon words. Then a Milton comes along and mixes them with the long Latin ones. Or take Shakespeare's 'seas incarnadine.' Speaking of which," he added, "Pound inverts words so badly in his version of that great poem, 'The Seafarer': 'May I for myself songs truth reckon . . .' "

I thought of Borges's *mot*, "writers invent their own fore-runners," when he next proceeded to tell me that a Southern soldier in our Civil War, Henry Timrod, "is one of the fine American poets."

"I finished *Doctor Brodie's Report* on the plane from Rio, Borges," I said. "I couldn't help wondering how you reconcile such overwhelming pessimism with such a hopeful statement as 'Some day we will deserve not to have governments.' "

"It's inconsistent, I admit," he said. "My father was an anarchist. I prefer to think that about future governments rather than abandon myself to the more probable fate of the Yahoos."

"You say in one of the stories, 'lost, as some day all things will be lost.' You believe that?"

"I *hope* all things will be lost?"

"Then why do you write?"

"What else have I got to do? Wasn't it Carlyle who said: 'Any human achievement is worthless, but the achieving is worthwhile'?"

"Shakespeare seemed convinced he would survive through his poems."

"*Aere monumenta*? That was a hoary literary convention. He stopped writing when he'd made enough money to retire, and he surely didn't expect that the 1623 Folio would ever be published. Writing was not taken too seriously then, and I don't take it too seriously."

"I was thinking as I drove over this afternoon—did you ever consider writing a story about one of these underground Nazis in B.A.? One who had finally become a decent human being, for instance, only to discover that society wouldn't let him?"

"No, I don't like the Germans," he said. "I went there six or seven years ago and found them so cringing, so wallowing in self-pity. I never heard one say a bad word about the German character—or even about Hitler."

"Your new stories are full of knife fights. Did you ever see one?"

"No. But I did see a man shot in a senseless vendetta once, in Uruguay."

My next question was triggered by a talk I had had the day before with Alastair Reid, about the lack of "motivation" in the characters of these new stories. "North Americans," Reid said, "have been brought up in a psychoanalytic world where everything must have an explanation—a rational one. Life, however, is what happens, not what can be explained. These are Borges's greatest stories because they are purified of motivational or metaphysical props. Borges likes to call Kipling's *Plain Tales from the Hills* the ultimate stories because they are the simplest. Latin American literature—whether Borges, García Márquez, Neruda—is written from the posture of humanity, and against theories of any kind which are death."

"Why does the protagonist of 'An Unworthy Friend' turn on his friend?" I asked Borges. "It seems an inexplicable act."

"The story is confessional," Borges replied. "When I was a student in Switzerland during the First War, a boy wanted to

32

be my friend and I rebuffed him—feeling that I was unworthy. So in the story I made myself a Jew boy, to dramatize it, and went further than rebuffing, to actual betrayal. But it's still a confession!"

"In 'The Gospel According to St. Mark'—"

"I think I should rewrite that one," Borges said. "The climax [when the boy who's been reading the account of the Crucifixion to the credulous peasant family is led to the cross on which they will re-enact the drama] is too abrupt and tricky. There are hints, but I think I should make it clear that he suspects what will happen, and then bamboozles himself into believing that he's safe."

"It's a great story as it is," I said. "Why cushion the reader's shock?"

"You think so? Then I won't tamper with it."

"It may be your best."

"I think 'The Intruder' is better. It's my most economical story. We aren't told about the way the woman is killed. That's better than melodrama, don't you think? You've noticed the older brother is the only one who speaks? It's always 'they talked' but 'he says.' So the reader is made aware that the decisions are his; the others have no authority. But people read into it such absurdities! Someone actually said to me 'Those two brothers were in love with each other.' Some people have to find homosexuality or incest or hidden meanings in everything. They can't accept a good story as a good story."

"What touched off 'La Intrusa'?"

"I'd just read Kipling's 'Beyond the Pale,' impressed by its terseness. I said to Vlady who happened to be with me, 'Now I'll write something . . .'"

"And 'Guayaquil'?"

"The point of that story is that the two of them *become* Bolívar and San Martín, and as it happened historically, the better man won. I was also taking a dig at the Argentine nationalists for their hero-worship of General San Martín. Why did his alter ego yield? He was a pompous fool from the start.

33

The story would have broken down if their conversation had been longer."

I took him home in a taxi about eleven. The driver dropped us quite a way from his door. He said he'd walk by himself, but I wouldn't let him. "How do you know we're even on the right street, Borges?"

"I know."

"You could see me, at the restaurant—in outline?"

"Only your hands."

"If I lie down on this doorstep you may see my face."

"Don't do it," he said, as his key slipped into the lock, "what *you'd* see would be even more ugly than what you see now!"

9

At the Library the next afternoon I read Borges the contents of my new British anthology and then those poems which he remembered or asked to hear. It was hard to wrench him beyond *Beowulf*. He liked my version of *Piers Ploughman*, and he said that Dunbar was an old favorite of his. He wanted to hear the one Shakespearean song he didn't know ("The master, the swabber, the boatswain and I . . ."). He approved my choice among the several versions of "Tom O'Bedlam." He quoted almost flawlessly Milton's "Sonnet on His Blindness." He speculated about the inferiority of *Paradise Regained*, quoting from memory,

. . . He, unobserved,
Home to his mother's house private returned.

"How could he? How could he! After the splendid conclusion to *Paradise Lost!* Surely it wasn't his blindness, for he was blind writing both poems."

Of Grey's "Elegy" he remarked: "Valéry's 'Cimitière Marin,' an inferior poem, is based on it, don't you think?

There really are no first-rate French poets—Hugo included."

"You almost convinced me of the contrary three years ago," I said. "Do you approve my large selection of Burns?"

"Burns was only a great song writer, and popular songs can't be judged any longer as poetry. For instance 'Drink to me only with thine eyes,' which may once have been thrilling."

I read him the bawdy 'Is there for honest poverty . . .' to see whether he'd be as shocked by the four-letter words as Norman said he would be, but he made no comment. When I came to Blake, he urged me to include the passage from 'Uthune' ('Uriel'?), intoning

> . . . But nets of steel and traps of adamant
> . . . Girls of mild silver or of furious gold
> . . . I'll lie beside thee on a bank
> in lovely copulation, bliss on bliss. . .

—repeating the last line over and over, with evident relish.

(I recalled that when a daring student in Oklahoma had once asked Borges, "Why is there so little sex in your stories?" Borges had replied, "Perhaps because I am thinking about it too much." And I remembered Norman telling me that Borges called this ditty which he'd found in a Buenos Aires men's room—

> La mierda no la pintura,
> El dedo no lo pincel;
> No sea hijo de puta,
> Limpiesa con papel—

"excellent didactic verse" and that he'd suggested to Norman that he write it on the wall of an American college lavatory "as a gesture of cultural exchange," which Norman gladly did.)

Among the poets of this century Borges, not surprisingly, showed little interest in Owen, Hardy, or Lawrence, but berated me for not having included Kipling's "best poem" ("Harp Song of the Dane Women") or anything of G. K. Chesterton at all.

As I was getting up to go I remembered what we'd been talking about yesterday. "I think you're of two minds about immortality, Borges," I said.

"Can you prove it?"

"In 'Delia Elena San Marco,' which I read last night for the first time, you say, 'Man invents farewells because he knows he's immortal," and in another of your poems, 'The Saxon Poet,' aren't you positing a kind of immortality when you say, 'Today you are *my* voice,' and then ask that 'some verse of mine survive on a night favorable to memory'?"

"Well," he said, after some thought, "I suppose *that* kind of immortality I do believe in. It's not personal. I won't be aware of it. And I certainly won't get a kick out of it!

"I wrote a poem yesterday," he confided, as we walked toward the door, "with a deliberately flat beginning. My idea is to work up to ecstasy at the end. The first part was very easy!"

10

"I spent a good part of last night in bed thinking about your anthology," Borges said when Norman and I met him in the park the following morning for some pictures. "Instead of poems that seem 'modern' I would have adopted the reverse principle. I mean I would have selected poems that seem completely *un*-modern: about old virtues like loyalty, and so on. We shouldn't be reminded of what we are—I mean like that stanza from Byron's *Don Juan* about the blacks, or Shelley's description of the London slums—but of what we were."

"But were we ever?" I said. "I'm more interested in the similarities. The constant is our common perversity and humanity. And the discovery of those ties will draw the reader from the new to the old, through what never changes."

"Well, maybe," he said dubiously, "but it wouldn't be my touchstone."

"It surely wouldn't," said Norman as we crossed the square, with Borges tapping his way ahead of us with his cane. "When Borges makes an anthology his criticism is narrower: he selects only what reminds him of himself."

"That Burns poem you read me," Borges said as we caught up with him, "is really nonsensical, isn't it?"

"Didn't I tell you," Norman whispered, "that he'd never accept those dirty words! It took him a whole day to come out and tell you!"

"Those figures you were giving me on the phone, Norman," Borges said. "It can't be possible—46,000 copies of our new book before publication?"

"Before any are even *bought,* Borges."

"Before anybody even *reads* them," I added.

"When they do, they'll throw the book away," said Borges, smiling.

"But it will be too late!" I said.

"Yes," he chuckled, "they won't be able to get their money back, will they?"

Top: Robert Frost at Ripton, Vermont, August 1949. Bottom: " 'What do you want me to do?' he asked. . . . He grabbed a clothesline running from a tree to the cabin, and managed to look perfectly natural doing it."

Chapter Two

ROBERT FROST

"The idealists . . . call me reactionary for settling for the writing of a few things the world can't deny—"

1

It was late in an August afternoon of 1949 that I climbed to the log cabin at Ripton and found the famous poet standing there as if carved in Vermont marble, staring into space.

I had a lecture to give that night at Bread Loaf in the valley below. A lecture that would become the introduction to *100 Modern Poems,* an anthology bringing "foreigners" like Mayakovsky and Brecht, Neruda and Rilke, Apollinaire and Saint-John Perse into a pantheon of poets peopled thus far by Anglo-Saxons. I'd heard enough about Frost's New England insularity and touchiness to be sure he wouldn't like it. And I loved him enough as a poet to hope that he wouldn't attend and count me among his enemies, though as the presiding genius of the summer seminar, and a nearby resident this particular season, I knew he *might.* So when the "command" came—he wanted to meet me before my lecture—I was elated: not only would I meet Robert Frost at long last, but I'd talk him out of attending!

I introduced myself and asked him what he was doing with the tin pail in his hand.

"Watering my beans—for the eight-hundredth time," he said.

"You looked to me," I said, "as though you were staring into space. I've always suspected that that's what you do, with a poem taking shape in the back of your head, when you're supposed to be farming. Is that your secret?"

His rugged face—the full lips slightly pursed as if to whistle, eyes under white visors as distant as frozen ponds reflecting a blue sky—relaxed. He looked at me quizzically.

39

"I'm not telling," he said. "One has to be secret in order to secrete . . . But come in. I have something for you," and from the cluttered table inside he took a copy of his *Collected Poems*. I read what he'd written on the flyleaf with a mixture of pleasure and guilt: "To Selden Rodman, with a debt of gratitude."

"I'm flattered, but what have I done to deserve it?"

"I have your two earlier anthologies here," he said. "I've been doing my homework. Perhaps I shouldn't be grateful for the Modern Library one in which you include only 'Two Tramps in Mud-Time,' though you were graceful in saying that the poem's all of me. It isn't really, is it?"

"No, of course not. No one poem could be. But it has that effortless quality swinging through its stanzas, with the rhymes seeming to just *be* there—"

"I call that 'hovering'—"

"—and the *loaded* feeling the line has in your poems, as though not another letter, much less a syllable, could be added . . . But as one who's been saying for years that great poems can't be written by professional intellectuals, academics, or even 'just poets,' I guess it's the philosophy of the last lines that clinched it for me. May I remind you:

> My object in living is to unite
> My avocation and my vocation
> As my two eyes make one in sight.
> Only where love and need are one,
> And the work is play for mortal stakes
> Is the deed ever really done
> For Heaven and the future's sakes."

"It's a funny thing," Frost mused. "They called me an escapist for writing that poem. (I do write out of invincible prejudices.) It infuriated the do-gooders—the very idea of my hogging the work, not giving it to the deserving poor, encouraging unemployment, and all that . . . But it was the preface to that anthology of yours that made me think. Your emphasis on humor in poetry, for instance. Not that the world's a joke, or that irony doesn't cover cowardice sometimes—"

"Maybe playfulness is the word for what you do in your poetry," I said, "like the lines about the bear sitting 'on his fundamental butt / With lifted snout and eyes (if any) shut'—"

" 'He almost looks religious but he's not'—?"

"—Which implies a sly criticism of preachers—?"

"Could be. I despise religiosity. But I have no religious doubts. Not about God's existence, anyway. They laughed at Harvard when I said, 'God can count on me never to be disappointed in him,' but I was only dissociating myself from the idealists, those who expect God to be on *their* side, reward justice, vote the straight New Deal ticket, punish our foes. I'm not an optimist—but neither am I a pessimist. I told them, sure, I wished for impossible things, even for perpetual summer sometimes. But I wasn't going to commit suicide if things just went on being the way they always are—longer winters, higher taxes, older age, death at the end. Life always ends badly. The idealists can't accept it that all ages since time began have ended badly. They resent my not thinking that *our* time is worse than any other. They damn me for taking it as I find it. They hate me for singing misunderstandings. They call me reactionary for settling for the writing of a few things the world can't deny—"

"You and Emerson—"

"I liked what you said about Emerson—"

" 'Not meters but a meter-making argument makes a poem'?"

"Yes. When I started this Bread Loaf business, I insisted that having something to say was what mattered, and that the discussions of poetry should begin with experiences. The professors didn't like that. It challenged their omniscience. They know all about prosody, metrics, spelling, and punctuation. They talk about the texture of the cloth, but how many can make a pair of pants? They eased me out."

"You're still here," I said.

He laughed. "Still here—but up the hill with the squirrels."

"And still making pants—"

"Patched, but wearable. What are you making these days?"

I told him of my discovery of the Negro self-taught painter, Horace Pippin, while I was in the army, and how this had led to my involvement with the Haitian artists after the war, and that now I was planning a book about Ben Shahn— "who paints America with the same intense concentration on observed detail and the same respect for remembered experience, letting the content dictate the forms—like the way you write your poems, never rebelling against tradition for the mere sake of rebelling, taking what's usable in the past."

He nodded, but he said he hadn't heard of the artists I was talking about, and I could see that he wasn't really interested in this alien terrain.

"And your poetry?" he said.

"I won't burden you with it," I said, "but *100 American Poems* [1] is new and you said you included it in your 'debt of gratitude.' "

"Well," he said with a smile, "you were kinder to me in that one. At least you included three times as many of my poems! And you said I wear better than Robinson, Masters, and Sandburg, which even my friend Louis Untermeyer might not admit publicly. I liked the way you countered Whitman and Henry James. The opposing commanders in chief, you might say, the Lee and the Grant of our perpetual literary civil war."

"You're conceding Henry (Grant) James the victory, then?"

"Of course not. I wasn't named for Robert Lee for nothing! And look what happened to Grant after he won. The losers have to be the winners in the war that counts . . . I liked the way you drew a line between the expatriates and the homebodies, too. I'm happy to be counted among the stay-at-homes —and to know I have a future!"

I got up to leave and asked him if I could return next

[1] First edition: New York, New American Library, 1948.

morning before my departure for New York, to take some pictures.

"I'll be here," he said, "still drawing water from this well to save my squash and beans. You can take me doing that and perpetuate my rustic image! But I may see you this evening. Ted Morrison says you'll be reading the foreword to a new collection, and that I should listen to it. Should I?"

"Certainly not," I said. "I was with Dick Eberhart and Dick Wilbur when you lectured at Harvard last fall. Your performance was so great that we all resolved never to get on a public platform again. At least not in your presence!"

"Well, if I come," he said, "you won't see me. I'll be a shade among the shadows."

2

I thought of that lecture by Frost in Lampson Hall, on the way to mine; wishing I were there, not here.

All the old clichés applied: he had us in the palm of his hand, we were rolling in the aisles; even when he paused, looking hard and saying nothing, it brought down the house. Simply by being himself . . . But what a self!

He'd begun by saying that poetry must be dissociated from the humanities. "The humanities are in a bad way these days, and besides, we've got to stop thinking of poetry as learning or tragedy. Poetry is play. Even *King Lear* is called 'a play,' isn't it? I'd even rather have you think of it as a sport. For instance, like football—though I hesitate to bring that up here [getting a big laugh for this reference to Harvard's current winless season] than as some kind of an academic solemnity.

"The people who tell you you have to memorize poetry are all wrong," he had continued, "because it's the poetry that memorizes you, if you have a weakness for it, sticking in your mind. That's the key word—'weakness.' I was stopped by a professor once who asked me why I walked in the woods. 'Why?' I said to him, 'because I have a weakness for it.' 'But what do you do in the woods?' he persisted. 'I eat bark,' I said. 'I have a weakness for trees.' "

And then he had told us about the scientist who assured him that science was on a higher level than poetry because science is exact. "I said to him, 'But poetry is exact!' And when he said 'No!' I got up from my chair and said to him, 'From now on we talk about the weather or we don't talk at all'—but I should have told him about the newspaperman who misquoted one of my stories once, because the misquotation perfectly illustrates the point I was making about poetry having to be just as exact as science." [Long pause. Cries from the audience: "The story! The story!"] "The story was about Granny reading her Bible all the time these days, and why? Because she's cramming for her finals. But the newspaperman wrote 'books' instead of 'Bible' . . ."

Chatting that way with his audience without ever raising his voice, flattering us with the illusion that we were a few intimate cronies, Frost had read his poems as casually. He remarked after one poem ("the Muscovite one")—"My, that's bad. I don't ever want to write like *that* again!" Or, lovingly, after a good one: "I *played* with that . . ." Or after the bridegroom couplets, wistfully: "I still wish I knew . . ." Or after another, simply: "That's that." ". . . And here's my only poem in free verse and it's only two lines long. [Long pause.] I never *could* remember anything that doesn't rhyme . . . I guess you'll have to look it up."

We had discussed his magic, walking across Harvard Yard afterward. "He's never pressed for time," Eberhart said, "he never glances at his watch." Once, at another overflow affair, when the power failed and the mike went dead, Wilbur had heard him cry out: "*I* never felt more powerful in my life!"

The will to power was certainly one of Frost's drives, maybe the central one. We'd chatted about sports yesterday while he was putting his tools away. "If I'd brought my racket along could I have lured you into a game of doubles?" I asked him. And he had answered with some asperity, "I still play a little *singles*. But how did you know?" And I had told him I could have guessed tennis was his game from his oft-quoted quip about free verse being like playing with the net down. "I've always thought of poetry," he said, "as something to win or lose—a kind of prowess in the world of letters played with the most subtle and lethal of weapons." And he had gone on to reminisce about his earlier aspirations to pitch in the major leagues—"I was good at it but not that good"—and to play college football—"I used to go at it so hard in school I sometimes threw up after the game!

"But to make it as an athlete," he concluded, "you have to go into training and obey the rules, and that I wasn't prepared to do. I was lazy. I enjoyed fooling around too much, drifting from one home to another, dropping out of Dartmouth, sampling one campus after another, investigating all the angles at my leisure, hiking and botanizing, having not merely thoughts but afterthoughts, writing only when I was elated—so elated that I *had* to write. I remember a boy at a writing seminar telling me once that he'd been told by his professor that the way to write poetry was to sit down and write it, six or eight hours every day. He asked me what would happen to him if he did that, and I said: 'You'll develop a magnificent handwriting.'"

3

He was right about being a shade among the shadows. I didn't see him at the lecture and only found out afterward when the lights were turned on that he'd been there in the back row and slipped out toward the end to cut through the woods to his cabin. "It's not like him," the professor said. "He either doesn't come at all or else he shakes hands with the speaker when it's over."

I decided next morning not to evade the slight. Why had he left, I asked him.

"I was a little hurt," he confessed, "by what you had to say. The pages you devoted to the likes of Rimbaud and Rilke—deserving poets, no doubt, but how can one be sure without being French or German? —Compared with the one sentence devoted to Robert Frost for being, what was the word?— 'flavorless'?"

I was horrified. I explained that what the offending sentence had said was that Frost's pastoral poetry "would be flavorless were it not salted with his characteristic dispraise of city folk." But I felt like the man who reads a retraction on page seventeen of the newspaper that unjustly accused him of rape on page one the day before. The whole lecture, I tried to explain, was part of an effort to enlarge the horizon of Anglo-American verse.

"I don't move forward easily," he said, shaking his head. "In fact I sometimes move two steps *backward* in order to advance a little."

"I know," I said. "As in the sonnet about the brook tumbling backward to its source—what are the lines I'm groping for—?"

"You mean—

> Not chiefly that you may go where you *will*
> But in the rush of everything to waste,
> That you may have the power of standing still—"?

"Exactly," I said, relieved to be taken off the hook. "The mainstream of modern poetry is so eager to get in step with the Second Law of Thermodynamics that it may boil over the brink and dissolve before ever meeting its unpanting public . . . Egged on by Ezra, of course."

He laughed. "You know Pound?"

I told him of our meetings, at Rapallo and more recently at St. Elizabeth's.[2] "What was Pound like when you knew him?" I asked.

"He was a flashy dresser," Frost replied, "but the Byron collars and Japanese dressing gowns didn't go with his shrill Idaho voice. He was full of generous enthusiasms, but possessive. Even before I'd met him in London in 1913 he was

[2] See below, Chapter 3, pp. 57–58.

eager to promote me. He made off with the first and only copy of *A Boy's Will*—it didn't matter that *I* was without one: I was only the writer of the damn book. And when he reviewed it he made offensive use of things I'd told him in confidence about my family. So that I ended by wishing he *hadn't* liked it. It was as though he were boasting to the world—his world, the literary world, the élitist corner of that world to be more exact—'Look! I'm so powerful I can take even this New England yokel and make a celebrity out of him!'"

"And he did, in a sense," I reminded him, "you wouldn't deny that, would you?"

"Whatever I was or am I would have been anyway. Should I be grateful because he hastened the process by a few weeks or months? Perhaps I should be . . . but I was never after that kind of success, the kind they call 'of esteem,' that meant so much to Ezra. I wanted to reach out to all kinds, and be read by people who didn't give a hoot in hell about Greeks and Provençals. I had no intention of sitting in a London club and looking down my nose—"

"Like T. S. Eliot?"

"Like Eliot who had the gall to sit there and tell me that Bobby Burns was only a passable writer of songs."

"You haven't skewered my particular bête noire," I said.

"Williams?"

"No. I love Williams as much as I do you, and for a lot of the same reasons. I was hoping you'd pay your disrespects to Wallace Stevens."

His eyes lighted up with wonderful malice. "Stevens and I ran afoul of each other in Key West years ago. He said the most cutting thing he could think of—'You write short stories in verse'—to which I answered, 'You write bric-a-brac.' "

"I had lunch with him in Hartford once," I said, "and said something that probably offended him more. I said, 'Why don't you write about the insurance business?' "

Frost laughed. "You hit the nail on the head—his head. That would be like asking Eliot to write about banking. Or Amy

47

about her bluebloods. The poetry is dry and bloodless as soon as you separate it from what you are—and do. It becomes poetry about poetry, or about something you know nothing about at all, like Ezra's funny-money quackery that got him in so much trouble. It's a mistake all young poets make . . . What was the first poem you ever wrote?"

"It was a ballad about a character in the Inferno, Piero della Vigne."

"There! You see? I did the same thing myself. My first poem was about Cortéz and the terrible things he did to the Indians. I'd never been to Mexico and I'd never seen an Indian. Perhaps MacLeish has, but I suspect that his epic of the Conquest came out of books. Out of two books—"

"Prescott?"

"And Saint-John Perse, whom you mentioned last night."

"Isn't that a little like damning Shakespeare for taking his plots from Holinshed and his style from Marlowe?" I said. "Milton was certainly a bookish poet, and so is Yeats."

"Yeats, like Milton, was up to his ears in politics; he wasn't trying, as MacLeish put it once, to be untimely. But Yeats was always *faking,* in his life and in his verse—like Ezra. Of course I agree with you that Ezra's poetry should be judged as poetry. And I think you were right during the war to refuse to let Random House cut his poems out of your anthology. But when Pound broadcast for the enemy he wasn't acting as a poet. He deserved to be hung as a traitor to his country—and got off easily."

I told him I had to leave and we walked out into the sunlight for some pictures.

"What do you want me to do?" he asked.

"Hang on to the nearest thing for dear life," I suggested.

He grabbed a clothesline running from a tree to the cabin, and managed to look perfectly natural doing it.

"Speaking of what we read," he said, "I told a reporter from *Time* the other day that my system was to stand in front of a bookcase, pull out books at random, and if one turned out to be interesting, sit down and read it. I guess that's the weak-

48

ness of my poetry. It's 'occasional' poetry, written out of pleasure in idleness, to give pleasure.

"The trouble with the United States," he went on, still hanging from the rope, "is the word 'happiness' in the Declaration. Why wasn't Jefferson honest enough to say 'wine, women, and song'? Happiness is a mirage. My life has taught me that much, or that little—look at what happened to my family, but I won't go into *that*. Wine, women, and song can be pursued and won. And the song—the poetry—must be soft but not flabby, hard but not like nails."

Top: Ernest Hemingway with his wife Mary at Finca Vigia, 1951. "The bottle of Haitian rum," he later commented, "was most *photogénique*." Bottom: "'If you ever write...don't say that I've ever been to any wars!'"

Chapter Three

ERNEST HEMINGWAY

". . . I'm simply a man trying to write well in the most difficult time we've had since the Dark Ages."

1

Hemingway's genius, like Lord Byron's, was essentially comic; but unlike Byron, Hemingway, though he died at sixty-two rather than thirty-six, never lived to write his *Don Juan*.

The parallels didn't occur to me when I was writing an undergraduate paper at Yale on the incest motif in Byron's poetry, but by the time Hemingway had gone to Spain a few years later they had become unmistakable. Recruiting, publicizing, trying to arouse the conscience of the world over the violated Iberian republic—as Byron had when the cause of Greek independence was similarly "lost"—Hemingway didn't find his Missolonghi, but he pursued it relentlessly in the world-wide extension of Spain's tragic conflict.

There are so many other parallels. Wounds of the body traumatized the minds of both writers, though the clubfoot Byron had to live with from birth seems to have undermined his assurance of manhood less than whatever Hemingway suffered at Fossalta. Both men invented a language in which to converse publicly, and both used it in letters which (until Byron made his comic breakthrough) were superior to their self-conscious creations. Both were amateur boxers. Byron's exploits as a swimmer hardly became the obsession that hunting was throughout Hemingway's career, but the image they sought to project—of the writer putting his very life on the line to quash the stereotype of the sedentary intellectual—was the same.

But the question is: Was Hemingway too long-gone in the destructive myth he had acted out to cover his guilts and fears?

Could he have exorcised them, as Byron did, in a comic masterpiece at his own expense? What I drew out of him, during the one day we talked at length, may give a hint of the comedy Hemingway was capable of.

2

It was perhaps the first really dark month of his life, that April of 1951. The darker ones were yet to come—Uganda, with the two near-fatal plane crack-ups; Spain, following the matadors to their gorings with more than a schoolboy's lust for murderous action; Rochester, Minnesota, seeking his own death openly, and in Ketchum, Idaho, finding it. April had been especially dark because of the euphoria that preceded it. He had come close to convincing himself that *Across the River and into the Trees* was his best book instead of his worst. He had told Lillian Ross boastfully: "It's sort of fun to be fifty and feel you are going to defend the title again." He'd even told his publisher that he was "trying to knock Mr. Shakespeare on his ass." And then had come the reactions to the *New Yorker* profile which everyone except Miss Ross (and Hemingway?) had considered a lethal exposure of posturing vanity. And the reviews of the novel—which almost everyone but John O'Hara had greeted with derision or sadness.

Only the publication in 1952 of the novella *The Old Man and the Sea* had kept Hemingway from sinking then and there into the pugnacious lethargy that was soon to engulf him. He must have known that the little book had recaptured something of the old magic, and if he didn't the hated critics were quick to tell him so. I was among them in a sense, for the Book-of-the-Month Club, hearing that I had left Haiti to visit Hemingway in Cuba, asked me if I would contribute a brief "profile" to accompany their selection.

I had met Hemingway twenty years earlier in Paris. I had just graduated from Yale and was traveling with William Harlan Hale, my roommate and cofounder of a brash and notorious college magazine. Hale had criticized the early

Hemingway novels rather sharply. I don't know whether Hemingway was aware of that, but he had heard that Hale had had an encounter in New York with a character at the Explorers' Club who was passing himself off as the famous author of *The Sun Also Rises* and *A Farewell to Arms,* and Hemingway wanted to hear about his double firsthand. I don't remember much about our luncheon at Lipps except that Hemingway introduced us to the *"distingué,"* a glass that must have held a quart of beer and several of which he downed while we were working over our first, and that he spoke of our publication with characteristic generosity.

From Haiti, where I was directing the mural painting of the Cathedral Ste.-Trinité, I had invited Hemingway and his wife to come over and see the work-in-progress, and stay with my (then) wife, Maia Wojciechowska, and me. I had a special interest in wanting to see his Miró ("The Farm"), for I had just included in an anthology those paragraphs from *Death in the Afternoon* which described Miró's Catalonian ambiance. Fortunately I could see the picture, for the Hemingways couldn't make it to Port-au-Prince but invited us to visit them in Cuba instead.

The Finca Vigia at San Francisco de Paulo has been described too often. Picking us up at the Havana airport in mid-morning, the Hemingways' chauffeur, Juan, drove us out to it, with a stop en route at the famous "Floridita" for ice cream.

Hemingway was at work but came out to greet us. Barefooted, he was wearing blue Bermuda shorts and a T-shirt, and I didn't think he'd changed much except for the grizzling and perhaps a thinness at the ankles which overemphasized his muscular calves. The beard I'd seen in recent pictures was gone. And gone too was the truculence ("Daughter, remember that I never carried Teddy bears to bed with me since I was four. . . .") that had accompanied Miss Ross from the Sherry-Netherland to Abercrombie & Fitch and back.

"Yes, I remember those *distingués* at Lipps very well," Hemingway said. "But now, on the *Pilar* when the fish don't bite, Mary and I read to each other from your anthology." He put an arm around my shoulder and whispered: "You didn't *pay* for that thing of mine, did you?"

"Of course," I said.

"Oh, shit! . . . But we'll talk about that at lunch, or after lunch in the tower."

We had a swim in the pool, picking leaves off the bottom, while he finished his writing. Mary, with characteristic insight and tact, brought us up to date on the latest chapters in the Hemingway saga. I wondered whether she had always had, or acquired from her husband, that genius for making guests feel immediately that they were intimates, almost members of the family. When Hemingway finally emerged and we sat drinking some of the Barbancourt we had brought them from Haiti, I decided to get the boring questions over with before lunch—and while I was sober enough to take down his answers. I asked him what he was working on now, and how he worked. The fullness of his answers surprised me, and his humility—in such glaring contrast to the public image—impressed me.

"I'm working on a very long project," he began, "made up of many books. I'll publish parts when they're ready, like this story of the big fish and the sharks that Scribner's has. I've worked on the project for years—and will for the rest of my life, I guess. Last year I rewrote and cut down from over 250,000 words to 186,000."

"The speed of light," I said, "and it's all about the Gulf Stream, like Santiago's episode—?"

"Selden," he interrupted, "I'm no good telling about what I'm writing, so you'll forgive me for not going into it now. It's always a bad sign when people talk about what they're writing. The worst sign is when they read parts of it aloud before it's finished. I hope to live a long time and if I'm lucky I'll try to write better. I have enough stuff planned to last me into my seventies. Let's say I'm simply a man trying to write well in the most difficult time we've had since the Dark Ages. I'm fully aware, too, that almost all the subjects have been written about before."

"Where do you do most of the work?" I asked him.

"I wrote *The Old Man and the Sea,* a sort of epilogue to the big project, standing up in the room we just left. But when I rewrite, it's in the library or the tower. I'd write in the tower all the time except that I get lucky sometimes writing somewhere else and then I hate to change. In the hot months I start at five or six in the morning and work until I'm through. Then I go down to the pool to swim. Sometimes you get it like a fever, and then you work through the afternoon too, and on into the evening. But I try to finish in the morning and then get enough exercise to keep in good shape and be tired enough to sleep to start fresh in the morning."

"Can you work anywhere else these days?"

"I've always loved Cuba and worked well here," he answered. "America is fine and so is Europe, but here you have the Gulf Stream right at your door almost. It's one of the last unspoiled places. You take Yoknapatawpha County, and I'll take the ocean. I love my own country and I love France and Italy and Spain and Cuba. I've loved to live and work in all of them, and I hope to live and work in all of them again. Right now I live and work here and I guess that's really because it's the closest to the place I love best and that moves me the most—the Gulf Stream."

"I've read that you get some of your exercise playing jai-alai and some of it sparring—with Kid Gavilan among others."

He laughed. "I'd have no occasion to spar with Gavilan Keed. He's a welterweight and I'm a heavyweight. I box, when I box, with heavyweights. You know what a thankless business *that* is. I'd be crazy to play *jai alai*. To be any good you learn that about the same age you learn ski-jumping. Before so many of our best friends among the *jai alai* players went to Mexico, they all used to come out here a couple of times a week to play tennis. We'd also box and play water polo. But now I get most of my exercise swimming or walking in the hills around here or fishing in the Gulf Stream. If I get a couple of big fish a week it keeps me in good shape. The main trouble is to avoid people interrupting you. That was what drove me out of Key West. I like people. But if they come in while you're working it ruins your work. Mary keeps them out, and when she goes north to visit her family I usually go down the coast somewhere on the boat and write on a drawing board.

"But all this must bore the shit out of you, since you know all the problems a guy has when he writes. If you work as hard and well as you can you're exhausted when you're through. If you're not exhausted you didn't work as hard as you could. Then it's necessary to get some exercise to be tired enough physically to sleep and not wake and think about what you're writing. Inventing from knowledge is the most fun I have, but sometimes it's rougher than a corncob. Naturally when you get through with a long period of writing you try and relax completely."

"That was when Miss Ross caught you," I said.

He grimaced. "If you ever write anything from the notes you're taking, don't say that I've ever been to any wars! Since that last book where I tried to make a portrait of a soldier, there's a school of critics that feels I'm a sort of thwarted (or practicing) militarist. I don't really think this is true and I'd like to correct it. One outfit believes I'm a victim of traumatic neuroses . . . But as I was saying, after writing you try to relax. Somebody sees you then and thinks, how can this relaxed oversized animal that won't be serious about anything be a good writer? They don't see you when you get out of bed at daylight and start working and won't say a word to anyone till your work is done. These people think a serious writer has to be solemn or pompous. They don't seem to realize that when you have to be serious is when you're *writing,* and that you're serious enough then so that you don't have to spend the rest of your life being an *homme des lettres.* Between us, did you ever notice that most of the writers who issue statements about how they never leave their homes, and so on, issue them at cocktail parties given by their publishers in New York celebrating publication of their books? They never go to cocktail parties, they say—at the cocktail parties. They never come to New York, they say—in New York. They wouldn't know a critic if they saw one, they say—to the critics. How come they are there, they ask wonderingly. They probably think they're in West Memphis and what's the party all about anyway? Books? What you mean books? They're just old dirt farmers. You'd never catch them at one of these New York cocktail parties.

"Of course," he concluded as we moved to the lunch table, "there are the other kind of beloved writers, the ones that claim they don't even know they're writing. They're just so natural they can't help it!"

Conversation during the meal was difficult. Hemingway and I sat together facing the Miró painting, but that was the least of the distractions. It was Mary's birthday and a troupe of guitarists were there to serenade her. They were invited to share lunch, and so was a burly Basque, Andres Untzain, the parish priest of Melena del Sur, who sang loudly throughout the meal to the incessant thrumming. The more red wine the padre drank, the louder he sang—and the louder he sang, the softer became Hemingway's voice as he spoke to me behind his right hand into my left ear.

"You've seen Pound at St. Elizabeth's?" he asked.

I said that Caresse Crosby had taken me to see him, along with Kenneth Rexroth, and that on our way out Rexroth kept muttering, "Crazy as a bedbug, crazy as a bedbug."

"He's that far gone?" Hemingway asked.

"I know you admire him," I said, "but he never made much sense to me, even in Rapallo where I went to see him long before his Fascist broadcasts. He had a great ear for poetry, and I know he was generous to other poets, but as far as what he ever had to say, Rexroth was right. And I have plenty of Pound's letters written to me during the Thirties to prove it."

"I have quite a few myself," Hemingway said with a smile. "But what was he saying at the hospital that was so crazy?"

"He was saying, 'Roosevelt's real aims? Ask Morgenthau.'

Or 'Truman's real aims? Read Meyer's sheet this morning.' Or 'Who's keeping me here? Ask Barney Baruch!' Or 'It don't matter what I say. Will people *never* learn!' "

Hemingway laughed. "I can hear him saying it! That was his favorite expression. But they shouldn't keep him locked up. He's harmless, and a great poet."

"I agree that he's harmless," I said, "and that he's paid the price for his treason. But a great poet? Influential, yes. Original, no doubt. Great, no. He's narrow, too full of bile, too bookish, too much of a faker." And I told him of the time in Florence I'd gone with Eugenio Montale to hear Pound lecture in Italian—"On *you*, I think it was! At any rate on the new novelists . . . I'd had a year of Italian at Yale and I turned to Montale after the lecture and said triumphantly, 'I understood every word Ezra said!' And Montale answered, 'Maybe you did, but I haven't understood a word of it!' "

Hemingway asked me about the Haitian artists I'd been working with—and what did I think of Joan Miró, pointing at the great picture in front of us.

"When Miró had so many of their qualities, as in your picture with its wealth of exact observation, I was crazy about him."

"Then you prefer Giotto, say, to Tintoretto or Goya?"

"That's different," I said. "None of them were primitives. And neither are you—though Lillian Ross sure makes you look like one!"

"It was a disaster," he said, shaking his head.

"And O'Hara's review in *The New York Times,* calling you 'the most important author since Shakespeare'—?"

"—A worse disaster," he said. "They shouldn't compare you to Willie."

His words coincided with a lull in the music. "Willie who?" said Mary at the other end of the table.

"Willie Mays," I said.

"I was saying," Hemingway said, "who would the Yankees trade to get him from the Giants?"

"Anybody but Yogi or Mickey," I said.

The conversation had leveled off appropriately, for some Cuban baseball players had now come in to pay their respects to "Papa." But Hemingway was intrigued by the way we were playing games with time, and when we climbed up into his tower after lunch and several more drinks, he was all set to pursue it. He had the *Journals of André Gide* lying open on his desk and asked me if I'd read it. I had.

"Do you think I could be an *homme des lettres*?" he asked.

"I think it would be out of character," I said. "Lillian Ross quotes you as saying you couldn't learn from Gide or Valéry, they were too smart . . . But you could try."

"How would you like to hear fragments from Ernst von Hemingstein's Journal?"

"I would."

He leaned over some notes on the desk but appeared to be improvising as he went along:

"Friday.—Saw Valéry. He looked very poorly. We both agreed Joyce's eyes were bad and that Gide is now impotent. Fargue is dead. A pity.

"Saturday.—Practiced all morning on the clavichord. Bach is more satisfying than ever. Poor Gide. Dinner with Sylvia and Adrienne. The food was never better.

"Sunday.—The Scribners (father and son) are publishing my *The Sun Also Rises.* It is a treatise on basic loneliness and the inadequacy of promiscuity. Perkins, the Scribners' editor is enthused. Not as much for the moral content but what he naïvely calls the dialogue. I must study how to eliminate this as well as the over-long descriptions of the Spanish countryside.

"Monday.—Lunched at Lipps with two young American writers, Rodman and Hale. Liked Rodman. Hale a bit over-promising."

"Tuesday.—Drunk with Joyce in the literal rather than the figurative sense.

"Wednesday.—Learn Fargue is alive not dead. Splendid. Another report on Gide, this time from *******. Most depressing. Learned that the young Hale was not the son of Nathan Hale as I had supposed.

"Thursday.—Commenced writing a new novel. It is to be called *A Farewell to Arms* and treats of the war on the Italian front which I visited briefly as a boy after the death of Henry James. A strange coincidence. Some difficulty about deciding how the book will end. Solved it finally.

"Friday.—Attended the Crucifixion of Our Lord. Tintoretto was there. He took copious notes and appeared to be very moved. Dined with Goya. He asserted the entire spectacle was a fraud. He was his usual irascible self but sound company. He says Joyce drinks too much and confirmed several new anecdotes of Gide. The unfortunate Gide, it seems, was refused admission to the Crucifixion as they have decided (officially) to call it. Goya offered me La Alba for the evening. Really charming of him. A well spent evening.

"Saturday.—Poor Goya is poxed again. A—— is furious. I worked all afternoon removing mold from old bread I had been saving to make penicillin for Goya. He says I am his only friend now that A—— has turned on him. Dined with A—— at the palace. What a lovely woman.

"Sunday.—Finished *Death in the Afternoon*. Did it in three days, including printing and developing the photographs. A—— says she is truly proud to see me working on something for a change. A change from what? I asked her. She answered, Don't be a damned fool. Her English is improving steadily and she is more charming every day. Tintoretto (Giacomo) has asked us both to Venice. There will be just the two of us, Giotto and himself. Giotto spent the evening drawing perfect circles. A—— says she believes this to be a monomania and that she would be happier if he drew an occasional ellipse. Goya rather depressed but says the improved penicillin is working wonders.

"Monday.—Pound turned up here. He is immensely popular because of some broadcasting he has been doing, in Greece I believe. Goya kept confusing him with Whistler and called him Jimmy. He kept telling him how much he enjoyed his Nocturnes. La Alba kept telling him, Nocturnes is Chopin. Flaubert kept interrupting to say Chopin was a consumptive

Pole and recounted a very drole incident with George Sand. Part of it was incredible. La Alba enjoyed it thoroughly. She has nicknamed Flaubert "Go-Go." Pound left during all this as he was lecturing for something called St. Elizabeth's. I had never thought of him as particularly religious.

"*Tuesday.*—We have all decided to go to Cuba. I completed *For Whom The Bell Tolls* and am hoping to qualify for a Guggenheim Fellowship. Guggenheim is an immensely important American millionaire who subsidizes American and Central and South American artists. Giotto has been trying for years for one of these fellowships but the story is that Guggenheim does not care for his painting. Also he is or is said to be Italian. With the writing of this last short book which is an attempt at analysis of certain aspects of the Spanish character, Goya says I may very well qualify for a fellowship. We shall see . . ."

"Well," Hemingway said, looking up from his notes, "what do you think?"

"I think you have a future as an *homme des lettres,*" I said. "In fact, I think you could work this up into a comic masterpiece. Especially if you keep the parts satirizing yourself, and make them even more pointed, as Byron does in *Don Juan.* Who now reads *Manfred?* Or *Childe Harold,* which made Byron a popular sensation all over Europe in his lifetime?" I would have liked to add that Byron stopped acting a part. But I didn't want to risk jeopardizing our very brief friendship. "Anyway," I said, "I hope you'll put this trial run on paper and send it to me."

He said he would. And he did.

Upper left: Pablo Neruda with his wife, Matilde, near Isla Negra, Chile, 1966. Upper right: En route to Valparaiso, 1969. " 'I love to pose like Mussolini,' he chuckled." Lower left: At the author's home in Oakland, New Jersey, 1966. Lower right: With Nicanor Parra at Isla Negra, 1970. " 'I'm so sure of myself now . . . I could live under Pablo's bed!' "

Chapter Four

PABLO NERUDA

". . . I can be realist and subjectivist, political and non-political, all at the same time, and sometimes even in the same poem. But if you have this sense of the totality of life, they say you are not free!"

1

The fact that Pablo Neruda has been a political activist for most of his mature life has had little to do with his popularity as a poet. Those who share his allegiance to the Soviet cause may read him more avidly on that account; but those who don't, shrug their shoulders, ignore the five per cent of overtly political poems, and happily go on devouring the rest of the Chilean laureate's stupendous *oeuvre*. One of the most popular of his books has always been *Veinte Poemas de Amor y una Canción Desesperada* ("Twenty Love Poems and a Desperate Song") written when Neruda had no political convictions of any kind; but no one would contend that this is his best book, or even that the startlingly original surrealist poems of *Residencia en la Tierra* ("Residence on Earth"), that also preceded his political conversion, are the whole Neruda; or even that his politics have not contributed substantially to the zeal with which he identifies himself with the common man.[1]

What makes Pablo Neruda's poetry uniquely universal in the world today is neither the youthful ardor, nor the surrealism, nor the Marxist philosophy, important though these have been in shaping it. Rather it is Neruda's capacity to project his own personality, unflaggingly over the years, as a particular person who feels, sees, eats, drinks, suffers, enjoys, loves, dreams, laughs, dawdles, gossips—one who invites his

---

[1] This chapter was written before Pablo Neruda's death from cancer in September 1973 and the fall of the Marxist government which he had represented in Paris. Our talks about politics, always in collision, and sometimes violently, were omitted at the request of the poet, and there was no time to reinsert them.

soul, as his idol Walt Whitman put it, and rarely lacks the magic (as Walt often did) to make his most inconsequential thoughts seem important.

Like Whitman, too, Neruda best manages to elude the vices of abstraction and rhetorical windiness associated with their kind of poetry by identifying himself with a particular place in a particular time. There is nothing quaintly regionalist about Neruda's love affair with Chile. Nor is he possessive about it, as Gabriela Mistral often was, identifying Chile with her sexual frustrations. Were that so, Neruda's poetry would appeal mainly to Chileans. On the contrary, he has always conducted his affair on such a plane that every reader tends to see his own country in the poet's intimate concern—sometimes brotherly, sometimes indulgent, sometimes chiding, sometimes despairing. Moreover Neruda ranges over the whole of Latin America in his search for what is common (and universal) in the Iberian experience; and sometimes even to Europe, North America, and the Orient, being at pains to point out that he is no flag-waver:

> They have talked to me of Venezuelas,
> of Paraguays and Chiles.
> I don't know what it is they say.
> I only know the skin of earth
> and that it has no name.

But it is to Chile, nevertheless, that the poet always returns, to his roots and for his substance.

2

In Lima on the eve of my first meeting with Neruda in 1966, I had had a talk with Clayton Eshleman, César Vallejo's translator, about these greatest of South America's poets. Eshleman contended that Vallejo's political conversion in 1938 was "impersonal" and "pure" whereas Neruda's (they were together in Spain, witnessing the debacle of the Spanish Republic) was "subjective" and "self-serving." What Eshleman was really saying, I thought, was that Vallejo was a poet's poet, too remote from everyday "reality" to make any connection between the political creed which he naïvely accepted and the metaphysical verse through which he identified his tormented alienation with the world's misery; Neruda, conversely, was the romantic poet, making poems as effortlessly out of his new-found religion of brotherhood as he had out of the despairing nihilism of his youthful *Weltschmerz*. So it was in part to test my preference for the Whitman-poet that I resolved to fly to Santiago.

I wrote Neruda a letter, mentioning the 1947 anthology in which I had included one of his early surrealist poems, and he invited me to visit him. The time could not have been more favorable. There was little to fan our banked political differences. Vietnam had not yet burst into flames. Khrushchev had exposed Stalin's mass executions so vigorously that Russian poetry itself was beginning to emerge from the underground. The tanks had not yet rolled into Czechoslovakia. And in Chile extremists of left and right were in disarray as the moderate Christian Democrat President, Eduardo Frei, gave the deceptive appearance of knowing how to curb the nation's foreign and native monopolists by legal means.

Neruda's mood was as relaxed. The first big book of his poems in English translation was soon to appear in New York. For the first time he had been invited to read publicly in the United States, and he contemplated accepting. His friend Nemésio Antunes, the painter, represented the Frei government in New York, and another close friend, Gabriel Valdez, was Frei's Foreign Minister. "There," he said, smiling and pointing at the Chilean Senate as his wife Matilde drove us from the airport in their Opel through downtown Santiago, "is where I spent the two dullest years of my life. Never again!"

At the airport I had had my first inkling of this poet's unprecedented role in a nation's society. I was standing in the plane's door with Bill Negron, who had accompanied me from Lima to make drawings. The Chilean hostess, observing our bewilderment as we contemplated the sea of faces, asked us whom we were looking for. "—Pablo Neruda?

Everybody knows Pablo Neruda!" and she pointed to a stocky figure in a tweed coat with a snap-brim fedora. Within a minute Neruda had greeted us in almost perfect English, introduced his Titian-haired wife, and rushed us through customs without inspection. The sixty-two-year-old poet had discarded his dimunitive hat by now, and I had a chance to study his features as he pointed out proudly the capital's blackened monuments profiled against the snowy Andes. His face is curiously Oriental. Sad, down-slanting eyes, in an almost square face, have drooping lids. He is virtually bald; and heavy without being fat, except in the beam. His eyebrows are perpetually arched, giving him a quizzical expression. There is a lurking almost childlike half-smile on his mouth, even in repose. As he shapes his thoughts, his eyes half close. He doesn't use his hands when talking, seeming too self-possessed to gesture. His conversation is like a soliloquy, but with every now and then a sideways glance to make sure the listener is listening. But Neruda listens, following a speaker's face with rapt attention. There is adoration in his look when Matilde speaks. He jokes, and laughs easily.

Since we had had dinner on the plane, Neruda suggested we spend the rest of the evening "at a very special *boîte,* 'La Peña de los Parra,' where you will hear the most authentic Chilean folk singing. The night club was started by Violetta Parra, Nicanor's sister, and our best folk singer and tapestry weaver." At the entrance, decorated by cork-float fishing nets and candles in bottles, the poet explained that this was his first visit and that we would slip in quickly "to avoid any demonstration." He was greeted, nonetheless, with much clapping and toasts in *vino rojo.* The walls were covered with graffitti and pictographs in drymark—Bob Dylan, the Picasso "Dove of Peace," quatrains, one of which went:

> Viva Chile and Peru
> And the valiant of Bolivia,
> But more valiant was my father
> For marrying my mother.

The music was sorrowful and Neruda explained that it was an amalgam of all Chile. "The flute is from the desert north, the guitar from the central highlands, the drum from Polynesian Easter Island—which we acquired, I like to say, when a Chilean sea captain spent the night with their queen and pleased her so much that she gave him the whole island next morning."

On the way to our hotel several hours later, Neruda suggested that we spend a week as their guests at Isla Negra on the Pacific. We explained that our families were stranded in Lima and that the weekly flight to La Paz, where we'd left our bags, would be leaving Arica the following night.

"If imperialistic Chile hadn't grabbed little Bolivia's only seaport, we could fly to Peru directly," I said with a smile.

"Then I'll pick you up at the Crillon tomorrow at nine and we'll spend the day talking—about more recent imperialisms!"

Neruda telephoned at nine to say that we'd have to come by taxi. "Matilde's brother died an hour ago and she's out making arrangements."

We expressed regret for his wife's loss. "Hell," he said philosophically, "we all have to die some time, don't we? Even *I* have to die. Come over and keep me company while I'm still alive."

The Nerudas' Santiago house is at the end of a curving blind alley at the foot of Cerro San Cristobal, a steep butte with a funicular, park, and zoo in the center of the capital. We heard lions roaring as we climbed. The house is built on many levels. The gardens, outdoor ovens, summer houses (one with wooden caryatids and a moldering upright piano) climb with it. There is also an aqueduct of rushing brown water winding through the benches and tables, shade trees, and a heavily laden grape arbor. A hose was spouting into the shrubbery as we sat down. "Rain is very important for poetry," Neruda remarked. "I was born at Parral in the center of Chile, a region of grapes and wine, but three months later my family moved to Temuco which is very dry."

"How did that affect you?"

"I don't know . . . Gabriela Mistral came from the north," he mused, "where there is only cactus and sand; but she survived."

"What triggered her poetry—and yours?"

"Rubén Darío was the great influence on all of us," he said. "—Not for what he said but for what he did to the language: the greatest transformation in Spanish poetry since Góngora. After Darío, Spanish America's greatest poets have been Vicente Huidobro—who imported a French way of looking at things, just as Darío had—Gabriela Mistral, César Vallejo, and López Velarde. Here, in the generation forty-five to fifty, Juvencio Valle and Nicanor Parra are very good. Enrique Lihn is thirty and very good too."

Matilde was back now and drove us to the local art galleries. In the car I asked Neruda whether he was still a Communist.

"Of course," he said. "I am a member of the Party's Central Committee, but I haven't been running for office since I was a senator in 1946–49. That was enough. We have two senators and twenty deputies now, but at that time we foolishly expected great things from the new President. I had been his propaganda chief during the campaign. But as soon as he was elected he began to persecute us. I called him a traitor and had to go into hiding. For three years I was in exile abroad. But today," he went on, "Chile's biggest enemies are not the politicians, or even the banks. They are the big American-owned copper companies that force us to fix prices at rates injurious to our economic health. Your State Department says to us, 'Reduce the price and we will give you that $10,000,000 loan.' We are not our own masters."

"Is Frei accomplishing anything?" I asked.

"Frei has good intentions and is honest," he said, "like Belaúnde in Peru. Belaúnde is the prisoner of the military. Frei is weak. He is doing a little to break up and distribute the big estates, but nothing at all to antagonize foreign capital. You can't make an omelet without breaking eggs."

As I got out of the car, I reached back in through the window to pick up my pen, almost losing my fingers as

Neruda rolled up the window. "You've put him up to this," I said to Negron, "so I'll have to play tennis next week with my left hand."

Neruda laughed. "If I injure you, your country will say: 'You see? That Communist Neruda is deliberately crippling our writers!' "

Back at their house, we had our first sumptuous Nerudian luncheon: fried albacore covered with tiny shrimps soaked in garlic sauce; chicken with rice; hearts of palm and tomato salad; white wine and red; peaches and grapes; smashed strawberries on sherbet; coffee and cakes. Neruda at the head of the table looked as Chinese as the watercolor hanging behind him, a man on a horse which he'd brought back from China; and on he talked as the hours passed, describing more exotic Chilean dishes we must sample, reciting poetry, joking, autographing a half dozen books he had had his publisher send over by messenger.

"Pablo," I said, "we have to leave in half an hour. Sit down with me over there under the arbor and tell me whether Latin American literature is in decline. Are the young replacing *indigenismo* with anything as vital?"

He thought for a moment. "For me it's very difficult to associate a writer's work with a movement," he said. *"Indigenismo,* realism, are only words. Writers like Ciro Alegría were important because they looked at their country for the first time closely—and with compassion. Before that we had volcanoes and strange animals but they had no names. The function of a surrealist here was to give names to things. Realists and subjectivists were too self-conscious to do that. The great writer, a Blake, a Góngora, a Quevedo, is not very conscious of what he is saying. He just has to say it—and in that particular way. For me, I can be realist and subjectivist, political and nonpolitical, all at the same time, and even sometimes in the same poem. But if you have this sense of the totality of life, they say you are not free! Nobody has ever *asked* me to write a political poem. If the subject didn't touch me, I couldn't. I haven't written a poem about your intervention in the Dominican Republic, for instance, but I am free to write one.

Poets like T. S. Eliot and Saint-John Perse are *not* free to. They are hobbled by conventions. Their conventions inhibit them, tell them that such a subject must wait a hundred years to be usable. After a hundred years the blood will be washed away by the rain. I prefer the blood to the rain."

"The Russians, the official ones anyway, claim to be social realists," I said.

"I don't believe in social realism," he said. "That label, that way of looking at things, is prefabricated. I want to taste the wine before it is bottled. You quoted from 'Song of Myself' at lunch. Did Whitman assume a label or justify a position? No! He was alive—with blood and life."

I asked his opinion of Vallejo's poetry.

"Vallejo was a great poet," he said, "and a good Communist as well. He brought to the Spanish language the structure and way of thinking of the Indians. Of his weaknesses he made a style. This is often the case, as with Gabriela Mistral—her faults were so strong, but she fought them so hard. So with Vallejo. I took him from Paris to the Writers' Congress in Spain. I discovered Octavio Paz on the same journey. Picasso never knew Vallejo; he made that famous drawing after Vallejo's death—that death from slow starvation in Paris. His poetry is lyric, idealistic, but not overtly Marxist."

"And Nicanor Parra—?" I asked.

"Parra is a mixture of the popular and the sophisticated. This gives a piquant unexpectedness to his idiom. He's the most inventive Chilean poet. He's not a Communist, but he is to the left—like all Latin American poets. The tension, the repression, the drama of our outsideness historically speaking, doesn't permit us the luxury of being uncommitted. Lihn is a Communist but is quite subjective in his verse. Here in Chile poets are more important than novelists. Manuel Rojas is one of our few novelists. But there are many Latin novelists abroad: Fernando Alegría, Alejo Carpentier, Miguel Angel Asturias, Carlos Fuentes. The painters, as you observed, can play games; but all literature in Latin America today is engaged."

On the way to the airport, Neruda renewed his invitation

to visit him at Isla Negra—"on the way back from Bolivia, perhaps?"

"I have to finish my book on Peru."

"Then come back next year and write one about Chile."

"Will Chile help me?"

"Of course. When you say 'I am the North American poet' they will give you everything you want." He winked. "Say the word 'poet' very softly."

"Can I get to Easter Island?"

"The Chilean Navy will take you. They go once a year, on January 6. They refuse to take me. But I will go as your secretary!"

3

What is most startling about Neruda, I think, when we compare him to Eliot or Dylan Thomas or Pound, is the great affection that accompanies his imagination. Neruda read his poetry for the first time in the United States in June 1966 at the Poetry Center in New York, and it was clear from that reading that his poetry is intended as a gift. When Eliot gave a reading, one had the feeling that the reading was a cultural experience, and that Eliot doubted very much if you were worth the trouble, but he'd try anyway. When Dylan Thomas read, one had the sense that he was about to perform some magical and fantastic act . . . maybe you would benefit from this act, and maybe you wouldn't. Pound used to scold the audience for not understanding what he did. When Neruda reads, the mood in the room is one of affection between the audience and himself.

The description is Robert Bly's, quoted by Clayton Eshleman as part of his continuing assault on Neruda as poet and man.[2] If one had not read Pound or Eliot or Thomas, (says Eshleman, counterpunching Bly) "one might NOT jerk back and exclaim, *But he is not saying anything about their work!*" And in so saying, Eshleman misses the point about Neruda again; for Bly *is* saying something relevant about all four poets, something that as a friend and admirer of all of them

[2] "In Defense of Poetry," by Clayton Eshleman, in *Review 72*, published by the Center for Inter-American Relations, New York.

and one who has heard them read their poetry, I have felt myself. Without implying any judgment of the poetic achievements of the four, Eliot read like a pedagogue, Pound like the polemicist he was, Thomas like a supreme performer, and Neruda alone with a sense that he wants to *share* with his audience the pleasure he has taken in creating something for verbal enjoyment as well as edification. It isn't the *way* Neruda recites his verse—I didn't like the way he read that night at the Poetry Center, in a kind of singsong monotone; it was the nature of the poems themselves that generated that aura of warmth that Bly and almost everyone else in that huge audience felt. As, for instance, in the "Ode to the Socks" which elicited laughs followed by cheers:

> Maru Mori brought me
> a pair of socks, knitted
> with her hands
> of a shepherdess,
> socks soft as hares.
> My feet slipped in
> as in two jewel boxes
> woven out of twilight
> on the skin of a sheep.
> Violent socks: my feet became
> two long sharks
> of ultramarine blue
> flecked with gold, two gigantic
> lovebirds, two cannon.
> My feet became so honored
> by those celestial socks
> that they seemed unacceptable:
> two decrepit firemen
> unworthy of the fire
> of incandescent socks.
> Notwithstanding, I resisted
> the sharp temptation of keeping them
> as schoolboys collect fireflies
> or scholars texts.

I resisted the impulse
of putting them in a cage
of gold, of giving them
birdseed and rosy melon chunks.
As discoverers in the forest
deliver green venison
to the spit
and eat it
with remorse, I stretched my feet
and put on those beautiful
socks, and then my shoes.
So this is the moral
of my ode:
twice can beauty
be beautiful
and that which is good
is doubly good
when it concerns
two socks
in winter.

My second encounter with Neruda had taken place the day before the Poetry Center meeting, when he had come out to my home in New Jersey with Matilde and helped me translate this poem. Apprehensive that the battery of translators provided by the Center would follow his recitals with renditions more scholarly than poetic, he had asked Alastair Reid and me to come to the stage at the end of the reading and give our versions of a few of his favorites. Reid's translation of a poem touched off by space travel is one of those rare miracles of the translator's art that loses nothing of the original—and perfectly exemplifies that casual, inspired quality of Neruda's art that so moved his audience:

> . . . In this time of the swollen grape,
> the wine begins to come to life
> between the sea and the mountain ranges.

In Chile now, cherries are dancing,
the dark mysterious girls are singing,
and in guitars, water is shining.

The sun is touching every door
and making wonder of the wheat . . .

My house has both the sea and the earth,
my woman has great eyes
the colour of wild hazelnut,
when night comes down, the sea
puts on a dress of white and green,
and later the moon in the spindrift foam
dreams like a sea-green girl.

I have no wish to change my planet.

4

Returning to Chile two years later, I had my first opportunity to visit Isla Negra. On our long drive to the Pacific I asked Neruda some questions about Gabriela Mistral, Chile's first Nobel laureate. "Her love poems, for instance," I said. "Why are they so impassioned but bloodless?"

"I saw her the last time in Rio," Neruda said, "when she fell madly in love with Vinícius de Moraes. Vinícius was a young man then and she was an old woman—too old to be in love in a fleshly way, if indeed she ever was."

"What about the young man in Cantera, her lifelong love, who committed suicide?"

"He was run over by a train. The post card to her found on his body may have been a later invention. But who knows? Gabriela, when I knew her, sublimated men into her poems about mothers and children."

"You think she is overrated?"

"I think she is a great poet, but only in a very few poems. The *Sonatas de la Muerte* are as good as Quevedo or any poet who ever wrote in Spanish. You must translate one."

(I did, later that week, with his help and Jorge Edwards's:

From the cold niche where men put you
I will take you down to the sun-drenched land.
Men did not know I would go there to sleep
and that we would dream on the same warm pillow.
In that sun-drenched earth I will bed you down
with the sweetness of a mother for her sleeping child,
and the hard earth will become cradle-smooth
to touch your body of a sleeping boy.
Then I'll go scattering earth and rose-dust
and in the powdery blue of the moon
those weightless spoils will remain forever.
I will go away singing my vengeful song
because to that depth the hand of no woman
will descend to contend for your handful of bones.)

I sensed a more personal feeling, and considerable hostility, when I asked Neruda what he thought of Borges, so I shifted the conversation to Borges's countryman, the late José Hernandez.

"Is *Martin Fierro* a primitive poem?"

"In a way," Neruda answered, "though the man who wrote it was no primitive. It's primitive like Chaucer."

I told him I'd noted this resemblance in the margin while reading the poem for the first time last month, but finally concluded that the Argentine epic had none of the subtlety and sophistication of Chaucer.

"You're right," Neruda said. "Chaucer had the whole Renaissance unfolding in front of him as he emerged from the Middle Ages; he was moved by the paradoxes of both worlds. *Martin Fierro* is no more subtle than the Gauchos; or than Argentina, a country which looks to Europe for its subtleties and is the least Hispanic in Latin America."

Our talk returned to Gabriela Mistral. Gabriel Valdez, at whose home in Santiago we had had an early lunch before leaving, had already contributed his memories of her. When Valdez was a child, the poetess had boarded at his family's house. "I was only eight," the Foreign Minister said, "but I knew she was a great woman though I was completely unaware she was a poet. Her personality was awesome; the grave, Greek gestures; the eyes sometimes passionate and sometimes dead; the mouth with a rictus, always down at the corners as if in grief."

"There was a very strange thing about Gabriela," Neruda said. "She had a memory like an elephant. She never forgot an insult, fancied or real. I'll give you two examples. When she taught school in the town where I grew up, Temuco, before I knew her, it seems that some of her pupils—or so it was reported to her—had made fun of her poems about childbirth—'How does she know, if she's never had one?' and so on. Later on, thirty years later when she was enjoying her triumphal return to Chile after winning the Nobel Prize, I happened to be back in Temuco. Down the Central Valley she went, as far as Puerto Montt and further, not stopping at Temuco. The people wanted to give her a great welcome at the railway station as she passed back through—one had to pass through Temuco in those days before the plane, nor was there any road—and they asked me to beg her to stop. I talked to her at Aïsen by radio-telephone but the connection was bad and I wasn't sure she had agreed. The people camped all day by the tracks but she wasn't on any of the trains. How did she by-pass Temuco? No one ever found out!

"The other story has to do with the tragic suicide in Brazil of her adopted and overindulged son. The circumstances weren't clear. Perhaps he was a homosexual, for he had at that time an inseparable friend of Syrian extraction. At any rate Gabriela developed a monumental distrust and hatred of *all* Arabians. Once at a poetry reading I remember commenting on the beauty of a woman in the audience, and Gabriela saying: 'Yes, but spoiled by the eyes. She could be from the Middle East.' "

Neruda is in his element at Isla Negra (Black Island), not an island but a rocky Pacific headland an hour's drive south of Valparaiso. When he acquired the property for thirty-five dollars after returning to Chile from his years abroad in the consular service, his only (then) neighbor, hoping to attract tourists, put up a sign renaming it Mar de las Golondrinas (Sea of the Swallows). "Every night," Neruda told me, "I went out and laid that sign flat on its face. After the fourth night my neighbor come to me and held out his hand: 'O.K., you win. Isla Negra it shall remain.' "

The whole Neruda personality could be described in terms of this house, how it grew, where it is going. But Matilde Neruda, who came out to welcome me at the time of this my first visit, is best described as the presiding genius by the poet himself:

> Your house has the sound of a train
>   in the afternoon:
> a buzzing of wasps, a singing of casseroles . . .
> while you move upward or down on the stairs,
>   walking or running,
> singing or planting, sewing or cooking
>   or nailing things down,
> writing, returning: or gone: when all the world says:
>   It is winter.[3]

My room was in the round tower. Nothing startling there except that the balcony rail had fallen the night I arrived, and I almost walked off into space. Perhaps I was a little startled (but grateful, for the night was cold) when a maid knocked at my door and came in holding a hot-water bottle wrapped in flannel: *"Un balsita, señor?"*

Under this room, and connected to it by a book-lined balcony, is the famous living room with its open fireplace and monumental ships' figureheads looming from the shadowy corners. Our friend Jorge Edwards, the novelist, was with Neruda in Paris when the poet saw one of these beauties for the first time at an expensive dealer's, and he remembers how upset Neruda was when he brought with him to the negotiations for its purchase the following day a friend who

[3] Translated by Ben Belitt from *Cien Sonetos de Amor*, in *Pablo Neruda: A New Decade: Poems 1958–1967*, New York, Grove Press, 1969.

happened to be a member of the French Communist party. Edwards remembers also a many-coursed luncheon with Ilya Ehrenburg at the Dôme, which Neruda topped off with a plate of several dozen oysters he happened to see passing on a tray while they were having coffee. The Russian writer looked at the Chilean poet with amazement and murmured: *"Pablo, tu es bar-bare!"* To which Neruda quipped back good-naturedly: "Ehrenburg, aren't we all victims of Western corruption?"

About being a *bon vivant,* a gourmet, an obsessive collector, a lover of handmade things and oddities, Neruda may have political qualms, but it is part of his persona. Ever since his surrealist days in Paris he has collected bizarre objects, and at Isla Negra they are concentrated in the bar. I catalogued them one afternoon when a family of autograph-seekers barged in and the poet was accommodating a girl who wanted hers inside a Swedish matchbox.

Antechamber: both walls glassed, with shelves containing bottles in the shapes of dogs, politicians, babies, violins, Eiffel Towers, dice. Other furnishings: a bidet painted with roses; outsize insulators and shoes; a small ice box covered with tarot cards; a poster issued recently by the Peking faction of Chile's Communists: NERUDA GO HOME! On the ceiling beams autographs of poets burnt into the wood: Federico, Paul Eluard, Alberto Rojas Jiménez. On the bar itself an ancient horned gramophone, a thirty-eight-inch bottle of cognac, a painted statue of a vaudeville Negro in a wooden chair.

Neruda's library and writing room are in a separate building a few feet from the main house, connected by an arcade with ships' bells and angled around the sand dune to provide fine views of the surf breaking on the black rocks below. There is a picture gallery with many oils, and prints of favorite poets: Whitman on a mountain peak in a loincloth (New York, 1870), Poe, Verlaine, Esenin, Keats, Baudelaire, Mayakovsky, Rimbaud. At the end of the gallery is a rotunda. A door to the left leads to a half-enclosed courtyard in which stands a stuffed horse, the nose of which Neruda loved to pat as a child when it graced a livery stable in Temuco (the people of that city presented it to him when the stable burned down some years ago). A door to the right leads to the little room in which Neruda writes his poems. The only object on the writing table, besides pen and paper, is a small daguer-reotype of Whitman.

5

> Valparaiso, what a blunder!
> How mad you are, mad port
> with your uncombed hills,
> combing yourself but never finishing it,
> dressing yourself, surprised
> by life, wakened
> by death, wearing
> long underwear
> with rags of color;
> naked
> with a name
> tattooed on your belly . . .

Driving up the coast the last day of the year to the raffish port Neruda thus describes, the car broke down. We were within walking distance of a gigantic tree root, like a sectioned airplane engine.

"You need it," I said to Neruda, "it belongs with the rusting steam engine and the thousand sea shells."

"I've tried twice to get it hauled to Isla Negra," he said, posing in front of it possessively while I took a picture. "I love to pose like Mussolini," he chuckled.

"Maybe that chain would be more appropriate," I said, pointing to a hitching post across the road. He walked over and hammed at pulling it loose. But when the car was fixed he found a better place: an itinerant photographer's vividly painted backdrop, with a wooden horse to which he lifted Matilde, holding the bridle for her. The photographer recognized him and so did a passing *carabinero*. Soon there was such a crowd of autograph-seekers that we had to move on.

Their Valparaiso apartment, perched on top of a movie house overlooking the city, was built, Neruda told me, "by a mad bird-loving bricklayer of execrable taste." But Valparaiso is like that: if you put so many bad tastes together you get, somehow, good taste—at least something highly flavorful. The whole city is built around a horseshoe harbor with an eighty-degree slope—shack piled on shack, buttressed, warped, cramped, and crippled to fit the ornery terrain. There are alleys of stone steps, ladders, cable cars, even an elevator one gets into by groping through a quarter-mile tunnel in the dripping, solid rock. In the gorges too steep to build on, roses and yellow bells dispute the slope with wind-blown paper and excrement. "Garlic and sapphires in the mud . . ." or *rosa inmunda* (filthy rose) as Neruda called it once. Valparaiso survives only thanks to the inertia of those who would improve it.

Neruda in his Olympian glacis overlooking this reflects something of the ambivalence. At the New Year's Eve party I couldn't find him among the elegantly attired guests, the tables groaning with king crab, lobster claws, turkey, and vintage wines. Finally the bartender, in his silk topper and shirt sleeves, said "Sel-den," and it was Pablo shaking Pisco sours and holding forth to his enthralled (and perhaps not overly bright) guests.

"Now," he said, squeezing out from behind the bar, "it is time to put more champagne in the punch."

"Champagne—?" I said in the tone of a mock accuser.

"—is the cheapest Chilean wine," he responded without batting an eye, ambling through the crowd to a small table by the picture window on which reposed a porcelain cow with a fitted lid in its back. There was about an inch of fruit punch at the bottom of this receptacle, and when he added a bottle of champagne, about three inches. "Come, let me help you," he said, but though I held out my cup hopefully for the ladle which he was sloshing around, he had turned to other guests with quips that delighted them, and five minutes later I served myself.

"Pablo has always been like that," said one of the guests with whom I prowled the waterfront after leaving the party at three A.M. "He has made the world revolve around him. That is one of the secrets of his success, his health, his longevity, his undiminished creativity. You notice he wouldn't commit himself about tomorrow or the day after? It has to happen at his rhythm. When it's siesta time he retires from the rest of the world totally. You've noticed that Matilde is the policeman. When he signals to her, the traffic in the world outside is permitted to move again and intrude—just a little. He didn't like it at all in New York when the poets didn't come to him, as they do here; that wasn't Pablo's style. And his poetry unfolds at the same pace as his life: deliberate, fecund, jovial, all-embracing, with Pablo at the center of it pointing out the places and things to be savored, the philosophical morals to be drawn."

6

Since the death of Gabriela Mistral in New York in 1957, Neruda has so completely dominated Chilean poetry that there have seemed only two ways for other poets to survive: to hate him or to join him. Pablo de Rokha, a poet of considerable power and ambition, tried hating Neruda. Unfortunately for him their politics coincided, so de Rokha felt obliged to write a whole book, *Neruda and I,* explaining the fine points of their difference, ranting and raving and calling Neruda everything from "an enemy of the workers" to a "bourgeois imperialist." Nobody took this seriously, so finally de Rokha committed suicide. The joiners haven't fared much better. Their imitative noises are lost in the roar of the Nerudian torrent. Only Nicanor Parra devised a strategy to maintain his identity. He defined it as "a wrestling match with the elements; the antipoet concedes himself the right to say everything without caring about the practical consequences . . ." When I met him, a couple of months after Neruda's New Year's Eve party, Parra was on his way to becoming South America's second best-known poet, and the idol of the younger generation. Our meeting took place at a dinner party in Santiago where Parra was amusing the guests by drawing little Thurberish pictures with one-liners attached. For instance, the Statue of Liberty under

USA
where
liberty is a

Or, when I told him about a rich man's cemetery I'd seen in Guayaquil:

LOS POBRES
que
son
realmente pobres
no
tienen
ni

```
     *              *              *
******     **********     *******
     *              *              *
     *              *              *
     *              *              *
```

"For five years, between the ages of twenty-five and thirty," he told me, "I was so bemused by Whitman I couldn't write poetry at all. I snapped out of it when I realized he was a sack of potatoes. Poetry's a funny thing. It's only a convention that we poets do it better than other people. The only really essential ingredient is madness. The case studies in Krafft-Ebbing are pure poetry." And then he quoted Vicente Huidobro's

Don't sing the rose—
make it open in the poem.

I talked to Parra about the suffocating influence of Neruda on the way to Isla Negra. He had offered to drive me from

Santiago to say good-by to Neruda my last day in Chile. "By his very presence," Parra said as we proceeded to lose our way in his Volkswagen, "Neruda forced Pablo de Rokha to be a windbag, straining to outdistance him. He compelled me to be a buffoon. I'm only beginning to get over that now. For the first time I'm beginning to write naturally about what really moves me. So now I'm going to start a new revolution—perhaps religion is the better word. I will no longer be the prostitute I had become in my desperation to achieve purity. In order to be pure you have to fight dirty. Fidel wanted so badly to be pure—and now he has to trade with Franco. No principles are worth dying for. Life is the only absolute value. To enhance life one must improvise, and solve problems little by little."

"Were you speaking ironically," I said, "when you remarked in *Discursos* that Neruda's life had been completely dedicated to the cause of humanity?"

"No," he answered. "Pablo has been the only Chilean faithful to his political credo, right or wrong."

"Then you agree with the sentiment he expresses in the poem 'To My Party'—'You have made me see the brightness of the world and the possibility of happiness.' "

"In those days," Parra replied, "I was close to the party myself. But my own spiritual development turned me toward skepticism, toward solitude, toward individuals who are actually there when you talk to them, not ghosts who are not permitted to invent. You could call me a sniper from the trees. Political poetry tends to become preaching. It ceases to be mad, and if poetry is no longer mad it is no longer poetry. It's a metaphysical impossibility to write a political poem. Pantomime is the supreme artistic form—"

"Pantomime?"

"Gesture—with meaning, and humor—farce. It probably comes from my childhood fascination with the circus clowns in Chillán. True seriousness is comic. Whitman's limitation, like Milton's, is that he had no sense of humor."

"Pablo has a great sense of humor," I said, "as in 'Ode to the Socks.' "

"Yes. His humor saves him from that metaphysical impossibility. He writes political poems and then forgets them. He returns to writing poems. He thinks about himself. He thinks about Chile, not as it ought to be, but as it is—"

"And you, Nicanor—?"

"I'm beginning to come out of my defensive position. I want to make people laugh and think and even cry. I'm even writing poems about Chile. Here's the start of an unwritten one:

> They're always fat before they're forty
> They go around hawking at the sky
> They don't recognize the merits of anyone.
> They claim they're sick but they're malingering.
> And worst of all
> They leave dirty paper in the park.

I laughed. "That's going to get you in trouble with some of your teen-age idolators."

He laughed. "I get in trouble with everybody. I shocked your friend Alfred Kazin at Stony Brook by saying, 'The more we read, the less we write.' Critics need to be shocked. I remember Robert Lowell once at a conference in Caracas turning to Kazin and saying quite dead-pan: 'Alfred, do you really like literature?' "

It was late in the afternoon when we finally got on the right road. We were approaching Neruda's gate when Parra pointed to a house right above it across the road, and said: "I almost bought that one."

"You mean," I said, surprised, "you could actually live that close to him?"

"I'm so sure of myself now," he said with a smile, "I could live under Pablo's bed!"

Neruda, who tends to idealize Chile more than Parra does, and to see the enemy outside rather than under the skin, had just gotten back from a long day inspecting nearby

84

school sites with Frei's Minister of Education. He greeted us cordially but his eyes were heavy with sleep. "Wait!" he said, lumbering up the stairs for his irreversible siesta, "Matilde will give you tea. I'll be down in an hour and then we can have dinner."

As we walked up and down the beach, Parra suggested we sneak out.

"Why?" I said.

"Because I know you want to keep our date in Santiago with Jorge Edwards and Enrique Lihn—you're an American, aren't you? And I know Pablo well enough to know what he'll say when he wakes up. He'll say, 'Jorge and Enrique are young men. I'm an old man. If you don't have dinner with me you may never see me again.' He's lonely and quite demanding, you know."

I asked him if he thought Pablo supported himself in his lavish style entirely from the royalties on his poetry.

"Impossible," he said. "Even though he's the best-selling poet in the Spanish language by far—impossible."

"Then how?"

"It's a mystery. Of course he writes for papers, including that regular column in *Ercilla,* and that pays better than poetry. Perhaps the University gives him a stipend. Perhaps the Communist party helps him—after all, he's their greatest asset—"

"And what will happen to this house and the grounds when he dies? Will he leave them to Matilde?"

"What would Matilde do here? He's bought her an apartment in Santiago, I'm sure. The house and grounds will be left to the Party, I suppose."

I left Parra walking on the beach, and on the way up to the house I thought of two things Neruda had said. The first helps explain why his individualism survives his Marxism. "My people, friends, neighbors, uncles, and parents in Temuco," he said, "scarcely expressed themselves. My poetry had to remain secret, strongly separated from its origins." The second observation testifies to Chile's sway over his emotions. It came when I showed him photographs I'd taken of Puerto Montt.

85

"My heart is still touched by those wooden houses," he said, "which sound like guitars when the wind blows through them. The rain on the roofs was the piano of my childhood."

Through the window I watched Nicanor striding up the beach, a half-smile on those rugged features that made me think of the tweedy, executive outdoorsman in the whisky ad, or Lee J. Cobb, but never a professor of physics or a poet. Or is that the way an antipoet should look?

Every real poet, Neruda included, is an antipoet part of the time, of course. But Neruda—like the compassionate internationalist Whitman, who was an outspoken hawk during our partition of Mexico in 1848—doesn't attempt to be consistent. The single-minded South American youth, that revolutionary who despises compromise above all else, hates Neruda for his party-line orthodoxy which makes him countenance the Soviet rape of Czechoslovakia, mistakenly assuming from this that the poet has no principles and that the poems are insincere. But like Shakespeare, whose amorality is notorious, and who has been accused of justifying everything from race prejudice to imperialism, Neruda goes right on writing poems that are universally popular.

Neruda came downstairs at last, and after trying unsuccessfully, just as Parra had predicted, to talk me out of being a good American and keeping our dinner date, he suggested we have one more cup of tea.

He was disturbed when I told him that Borges resented his not having included Perón in his inferno of villainous *caudillos.*

"That is ridiculous, Selden. I have held many mass meetings here against Perón, and I have written against him too. Perón disturbs Borges because Borges is part of the upper class Perón disturbed. Perón was a special kind of politician, like our Alessandri—the old Alessandri. He did many things that had to be done, good things; and of course many bad things, too, because he was a dictator. But Borges despises and dislikes him for the wrong reasons—for the good things he did against the landowners and oligarchs."

I told him I'd be off to Easter Island tomorrow, and he

regretted that he and Matilde wouldn't be able to accompany me as they had planned. I told him I'd heard that Yevgeny Yevtushenko had flown there from Santiago last year, and I asked him what his impression of the Russian poet had been.

"It's difficult for me to judge how good a poet he really is since I don't read Russian," he said. "Some Russians say that Voznesensky is a better poet."

"But as a man—?"

"Yevtushenko seemed very nervous when he was here," Neruda replied. "Very worried that he wouldn't have a big enough audience. I was talking and reading poetry with him in the same hall but he was still worried! He kept counting the heads and taking pills—tranquilizers, I suppose. There was no need. We had a bigger audience than the hall would hold. When he began to recite he forgot his nervousness."

It was at Easter Island, two days later, that I heard the story of another poetry reading in Santiago, a story that brought out another dimension of Neruda. It seems that he had just returned from the Soviet Union, some years ago, and the overflow audience that came to hear him expected sensational pronouncements. But he opened up by saying that it would bore them, and him, to say the usual things; he preferred to talk about the way they catch fish in the Volga River—and proceeded to talk about nothing else for the whole two hours, holding them spellbound.

"That's Neruda's genius," said Edmundo Edwards, Jorge's young cousin who told me the story, and who had been there—"to talk about the simplest things with the greatest penetration." A pretty good definition of poetry . . . to which Neruda, in one of his poems, adds:

And I sing because I sing because I sing.

As election time neared Santiago was sizzling with wild rumors, some of them involving Neruda. One close friend insisted the poet would vote for Alessandri, the aging candidate of the Right—"secretly, of course." When I said that was beyond belief, our friend said: "Pablo has always disliked and distrusted Allende, you know; and he might think a vote for Tomic would make Allende's victory certain. The Left has been riding Pablo very hard for his luxurious life-style. Maybe he thinks they might expropriate Isla Negra! And they would, if the MIR and others to the left of the Communists gained control."

Driving to Isla Negra on election day with a Peace Corps friend, most of those on their way to the polls waved two fingers (Alessandri). They could have been saying: That's the way you Americans hope we'll vote. Neruda expressed no doubts. "When I come down from my siesta, Allende will be President of Chile."

We found him behind the bar in his shirt sleeves, regaling two American guests with the story of how he'd tried to tip us off about Pearl Harbor in November of 1941. He'd been consul in Mexico and had observed five Japanese businessmen returning home via Valparaiso rather than by the shorter northern route. He'd gone to Jacques Soustelle, among others, to try to have the Mexican government arrest them for questioning, but without success. "And now," he said, flourishing a bottle of fifty-year-old sherry, "I think Japan and Germany are preparing another war together."

"Against whom?" I asked.

"It doesn't matter. They corner the scrap-iron market again. The target will be announced later."

I told him I'd seen the criticisms of Nicanor Parra in the leftist Chilean papers, denouncing him for being photographed at a White House reception with Tricia Nixon. "Isn't that rather cruel?" I asked him.

"No. Why cruel? He tries to sit on two chairs."

I asked him what he thought of Castro's admission of "failure" yesterday.

"It's been greatly exaggerated in the reactionary press," he said. "A great man can afford humility. Castro has to rank

88

with Bolívar and Lincoln. Have you had any great men since Lincoln?"

I mentioned Kennedy. "At least he gave promise of being one."

"Kennedy was a playboy. A rich banker's son."

"I think he was more than that—"

"Well, he was a privileged son who woke up after the Bay of Pigs and realized that the CIA and the Pentagon were misinforming him."

I gave him Mazur's biography of Bolívar which I'd brought as a present.

"I'm anxious to read it," he said. "I don't trust Madariaga or any of the other Spanish biographers. Like the Colombian ones, they're interested only in facts. Gossip is so much more important, don't you think, in estimating a great man's significance? Take O'Higgins. The key is that he was the Viceroy's bastard son who got his ideas from General Miranda. Why don't you write a biography of Simón Rodríguez, Selden?"

I laughed. "With my Spanish, Pablo?"

"It doesn't matter, I'll help you. I'll give you access to all the archives."

My Peace Corps friend asked who Rodríguez was.

"He was the hippie of Independence, wouldn't you say, Selden?"

I told them about the classes Rodríguez conducted in the nude, after Bolívar put him in charge of education in La Paz. "Speaking of hippies," I said, "I hear that young Sergio Larraín, who was with us New Year's Eve, has joined a Zen Buddhist cult in Arica."

"It's typical of the rich men's sons of this generation," said Pablo disapprovingly. "His father, the Ambassador, gave him everything—better cars, bicycles, cameras than the other boys. Result: he dumps it all, including the camera which he'd learned to use well, to defy his benefactor. They lose their sense of class and struggle, these rich young men. How do you say it? They drop out?"

I asked him on the way to the dining room why he wasn't

in Santiago, voting. He made a broad sweep of the Pacific with his hand: "I prefer the sound of the waves."

It was another of those Nerudean banquets: *mariscos*, Italian cheeses, Chilean wines, squabs with rice and mushrooms. Neruda wanted to hear some of the Bob Dylan lyrics with which, I'd told him, I was concluding the new *100 American Poems*.[4] He kept time with his foot to the early ones, remarking on their "folkish" quality and conventional metrics; but when I read him "Dear Landlord," "The Immigrant," and "Gates of Eden" he was entranced, translating each lyric into Spanish after I'd read it. He hadn't heard of Dylan, he said. Did he know the Beatles' lyrics, I asked him. He couldn't believe that they were of this quality. No? I sang "Eleanor Rigby" quite slowly, enunciating carefully. He translated again:

> Gente solitaria . . . gente sola . . .
> Lavando la mugre de las manos . . .
> Se compone la cara de un frasco
> que guarda in la puerta . . .

He made me promise to send him the Dylan lyrics. "I want to be the first to translate and publish them in Spanish."

"And when will you be visiting us again, Pablo?" I asked as he walked up the stairs, siesta-bound.

He leaned over the balcony with a half-smile. "Not for a long time. Not until Nixon and Johnson are dead and you are out of Vietnam!"

7

Two years later, while serving as Allende's Ambassador to France, Neruda returned to New York and I had my last meeting with him. Since the Nobel Prize for literature had been awarded him at long last, a second round of poetry readings was called for. He asked me to accompany him to Colum-

[4] Revised edition: New York, New American Library, 1972.

bia University and read my translation of the "Ode to the Socks." We had lunch at the Algonquin, where he and Matilde were staying, and I reminded him of his answer when I had asked him at Isla Negra who the next recipient of the Prize should be and he had answered, "Marianne Moore." He was saddened to hear that she had died. I came close to falling into the Eshleman trap by asking him a pointed question about Mandelstam that angered him; I reflected that my question was less dictated by concern for that great poet's tragic fate than by my momentary desire to discomfort Neruda, to make his politics conform to mine, perhaps even to put him down as a poet for his political consistency.

During the question-and-answer period that followed the reading I was pleased to hear Neruda answer a question about García Márquez by calling *Cien Años de Soledad* "the most important novel in Latin America's history." (That García Márquez is an outspoken critic of Soviet foreign policy Neruda was surely aware.) "The novel is as important as *Don Quixote*," he added, and went on to say kind words, though without superlatives, about Borges and Amado, Cortazar and Onetti. "But among American writers, Whitman and Dreiser, for their honesty and courage, are the ones we have most to learn from."

On the way back to his hotel in the car I turned to him and asked him what he'd been doing in New York besides making speeches. He smiled.

"You'd never guess," he said, "but I've been trying to buy sea shells for my collection. There's a rare one, especially, that used to cost in the thousands but that may now be had— thanks to skin-diving—for a few hundred. It's still too expensive," he sighed. "I wish I had time to look for rare books too, like a pirated *Leaves of Grass* I once saw and regret not having bought. But most of all I wish I had time to visit Nantucket Island. I feel I know it so well already from Melville. I'd be comfortable there and could spend all my time asking questions instead of answering them."

Upper left: Stanley Kunitz at home in Provincetown, Massachusetts, summer 1971. Upper right: New England Gothic. Lower left: The poet with his wife, the painter Elise Asher. Lower right: " 'Poetry can be the poet's ultimatum, his defiance of Chaos and Old Time,' Stanley continued."

Chapter Five

STANLEY KUNITZ

"The poem is the battleground between the conscious and unconscious life."

1

"I did not choose the way,
  the way chose me."
You have tasted the fire on your tongue
till it is swollen black
with a prophetic joy:
"Burn with me!
The only music is time,
  the only dance is love." [1]

I was not the first to discover that Stanley Kunitz is an important poet; but I take pride in having made the belated discovery on my own. Theodore Roethke and Robert Lowell, who seem to have been in on the secret long before, never mentioned Kunitz to me. Kunitz himself says that Harriet Monroe of *Poetry* once had us for lunch together in New York when we were fresh out of school and just beginning to publish, but my memory is not so good. Around 1950, when he was compiling the first supplement to *Twentieth Century Authors* for The H. W. Wilson Co., Kunitz wrote me a characteristically generous letter about my poetry, but I remained ignorant of his. And my ignorance, considering the five anthologies I had put together between 1936 and 1946, was inexcusable. I can't think of another deserving poet who wouldn't have regarded me as an enemy or a fool; but not Stanley. Neglected though he was during those decades—and about every other anthologist

[1] From *The Testing Tree*, Boston, Little, Brown, 1971.

neglected him—he continued to grow in stature with a self-lessness and inner confidence that can only be called heroic.

It was during the evening of February 9, 1956, that my eyes were opened. Following a lecture and poetry reading I had given at the University of Washington in Seattle, I missed my plane to San Francisco. The poet Carolyn Kizer gave a party that night. It was attended by Mark Tobey, and by the galaxy of young poets, James Wright and David Waggoner among them, who made up Carolyn's "salon." And among them was Stanley Kunitz, then filling in for the unexpired poetry professorship of Ted Roethke, who had gotten married and gone off to Europe. I remember being excited that evening by Kunitz's recitation of poems by Christopher Smart and John Clare, poets who had impressed me little before. I remember wondering whether he had a sense of humor or any interests outside books. And I remember his telling me, when I asked him whether his own two volumes of verse were available, that both were long since out of print. It was after he left the party that Carolyn gave me a Xerox copy of some of his recent poems, which she had struck off for her friends. Kunitz had not been able to find a publisher for them, she told me.

On the plane to San Francisco the next morning I read "The Road to Thebes," "Off Point Lotus," "For the Word is Flesh," "The War Against the Trees" and that marvelous short one that goes:

> Within the city of the burning cloud,
> Dragging my life behind me in a sack,
> Naked I prowl, scourged by the black
> Temptation of the blood grown proud.
>
> Here at the monumental door,
> Carved with the curious legend of my youth,
> I brandish the great bone of my death,
> Beat once therewith and beat no more.

The hinges groan: a rush of forms
Shivers my name, wrenched out of me.
I stand on the terrible threshold, and I see
The end and the beginning in each other's arms.[2]

I read the poems with tears in my eyes. I was overwhelmed.
So much so that that night, at the Poetry Center of San Francisco State College, where Kenneth Rexroth had arranged a
reading for me, I scrapped the group of poems by Yeats,
Williams, Thomas, Lowell, Bishop, and others that I had
chosen, reading instead nothing but the unpublished poems of
Stanley Kunitz. My friendship with Rexroth, who insisted
that Kunitz was no poet, came to an abrupt end. I returned
to New York and put the precious Xerox in the hands of every
publisher I knew—without success. But my conviction has
never wavered that Stanley Kunitz is the finest American poet
of the postwar period.

2

We met in New York once or twice in the years that followed, and in New Haven, but it wasn't until the summer of
1971 while visiting my sister on Cape Cod that I got to know
Stanley Kunitz. My fear that he lacked a sense of humor was
quickly dispelled. I'd been thinking back to the academic
atmosphere of Seattle, rather than judging by the unmistakable evidence of the poems (those squirrels in the Pennsylvania attic playing their "nutty games," for instance, a connection that Kunitz's model and equal, Yeats, would not have
seen). And there were other unsuspected dimensions of the
poet—his horticultural expertise, his cooking, and his ag-
gressive tennis—that delighted me.

But what facilitated our rapport most, perhaps, was the
discovery of parallels in our lives: both fatherless, virtually
from birth; both lonely and miserable in childhood; both

2 "Open the Gates," from *Selected Poems: 1928–1958*, Boston, Little,
Brown, 1958.

obliged to play the violin; both finding our identities in college; both several times unhappily married before our present beatitudes; both desperately "lost" in the World War II army where we had been falsely pigeonholed as "subversives" until fortuitously thrust into "political orientation"—even to the locale of our deliverance from Purgatory in Washington: he at the Air Transport Command, I in the Office of Strategic Services.

The Kunitz house is on Commercial Street in Provincetown, at the far end of the tourist honky-tonk with its owl-faced girls in hip-huggers and bearded men in patched dungarees looking like unemployed Christs. The house is set back from the street and above it, the steep slope ingeniously terraced with railroad ties to provide beds for the poet's potentillas, pink-eyed Susans, and lilies, a cataract of blossoms.

I began by asking Stanley about his boyhood. It wasn't biography I was after, but the story he told was so fascinating that I encouraged him to go on. He was born in Worcester, Massachusetts, in 1905. His immigrant parents were from grain merchant families in Lithuanian Russia—"though perhaps my father, who killed himself six weeks before I was born, came from East Prussia: I've never known much about him because mother made it a forbidden subject. Why he killed himself wasn't clear. The dress manufacturing business they'd started together was going bankrupt; but there must have been another woman, too, or mother wouldn't have made the subject taboo. Not even his name could be mentioned. Mother was a great seamstress—and business woman—so after the double catastrophe she opened a little dry goods store and for years worked day and night to pay off the debt—though she wasn't obliged to legally.

"I was farmed out, or in the hands of nursemaids."

> At breakfast mother sipped her buttermilk,
> her mind already on her shop,
> unrolling gingham by the yard . . .

"When I was ten we moved to the outskirts of the city. Our house was the last in town, bordering the old Indian trail, which I proceeded to explore in deep loneliness.

> On my way home from school
> Up tribal Providence Hill
> past the Academy ballpark
> where I could never hope to play
> I scuffed in the drainage ditch
> among the sodden seethe of leaves
> hunting for perfect stones
> rolled out of glacial time
> into my pitcher's hand;
> then sprinted lickety-
> split on my magic Keds
> from a crouching start,
> scarcely touching the ground
> with my flying skin
> as I poured it on
> for the prize of the mastery
> over that stretch of road,
> with no one no where to deny
> when I flung myself down
> that on the given course
> I was the world's fastest human . . .[3]

"I didn't return to Worcester," Stanley continued, "until 1963 when Clark University gave me an honorary degree. And just last year I ventured back for long enough to re-explore my stamping grounds and let my memory simmer. It was terribly depressing to see the degradation of that once wild and free countryside where I'd once walked all day long without seeing another soul and tested myself by climbing the quarry's sheer rockface.

"I was lonely and fatherless, but my father *had* left a library

[3] From "The Testing Tree" in the book of the same title. The previous three-line quotation opens "The Magic Curtain."

—fairly substantial sets of Dickens, Thackeray, Tolstoi, and the like—and once I had gone through it I could take the daily four-mile walk to the big library. I would take out my quota of five books a day. I discovered poetry. A lady gave me her complete Wordsworth—perhaps one reason I never developed your distaste for Wordsworth!

"My two older sisters died young. Mother was just forty when I was born. When I was eight, she married again. My stepfather taught me most of what I know about love and gentleness. He was an Old World scholar, of no practical help to my mother, but she revered his learning and the sweetness of his character. She anticipated the modern liberated woman, being perfectly capable of managing by herself what had developed into a flourishing business, based on her dress designs—I can still see the loft with its cutting tables and long rows of girls bent over their electric sewing machines. Mother never trusted anybody else to repair the machines when they were out of order. But she was always tired at the end of the day. When my stepfather died suddenly in my fourteenth year, my world was shattered. It didn't leave me with much sense of family."

"You have a great sense of Worcester," I said, "so Worcester must have had something. What with you and Charles Olson and Elizabeth Bishop all having been born there in the same decade—" and I told him of my adventures five years before, driving through Worcester on the way to visit the Cummingses in Silver Lake.

"Cummings and I met late, but we had an understanding," Stanley said. "In a curiously disturbing way I am involved with his death. You known he was very naïve in many ways; there was something childlike and beautiful about his presence. Marian told me afterward that on his last day at Silver Lake he was being driven around the countryside by a friend. The conversation turned to contemporary poets, and Cummings spoke warmly of me. The friend betrayed his surprise: 'Isn't he a Jew?' Cummings was indignant and replied vehemently: 'How can you possibly call him that?

He's a gentleman! He went to Harvard!' And on his return home he was expressing this same complicated feeling of outrage to Marian when his heart failed him. At Marian's death I came into possession of their Victorian chairs and their house plants—keepsakes I treasure."

I asked him to resume the story of his mother.

"What finally destroyed her," he said, "was that she couldn't bear to fire anyone. So she went bankrupt again in the Depression, and that was the end of her business career. She had fought for money and power, and she had failed—for which she could not forgive herself. She died, alert and intransigent, in the early Fifties at the age of eighty-six.

"I had already graduated from Harvard (1923–27), where I won the Garrison Prize for a dreadful poem called 'John Harvard.' Very romantic-melancholy, but I suppose it anticipated my themes of Time and Mutability. The decisive moment came when a visiting professor, Robert Gay, wrote on one of the daily page-essays of 1925: 'You're a poet. Why don't you write poetry?' Of course I'd written some, for years, but I was then deep in a novel, which fortunately never saw print. At Worcester Classical High I'd edited our school magazine and contributed light verse. I saw some of those verses recently and was surprised by their technical competence—with no instruction. The great experience of those high school years was hearing Martin Post, my English teacher, read Herrick's songs—definitely not in the curriculum. On one occasion, after telling us that sounds had color, he asked us what the treble notes on the piano made us think of. I answered 'White!' And when he struck the bass: "Deep purple turning to black!' Whereupon he announced: "Stanley, you're going to be a poet!'—a prophecy that still astonishes me.

"In 1928 I had good jobs reporting and night-editing for the *Worcester Telegram,* but quit to try my luck writing in New York. I almost starved. Finally The H. W. Wilson Co., reference publishers to the library world, offered me a job—which I still have, sort of! It didn't take me long to discover I couldn't survive in an office and they went along with that, letting me drop out little by little, after I'd founded their *Wilson Library Bulletin* and initiated the Authors Biographical Series, of which I am now advisory editor. In 1929 I went abroad for a year. And in 1930 my first book of verse, *Intellectual Things,* was published."

"The title would have put me off even then," I said, "but how could the poems have escaped my notice completely?"

"Quite easily," he said. "There were only five hundred copies in print. But it did get some quite marvelous reviews: Zabel in *Poetry,* Yvor Winters in *The New Republic,* William Rose Benét in the *Saturday Review,* and so on. Marianne Moore had already published some poems from it in *The Dial.* But then I more or less dropped from sight, living in the country, far from literary circles, and not emerging with another book till fourteen years later—in the midst of World War II, the least propitious time for my kind of voice.

"My hundred-acre farm in Connecticut, 'Wormwood Hill,' absorbed me. I restored the old house, raised herbs and vegetables, ploughing my fields with a yoke of white oxen, and earned enough, besides, out of free-lancing for my subsistence. *Our* subsistence, I should say, for my first marriage, a most painful one, was then running its course. She was a poet, Helen Pearce, a great beauty. I'd met her at Yaddo in 1928—"

"Is she still alive?"

"Nobody knows! She simply disappeared."

"You have a daughter, Stanley?"

"Yes, out of my second marriage, which occupied my middle years—a good marriage, to a fine person, though it ended in divorce. Now, as you know, I'm married to Elise Asher, who's a painter and who links me to that other world, of art, where I have so many friends and where I feel so much at home. Do I regret not having children in my later years, as you have, Selden? —No, because I am so close to the young anyway through my poetry and my teaching and my editorship of the Yale Series of Younger Poets."

We took time out for tennis and lunch, and he concluded his biography in the few minutes left to us that afternoon.

"After beating Frankie Parker in his prime," I said, "as you claim—but I still think you're pulling my leg—I'm surprised you didn't settle for tennis as a career."

"I forgot to tell you," he laughed, "that my earliest training was as a *violinist*! It ended at Harvard where I played under Walter Piston in the Pierian Sodality—only Harvard could call an orchestra *that!*

"It was in 1936," he continued, "after the Hurricane had uprooted my sugar maples, blowing my first marriage away with them, that I moved to an old stone house in New Hope, Pennsylvania. That's where Ted Roethke 'discovered' me. He had driven down from Lafayette in his jalopy in search of me. There he stood on my doorstep one evening, enormous in his raccoon coat, clutching a copy of *Intellectual Things,* the book I thought everybody had forgotten.

" 'Are you Stanley Kunitz?' he said.

" 'Yes.'

" 'Well—I just wanted to say—you're—one hell of a poet!'

"When Ted was fired from Bennington ten years later, after a breakdown, he got me the job to succeed him by saying, 'I'll go quietly, if—' I was nearing the end of my army career then, having accepted conscription as a Conscientious Objector, refusing to kill or bear arms, but agreeing to be a Medic. Once they had me in their grip, they denied there was any such agreement. It was a nightmare. I went through Basic Training three times. I was down to one hundred pounds, doing nothing but KP and latrine duty for more than two years. Finally I went South to Camp Monroe, where the racial tensions were fierce and I was accused of being a 'nigger-lover,' but somehow, finally, I got to the commanding officer.

" 'What do you want?' he said.

" 'I want to tell you the morale at this camp is terrible—and so is mine—sir!' I told him also that I was constantly under surveillance, falsely accused of being a Communist—as if I were the kind of person who would ever have submitted himself to Party discipline. I proposed editing a camp news-paper for them.

" 'Why are you qualified, Private Kunitz?'

" 'Look up my history—sir!'

"Amazingly, he let me. And more amazingly, our publication won first prize for army publications four months later. I was transferred to Gravely Point, Washington, headquarters of the Air Transport Command, to take charge of Information and Education. But I refused to be commissioned as an officer."

3

"Poetry is not necessarily involved with statement," Stanley began the following morning when we resumed our talk. We were taking up an argument we'd been having in Seattle, where I'd spent most of my time talking to Mark Tobey, arguing that the major artist's major commitment is to his 'message.' " [4]

"Poetry can be the poet's ultimatum, his defiance of Chaos and Old Time," Stanley continued. "Rothko *does* communicate grandeur, a poignant sense of the colors of the world removed from the flux, so that they *stand* and are true. They embody a vision of tragic reality."

"If Rothko had had any sense of humor at all," I said, "I'd have said 'Smile when you say that' when he tried to justify what he was doing in almost those words . . . Tragic? How?"

"As opposed to flux, resistant to mortality, refusing to surrender to mere *motion* . . . and yet ultimately doomed. We mustn't look here for the dialectic implicit in language."

"And why not, Stanley, why not? There isn't this abyss between Goya and Blake that you tolerate between Rothko and yourself."

"Painting is essentially a medium of forms and pigments, as music is of sounds, as poetry is of words."

"Bullshit! Tell that to Beethoven . . . Not that I'm denying the accuracy of your description of the bloodless little world

4 *Conversations with Artists,* originally published in 1957 and reissued as a Capricorn paperback, also includes talks with Rothko, Pollock, David Smith, Frank Lloyd Wright, and others.

painting has settled for, but your tone implies that you acquiesce in the limitation. How can you? Obviously you don't accept any such formalistic strait jacket when it comes to using *words*—"

"The difference is that the nature of language is conceptual."

"Couldn't we all write poems like 'Jabberwocky'?"

"Even Carroll's nonsense poems have logic and sequence— 'Jabberwocky' included. Poetry cannot escape meaning. But painting, even in the ages and cultures where it is expected to be representational, is always converting its themes into a convention—subject matter does not explain greatness."

"But Stanley! Your own poems! Surely they don't deviate from this sterile abstract formula by having logic and sequence? Take such a great one as "The War Against the Trees" with its tremendous lines:

> They struck and struck again
> And with each elm a century went down . . .

Isn't that whole poem, apart from its transcendent language, a primer of ecology?"

"Thanks. I'm grateful for a medium that can catch the mind in motion. Painting deals with broader aggregates—quanta of perception. What is common to all the arts is the struggle to achieve an imaginary order out of the real disorder of life. One of the measures of art is the amount of wilderness it contains.

"I call poetry," he went on, "a metamedium—metaphoric, metamorphic, metabolic. It articulates shifts of being, changes and transfers of energy. This has always been so, of course, but we are much more aware of it today."

"Metabolic—" I interrupted. "Is that the meaning of Blake's

> The caterpillar on the leaf
> Repeats to thee thy mother's grief. . . ?"

"Yes. He is saying that the universe is a continuous web. Touch it at any point and the whole web quivers."

"Your recent poem on the Apollo flight," I reminded him, "with its ending:

I was a stranger on earth.
Stepping on the moon, I begin
the gay pilgrimage to new
Jerusalems
in foreign galaxies.
Heat. Cold. Craters of silence.
The Sea of Tranquility
rolling on the shores of entropy.
And beyond
the intelligence of the stars.

—what's going on, Stanley?" I said, with a smile. "Don't you believe in the Second Law of Thermodynamics?"

"One of the first questions I can remember asking," he said, "was, 'Where does space end?' Later—as if I didn't have enough problems on earth as an adolescent to concern me— I began to worry about the running down of the universe. I still do. When I read about the latest galactic probings, I get a feeling that can only be described as a metaphysical shudder. I don't need to partake of the magic mushroom to see Shake- speare, Mozart, Michelangelo, Jesus, Buddha, you, me, everything we love, all the works of man, his cities and his dreams, pouring through a black hole in the universe, hell- bent for eternal annihilation. Time is shorter than Newton knew. What do you suppose motivates our space explorers? They may not admit it or even realize it, but they are trying to find a way to escape from the solar system before it is too late. It is the greatest of all human adventures. And the odds are all against us."

"What if we don't make it," I said, "has it all been a waste of time?"

"The act of imagination, of self-assertion, justifies itself. Do we really need a posterity of witnesses to give meaning to our existence? And who knows?" He smiled slyly, with the crows'-feet around those sad, bulging eyes contracting, "—some great salvage operation may carry our best to another galaxy. Say—twelve books?"

"Which twelve?"

"What a torment to have to choose between poetry and information! Shakespeare, Homer, Virgil, Dante, of course. But what about books of reference? Dictionaries, encyclopedias, histories, Bibles, anthologies? I'm afraid I'd have a nervous collapse before rocketing off."

We got to talking about painting again, and I asked him whether any of the figurative moderns satisfied him. "Bacon—?"

"Part of me is tuned to Bacon, but in the end that compulsive pitch of hysteria turns me off."

"What does his art say to you?"

"It says, 'I suffer, I'm scared.' Art at its best has freshness and sanity—"

"Like Matisse?"

"Like Matisse. I know you don't care for him. I'm restored and glorified. Picasso's *machismo* overwhelms me without moving me as much. But I recognize that our age responds more readily to a muscleman."

"To come back to poems," I said, "why are yours so uniformly good?"

He didn't bat an eye. "I think of every poem I write as my *last*. Even so, I have my share of duds. Most poets write too many poems."

"Galway Kinnell, to mention one of the best, doesn't, yet the 'complete poem' never seems to emerge. Why?"

"He's still young. He needs to reconcile his myth with his life, his animal-sense with his humanity. Give him time."

I told him that I'd be seeing Mailer later that month in Vermont. Did he know him?

"We've both owned homes in Provincetown for well over a decade, at opposite ends of the town—which may be symbolic!

He and I had what was billed as a public dialogue in the Universalist Church a few years ago—we did it for some worthy cause. It didn't go well. As two radical types—though how different!—we couldn't find enough areas of disagreement, and that's bad for Norman, who's a counterpuncher. He couldn't manage to commit an act of aggression."

"You think that's his limitation as a writer?"

"He disappoints us more than other writers, because he has conditioned us to expect so much from him. Now his ego's in the driver's seat, stepping on the gas of his obsessions. The nature of his genius is to find itself by *going*. If only he could stop, reflect, take stock of himself . . ."

4

We all had dinner at the Kunitzes' our last day at the Cape, and while Carole and the children went shopping down Commercial Street with Elise, Stanley and I talked alone for another hour. He mentioned his debate with Mailer again. "He was in the prize ring with me, waiting for me to lead. But I was playing tactical tennis, with chops and lobs. We never got into the same game!

"I was thinking of something else yesterday," he went on, "how Ted Roethke once said ruefully, 'Stanley and I are the oldest younger poets in America.' Now I'm the oldest younger poet, I suppose. It's a long haul. America does one of two things to its poets. It either withers them with neglect or kills them with success."

"Frost included?"

"Read Thompson's biography. He was always playing a role. Something had happened to his heart."

"And Borges?"

"I was talking about U. S. Americans. But Borges's career is fascinating. It's almost a fairy tale of an old man's triumph. Ten years ago who would have believed it? The explanation is that we were ready for this turning away from naturalism to fantasy, this rejection of the grandiose to focus on small scale.

Kafka and Hiroshima prepared us for such a writer. The influences Borges admits to you—Stevenson, Kipling, Chesterton—are figures in a charade, part of his mystification. At his best Borges has refined the drama of his inner life to the point where it can be acted out in miniature at another level. I find his fiction more interesting than his verse. In my one conversation with him he told me that his poems 'lose nothing' through their translation into English because he writes them in Spanish—a language too mellifluous for his taste—only in order to have them converted into English. I'd like to hear Neruda or Paz comment on that remark!"

"As long as we're talking about poets who are going into this book," I said, "give me your impressions of Ginsberg. You told me you met him in Seattle in 1955, the year before I was there?"

"I was sitting in my apartment reading one night," he said. "There was a knock on the door, and there were those two slim young men in blue jeans and tennis shoes. One was Gary Snyder. The other, the one with thick glasses, handed me a manuscript and said abruptly: 'I want you to read the greatest poem of the century.' It was *Howl*, then unpublished. I read it, not without astonishment, that night. Allen's recollection, by the way, differs from mine, for he contends it was not in character for him to be so brash. For the sake of the legend I hope I'm right."

"Did they give a reading?"

"Yes, next day at the university before a small audience. Allen read *Howl*. Gary read from his *Riprap* manuscript. Some members of the faculty walked out on them. They thought the barbarians were loose."

"How important was the Beat movement?"

"It signified a good deal as a social phenomenon. And it did shake up the literary scene for a while, gave it a new infusion of blood. But most of the stuff it spawned was trash—those tons of rant! Not much remains of it. Snyder has had a more interesting development as a poet, but Allen, in his own way, has shown surprising stamina. His emergence as a cult figure is a curiously edifying example of the American success story. One of the great things about Allen is the way he gives himself wholeheartedly to his causes—drugs, Bangladesh, homosexuality, whatever. His shamelessness is a kind of nobility."

I asked Stanley if he thought poetry could be taught.

"No. But poets can be. Poets learn from poets. One of the deficiencies of American life is the poverty of communication among artists. For young writers a workshop provides a testing ground in the company of their peers. You can't give a would-be writer imagination or vision; but poetry is also a *craft,* and the miracle is that the exercise of craft can release hidden powers. The poem is the battleground between the conscious and the unconscious life. The poet must never surrender *either,* for if one or the other takes over, the tension is lost. The automatic imagination is a delusion—and a bore. A poem is a sum of triumphs over unpredictable resistances."

"Do you think youth's separation from the Establishment will be good for poetry? Good for the country?"

"It's already a tremendous effect. The power brokers fear the young, and they have good reason to. And they would fear poets, too, if they understood them. Poetry has been a counterculture since the dawn of the Industrial Revolution. Indeed, some of us have been too comfortable in our adversary status. The treason of the *avant-garde* was in becoming fashionable."

"What about drugs?" I asked.

"I belong to the generation that looked for ecstasy and oblivion in the bottle. My experience with drugs has been desultory, but on the whole disappointing. The writers I know who depend on drugs for their visions are a sad lot. Not that you need to be a saint to have visions worth talking about. The most effective prescription, I suspect, is to be a disciplined sinner. Perfection, as Valéry noted, is *work.*

"Imagination," he continued, "often follows a deep fatigue. You catch your second wind and suddenly you're free, all your meanings adrift on a sea of language. Incidentally, this is the exact opposite of the cold manipulation of language, for ulterior motives, by advertisers and politicians. I think that Confucius was on solid ground when he argued that civilization and right language go hand in hand. Look at the decline of our public speech since the time of *The Federalist Papers.* Since Lincoln we've had no transcendental figure in the White House, and no one—with the exception of Woodrow Wilson—who could write a decent prose sentence. In fact, hypocrisy is so ingrained in the State that our Presidents do not even write their own inaugural addresses."

"Do you feel more hopeful about Israel?" I asked.

"Israel began so idealistically. But she seems to be hardening into a military posture, by force of circumstances. Like us they need an act of imagination to save them. I wish they would dare to make the impossible gesture to the displaced Palestinians, a sincere offer of repatriation. Nothing less will do. It doesn't matter how many wars the Arabs lose. If they win just once, it will be the Final Solution."

"Do they think of you as one of them, Stanley?"

"Strangely, I've never been invited to Israel. Maybe it's because I'm not usually considered to be one of the Jewish writers. I have no religion. And my interests are not parochial. But that could be said of others. Anyhow, they'd better hurry up!"

"Do we lack a tragic sense of life, Stanley? Is that one of our liabilities?"

"There's a dark strain running through the American imagination, but the mass of our people are content with their success fantasies, their sports entertainments, and their soap operas. The children of immigrants from Europe— fugitives from the Old Country's poverty and persecution— have helped make our literature serious. And now the Black and Hispanic cultures are contributing their rage and their ancestral pride. In Seattle where you and I first met, I had a wonderful sense of being a stranger in a new land, facing toward the Orient—"

"A sort of Wandering Jew?"

"I could spend the rest of my life wandering from campus to campus—if I weren't so *heavily* married!"

The jesting word was for Elise who had just come in and was smiling at him from the doorway, with Carole behind her. My son, Van, five, settled down for the evening with the bucket of hermit crabs he'd collected; while Carla, seven, composed her first poem:

THE BEAUTIFUL HOUSE
HAD A TABLE WITH FOUR LEGS
Shandoleers all over the celing
chairs and trapdoors   all over.
Lamps and Lights.
Gold all over and silver too.
thinngs all over the celing
love   Carla   to stanley & elise

Stanley tacked the poem to their kitchen bulletin board.

The children were enchanted with his story of the five owls he'd domesticated in Connecticut and of the woodchuck, Slop, who forced Musing, the cat, off her favorite perch on his right shoulder, obliging her to move to the left one. "The battle took place on my back," Stanley said, "and Slop won. But from then on I couldn't get any work done at all. Could you, with *both* shoulders occupied, morning and night? . . . Well, finally Slop died. He'd gotten to love marshmallows so much he couldn't eat anything else: he swelled into a butterball, could scarcely waddle around, so finally, one day— it was inevitable—he dug a hole for himself under the back porch and climbed down into it."

He and Elise had bought the house nine years ago from the estate of a semiretired Boston madam. After dinner while the children were playing he took us downstairs to show us his study, Elise's studio, and a whole row of sparsely furnished workshops that had once been bedrooms.

While we were inspecting Elise's latest paintings, I remarked how much easier it is to enjoy this art than ours. "Except for children," I said, "there are no primitive poets. And a college education seems to be more of a hindrance than a help in putting a picture together. Are you happy with your teaching?"

"From my kind of teaching," Stanley said, "I learn as much as I give—maybe more. In a curious way, I feel that this generation is the first I'm close to. I'm certainly not close to my own! Are you?"

"Jim Agee was the last member of my generation I felt close to," I said. "And that was more than twenty years ago."

"This new generation," Stanley said, "shares my long-time distrust of institutions, even those that profess to love me. Not to congeal in a generational pattern is so important. Not to feel that wisdom or art has already reached a climax. As with you, my closest friends today are painters. I love their *élan,* their openness, their gregariousness, their physicality. Poets are such difficult people, so tied up in knots—an occupational affliction. The young know that you can't live in a trap of words. A kind of romantic pantheism is in the air. I can hear the windows opening on a world of affections."

As we drove away down Commercial Street—so aptly named!—and I caught a last glimpse of Stanley and Elise at the gate behind us, waving, I thought of the ending of "The War Against the Trees":

> I saw the ghosts of children at their games
> Racing beyond their childhood in the shade,
> And while the green world turned its death-foxed page
> And a red wagon wheeled,
> I watched them disappear
> Into the suburbs of their grievous age.
>
> Ripped from the craters much too big for hearts
> The club-roots bared their amputated coils,
> Raw gorgons matted blind, whose pocks and scars
> Cried Moon! on a corner lot
> One witness-moment, caught
> In the rear-view mirrors of the passing cars.

Top left: Gabriel García Márquez at Barranquilla, 1971. Top right: The novelist's father, Gabriel Elígio García. Bottom: With the author. " 'I divide my admirers . . . between those who jumped on the bandwagon when *Cien Años* became a bestseller, and those who were already there.' "

Chapter Six

GABRIEL GARCÍA MÁRQUEZ

"I like to live my characters before writing them. I spoke the lines of the people in Cien Años *for years before writing the book. I got to know them that way."*

1

Noble corner of my forefathers: Nothing
Evokes like intersecting alleys
The times of the cross and the sword,
The smoking candle and the sulphur match.

Gone utterly . . . City of massive walls,
Age of chivalric tales, your caravels
Have sailed through the neck of the bay for the last time,
And oil is no longer stored in leathern bottles.

You were heroic in those colonial days
When your sons had the shape of well-heeled eagles
Before becoming a swarm of swifts . . .

But today, crumbling in rancid disorder,
You inspire only in the tolerant heart
The affection one feels for a pair of old shoes.
                    —LUIS CARLOS LÓPEZ

Where is that solitude the poets sing of? Those butterflies like translucent shadows, the magic birds, the singing streams? Poor fantasies of those who know only domesticated retreats. . . . I am aware only of crunching jaws, warning whistles, belching beasts, dying wails . . . All for the brief joy of a few more hours of life. . . . Civilized man . . . the champion of destruction, destroying millions of trees to defraud the future.
                    —José Eustácio Rivera

My search for Gabriel García Márquez began in 1968 in Cartagena, Colombia, at the base of a pair of gigantic bronze shoes to which the poem above, "To My Native City," is affixed. I translated it on the spot. I was carrying in my pocket a copy of José Eustácio Rivera's Colombian novel, *La Vorágine*, which focuses with traumatic intensity on a journey through the Amazon jungle, ravaged in the Twenties by imperialists of the international rubber boom. Garciá Márquez's masterpiece, *Cien Años de Soledad*, had not yet been translated,[1] but much had already been written about the young Colombian novelist's debt to William Faulkner.

I believed, on the contrary, that like all good regionalists and poets of the picaresque, García Márquez's sources were home-grown: in his case the forgotten "surrealist" poet of Cartagena and the almost equally neglected novelist who had died of jungle fever in a New York hospital in 1928. García Márquez lived in Barcelona, Spain. And it would be four years before I would catch up with him in Barranquilla, when our paths crossed during a fleeting visit we both made to that Colombian port. But meanwhile I was determined to learn as much as I could about the novelist from his friends and relatives in Colombia, and to visit his birthplace, the village of Aracataca, where the United Fruit Company exported bananas during the novelist's childhood, and which he was to make the scene of his legendary Macondo.

Rivera's sensational novel shows the deterioration of a neurasthenic hero, for perhaps only neurasthenics venture into such geeen hells as that which the rubber boom was making of Amazonia. Like the Spanish Conquest, the experience was too brutalizing to yield anything but melodrama. There were no "good guys"—only butchers and their primitive victims. But the symbol of the devouring jungle, Rivera seemed to be saying, was all that can be expected from the mass exploitations and wars of the future.

García Márquez's world of fantasy is the opposite side of

[1] The book was published as *One Hundred Years of Solitude* in 1970 (New York, Harper & Row), translated by Gregory Rabassa, and brought out as a paperbook the following year by Avon (New York).

this coin. The creator of the mythical Macondo is less of a nihilist than Rivera only in the sense that he regards *all* life as without purpose or continuity: the fantasies imagined by the damned are the only true reality. But the effect of carrying one's despair that far is salutary. One emerges from Rivera's desperate journey with a sense of suffocating depression. One emerges from García Márquez's books with a reassuring sense that a world so full of lusty adventurers, irrepressible louts, and unconscious poets can't be as bad as he is at pains to say it is. It is the triumph of the artist over the sociologist. The alienated Colombian, the bitter exile, the Marxist existentialist in Barcelona, set out to write a book that would strip the pretensions from whatever calls to arms, whatever rhetorical idealisms might be left: a novel so fatalistic that all the actions of its characters during their "hundred years of solitude" would be shown to be no more than the fulfillment of a prophecy made at the beginning that it must end in a "fearful maelstrom of dust and rubbish."

In other words while Rivera, the conscious artist, succeeded in doing exactly what he set out to do—horrifying his readers —García Márquez, the unconscious artist and the better one, created a world that gives delight. His characters, with a life of their own, refuse to be manipulated. They may fulfill their tragic destiny, but in the course of doing it they behave with so much spontaneity and good humor that we remember them as the better parts of ourselves and accept their world of irrational "happenings" as the real one.

2

The parents of the novelist were out of Cartagena for a few days, so Bill Negron and I decided to visit Santa Marta and then come back.[2]

2 Bill Negron was doing the illustrations for my *South America of the Poets* (New York, Hawthorn, 1970) in 1968. Some of the first three parts of the present chapter are taken from that book, and a few paragraphs from *The Colombia Traveler* (Hawthorn, 1971), written a year later.

"So which would you gentlemen like to see first," said an enterprising representative of the Santa Marta tourist board in the Hotel Irotama's lobby, "the beaches or the house where Bolívar died?"

"Neither, thanks just the same. We only have a day here this time, so we'd like to spend it all in Aracataca."

"Aracataca! No one in the world has ever asked to visit Aracataca . . . Why?"

"Because García Márquez was born and grew up there."

"García Márquez? Ah, yes, García Márquez . . . Macondo? But you'll see nothing of that in Aracataca. It's a run-down village off the main road, left to go to sleep after the banana company moved out thirty years ago."

"I know," I said, "but it was asleep then, too, so it must have something. Anyway, until we see for ourselves we won't be happy."

There is a paved road part of the way now, because cotton has taken the curse of unemployment off this cactus-studded region, but the village itself, at first sight entirely depopulated, can't have changed much from the time the novelist lived in it. One can detect a touch of hope in the air—or did we falsely deduce this from the naturalness, hospitality, and infectious good humor that emanates from any Latin American village untouched by tourism and modernity?

Who could have blamed these simple people had they received us sullenly as the well-heeled snoopers (with cameras and writing pads) we were? How foolish we felt—and must have looked—getting out of our comfortable rented car in the unpaved main street of this still poverty-stricken village, asking one passer-by after another if he or she might be familiar with their famous native son and his books. Could they direct us to the house he lived in as a boy, find people who might remember him? Yet in a matter of minutes we were surrounded by a crowd of friendly well-wishers of all ages who accepted our bizarre mission as though it was the most natural thing in the world. Everyone had a friend or acquaintance who might help, and ran to get him. And everyone—except one old crone who had vowed to the Blessed Mother not to be photographed—wanted to pose for pictures. A girl assured us that the Buendía family, perhaps even the redoubtable colonel himself, really existed and might be located—such is the power of the novelist's pen! And there was, amazingly, a "Buendía"; but he had never heard of the author or his books —"regretfully, *caballeros.*" Another bystander scoffed at the idea of a man of eighty still being alive. "Only women live to be that old in this town!"

In the house where the novelist was born, which still exists behind a modern front, we found an old man, the present owner of the whole collection of wooden shacks with thatched roofs. Standing among his pigs with great dignity, he told us the little he remembered of García Márquez's childhood, and pointed with considerable pride to the gnarled stump of an almond tree which (he had been told) "figures in that big book about us, the name of which slips my mind, and was planted by the author's grandfather." He offered to introduce us to Tomasa, García Márquez's nurse.

Tomasa, a white-haired Negress bent with age, came out to receive us with a caustic wit. When Bill asked her age, she replied: "Three hundred!" She would not only be glad to help us any way she could—she was understandably vague about her charge of forty years ago, one of many, no doubt— but she would be glad to go for a ride in our car—"Anywhere you care to take me, and for as long as possible. I have plenty of time!" A schoolmate of García Márquez, now principal of the village school, told us that Tomasa had been photographed for hours some months ago by a magazine called *Flash!* without receiving a cent for her trouble. We made up for that discourtesy. The novelist's friend also told us that García Márquez frequently visits Aracataca, and that when he does he gives a traditional feast of *sancochos* for his friends, who are legion, and stays up all night dancing with them to the music of the guitar and accordion. His wife and children came with him once, and apparently he feels as comfortable with these people—perhaps more comfortable—as when he was a serious lad of twelve about to go forth into the world to seek his fortune. The schoolmaster showed us the two modest memorial markers to local heroes in the village square, both so worn by wind or touch that the lettering could not be read.

A key to the difference between García Márquez and Faulkner is Aracataca. It is not a sick place though it may be as poor as any village in Mississippi. There are no neurotic aristocrats with ante-bellum memories of lost grandeur, no victims of racial bigotry. As the sun went down, we saw blacks and whites playing together happily in the streets with bits of framed cardboard on strings, and their elders on the porches shaking *dados* or moving dominoes. And in Santa Marta (we discovered that night) Aracataca is as famous for its superstitions as for its poverty, the latest evidence of its credulity, quoted in *El Informador*, being a pig that had been heard to talk. It was encountered grunting from house to house, *"Mirame mi zapatillas rojas!"* ("Look at my little red shoes")—a likely enough situation and title for García Márquez's next story.

3

Gabriel Elígio García and his wife, Luisa Márquez, have eleven children, of whom the eldest, the novelist, was born in 1927, and the youngest, a son just twenty, is beginning to publish papers on physics. Señorita Margot, the only un-married child, works in the local treasury office, and it was she who guided us to the house of her parents in the suburb of Cartagena called Manga.

In a matter of seconds we were in an (enclosed) mirror image of the Aracataca scene. The same innate hospitality of adults; the same happy proliferation and integration of children. For though the Señora is as white as samite, and the Señor quite dark but square-jawed with Spanish features, the nineteen grandchildren milling around us ran the gamut from

African to Indian and even Oriental. Or so it seemed, though some of the children in this indoor-street-scene could have been friends from the street. There was a constant circulation, curious but respectful, during the hour we stayed. Every time I looked around I saw a new face, or faces—the *nieta* on Grandmother's lap, falling asleep and being quickly replaced by another three- or four-year-old; a boy looking over Grandfather's shoulder at the scrapbook with the clippings about the famous uncle in Barcelona; far down the corridor, a knot of children, appearing and disappearing; a boy of seven with big round eyes, stretched out on the floor, his chin cupped in his hands, regarding us unblinkingly. Nor was it easy to ask questions and get coherent answers, for everybody over twelve was eager to help and sometimes four or five voices were answering at once.

I felt sure enough of the Buendía hoax at Aracataca to want to scotch that first. "Of course there was no such name," the novelist's father said. "It was invented. But my wife's father was a colonel, and he gave Gabriel some of the features of the portrait. You want to see him?"

He gave orders to a youngster who rushed out of the room and back with an outsize tinted photograph in an oval frame. The picture, taken in 1916, was of a very proper old gentleman with pince-nez.

"How does he look?"

"Prosperous," I said, "and more like a small-town banker or mayor than a colonel—and certainly not the commander who ordered his best friend hanged for insubordination."

Gabriel Elígio García smiled and said: "My son added many features, but his grandfather did see action in the Thousand Day War of 1899."

Luisa Márquez smiled as proudly and said nothing. She said nothing all evening, and yet her presence, contented and assured, held the family together as masterfully as her husband's, I felt sure.

The house is spacious but sparsely furnished. The principal decoration is a large store-bought mural of pirate galleons setting fire to one another in Cartagena Bay. On the table in front of it was a vase with three feathers and a china figure of a peasant girl stroking the back of a goose. At the far end of the corridor off which the bedrooms open was a color print of Christ, and a phonograph on which the proud parents played for us a recording of their son reciting a part of *El Coronel*.

A picture of the novelist's development was beginning to take shape. As a child in Aracataca—they left the village in 1937, about the time of his tenth birthday [3]—Gabriel had been quiet, curious, absorbent. "He liked to be with other people," his father said, "but in his first year of high school he won eleven medals for excellence. *Cien Años de Soledad* proves that he never forgot anything he saw or heard."

"When did he start to write?" I asked.

"Later, when we moved to Barranquilla and he went to school there, he began writing poems."

"Which of his books do you like most?" I asked.

He misunderstood me and said *Cien Años* had sold two hundred thousand copies to date, twenty thousand in Argentina on publication day, but that it was not easy to find in Colombia—"because they can't keep up with the demand, I guess." Then correcting his answer, he added that he preferred the earlier *El Coronel No Tiene Quien Le Escriba*.

"Why does Gabriel live in Spain?"

"Because he likes to travel. He knows six languages."

"And has success changed him?"

"Not at all. He visits home often—most recently in August of 1966—and I think he will live in Colombia one day, in Barranquilla probably, because he grew up there."

"Who is your son's favorite writer?"

"Faulkner."

[3] In Aracataca they had said *twelfth*. In Barranquilla a boyhood friend, now editor of the city's *Diario del Caribe,* told me the family moved to Cienega when the novelist was *two*. I felt this was the way García Márquez would like it—elusive.

"And among the South Americans?"

"I don't know. Borges and Neruda perhaps."

"And his closest friends?"

"Fuentes and Vargas Llosa. But in Barranquilla it was Alvaro Cepeda Samudio, who now edits Barranquilla's leading newspaper."

I asked Gabriel Elígio when the United Fruit Company had pulled out of the Santa Marta-Barranquilla region, and how this had affected Gabriel—if indeed it had. He said that there had been a bloody strike in 1928, in which many Colombian workers on the plantations had been killed by Colombian police, and that it had been as a result of this that the American company had decided to liquidate its holdings. *"Cien Años* is about that strike, which my son remembers in every detail though he was only two at the time. I'll give you an example of his memory. When he was in Aracataca in 1966 he encountered an old man who had been very friendly to him in 1928. Gabriel addressed him instantly by his nickname, *Hebilla* [belt buckle]."

I asked the father how many grandchildren he had. He counted to himself. "Thirty-eight," he replied, "including the offspring of my four legitimate children and the seven illegitimate ones." (I felt sure that unlike the Buendías of *Cien Años,* they knew they belonged to the clan.)

4

Sister of light, first unawakened breath
of a life to put this life of ours in shade;
season where hunger is delayed
to hide its rendezvous with death;

bride of my song, ear of wheat, knowing
that your great weakness is your strength,
that luck in love will go to any length
to make the dawn go where it's going;

highway of drought, way of the wind,
I look (and catch) your image in my mind
and by your shadow measure what you'll be;

but to surprise you in this verse
would be in vain, and to detain you worse,
in the first flour of your infancy.

Returning to Bogotá from Cartagena, I translated (puns and all) this somewhat labored conceit by the young García Márquez and a second poem (below) that may well constitute the complete poetical works of the novelist. Both poems were written in 1943 during school days in Zipaquirá, when García Márquez was seventeen. The originals were given me by the novelist's friend Daniel Samper, a young assistant director of Bogotá's influential *El Tiempo*. The second poem, dredged from a yellowing back file of the daily newspaper, was entitled: "Elegy for Marisola":

You have not died.
You have begun your late afternoon journey.
At two in the afternoon
you will find San Isidro
with his gentle oxen
ploughing the limpid sky
to sow the lights:
the stars in their clusters.
At six in the afternoon
the Angel of the Service
will come out to hang the moon.

Samper, who had just returned from Barcelona, was full of revealing side lights on the personality, methods, and hang-ups of his friend. "He needed to live in Mexico," he began, "and now in Spain, in order to feel homesickness. It was the fuel of homesickness that set *Cien Años* ablaze. But when he finishes his next novel, which will be his last, he says, he will come back to Colombia for good, settling down with Mercedes and the two boys."

"What will the final book be about," I asked curiously.

"A tropical dictator, one hundred and nineteen years old, who has been in the saddle so long he's forgotten how he got there."

"Sounds like Gómez of Venezuela," I said, "and a far cry from the almost apolitical *Cien Años*. Does everybody in South America love that book?"

"Everybody except Gabo's father, who must have been on guard when you asked him. According to Gabo, the old man told him: 'Don't write any more of that shit.'"

"Was the novelist offended?" I asked.

"Of course not. He was amused. He's very fond of his parents. He told me his letters to his mother would make a fine book. In fact, a Spanish publisher heard about them and offered him a house in Palma de Majorca for the publication rights."

"And—?"

"Gabo said: 'Go to Hell! What you think I am, a *puta?*'"

One out of every three words the novelist uses is four-letter, Samper added. "Even in front of his wife and children. After all, he was born on La Costa, where everybody talks that way."

"And he'll live on La Costa when he retires?" I asked.

"In Barranquilla. Since Aracataca, he's always lived in cities."

"But what will he do in this premature retirement?"

"He says he'll study classical music, and compose a concerto for full orchestra and a triangle."

"Triangle—?"

"He calls it the most neglected instrument. To illustrate he sings a series of ascending notes concluding with a 'PING!'"

"He's pulling your leg."

"You never can tell. Maybe he'll do exactly what he says. It would be more like him than *not* to."

"I've heard that he's upset by reporters and publicity."

"True. He went to Barcelona to escape them. But since *Cien Años* came out, it's worse than ever. He told me about a girl reporter who wanted him to answer two hundred and fifty typed questions. Gabo glanced at them and said: 'In *Cien Años* I've written three hundred and fifty pages of opinions. That's all the material reporters could wish for.' While I was with him an editor came to propose a prologue for the diary Che kept in the Sierra Maestra. Gabo said to him with a straight face—as straight as he can manage with that sly low-browed peasant's look of his—that he'd need eight years. 'After all,' he said, 'I'd want you to have a well-done piece of work.' He thinks Colombian literature has a bleak future because the young writers write to get published instead of just for the sake of writing, and that the old song-and-dance about editors not being willing to publish them is for the birds because, as he puts it, 'They're sweeping around under the beds looking for writers.' He himself never brought a book to an editor. He calls all editors parasites who live off writers and readers, and he says that with Fuentes and Cortazar and Vargas Llosa he's preparing a deadly remedy."

"Did he tell you what he did during those school years in Zipaquirá?"

"He said he avoided the sadness and cold of this area by staying shut up in his house reading the books of Jules Verne and Emilio Salgari. Evidently, after the hot climates of Barranquilla and Aracataca, Bogotá's altitude got to him. Here's something I quoted from him in an article for *El Tiempo*:

> I was a little boy when I came to Bogotá for the first time. I'd left Aracataca with a scholarship for the National College at Zipaquirá. The trip was cursed by the river and by the train's ferocious climbing of the mountains. When we finally reached the capital, that railroad station was like another world. I remembered immediately that those who come here from La Costa die of pneumonia. But I climbed into a cart with the "aide" they furnish distant students and had my first view of that cold, gray city at six in the afternoon. Miles

and miles of ruins. No sound of the familiar joy of the *barranquilleros*. The buses passed with their dead weight of human freight. When I crossed in front of the governor's mansion, all the *cachacos* were walking in black, under their umbrellas and hats and mustaches, and I couldn't resist it: I sat down and cried for hours. And from then on Bogotá has been for me apprehension and mourning. The *cachacos* are dark people. And for years I choked in the atmosphere one has to breathe in this dark city, only learning three points and the distances between them, never climbing to Monserrate, never visiting the Quinta de Bolívar, and having no idea to this day where the Park of the Martyrs is.

"And in Barcelona—?" I asked Samper. "Is your friend a changed person?"

"Transcendentally! He never wears a tie or hat. He always has the same black woolen shirt on, and horrible red socks. On the avenue of the department stores he looks everywhere for a shirt with a long collar and fine stitching, but not finding it he settles for those socks which Mercedes has to pay for because he never handles money. The family lives on the steep street called Lucano. There's a fifteen-year-old receptionist, a few flights of stairs, a Carmelite door. The living room has three chairs, a tape recorder for classical music, and a very modern electric typewriter. The typewriter writes so fluently, Gabito says, that it writes the novels by itself. At four in the afternoon the boys are back from school, either looking at the monkeys before Mercedes sets them doing their chores, or covering the black sofa with comic strips of Tarzan, Mickey Mouse, and Donald Duck. There are very few books in the house and for a simple reason: Gabo throws out every book he's finished reading. Once, when his wife asked him to finish one so she could start it, he tore it in two and gave her the part he'd already read."

5

It was three years later, flying through Barranquilla on my way to Bogotá, that I read in *El Tiempo* that the novelist had just arrived on La Costa for a very brief visit and was staying at the home of *El Caribe*'s editor. I telephoned the novelist there and flew back to Barranquilla the next day, arriving at six in the evening and knowing that I'd have to return to Bogotá at dawn the following morning to make connections for a scheduled flight to Lima. I'd spoke to Cepeda on the phone too, and tried to contact Alejandro Obregón, the painter and an old friend, but he had just left for Cartagena with Dominguín, the bullfighter. Cepeda never showed up, and Señora Cepeda, whom I'd met before, retired quickly without offering either food or a bed. I mention this because in Latin America the gap between the kind of hospitality one encounters among simple people like the Aracatacans and the boorishness of the elite is notorious; and because the son of Gabriel Elígio García and Luisa Márquez was embarrassed by it from the moment he received me at the door.

"How about being my guest at a restaurant?" I said, when Señora Cepeda had retired, leaving us with two cans of beer for the evening.

"How can I?" he said, grimacing and throwing up his hands. "They give me no key. I'm a virtual prisoner here, the keyless kind."

"Well," I suggested, "couldn't we leave the door or the gate unlocked for a few minutes?"

"In Barranquilla?" he said, throwing up his arms again. "They'd have the whole ground floor stripped before we got back! Where will you sleep?"

"On a bench in the airport, I guess—unless this couch is available?"

He threw up his arms for the third time. "How can I say yes? If it were *my* house you'd have my bed and I'd sleep on this couch."

I gave him a copy of *South America of the Poets,* which had just been published, and he read the chapter about him while I took some pictures with the aid of a press photographer who had driven me over from the airport and wanted us together for his paper.

"I divide my admirers," García Márquez said, "between those who jumped on the bandwagon when *Cien Años* became a bestseller, and those who were already there. You were there. You can call me Gabo."

"I was barely there," I said, "but I'll take credit for two things: printing your first and only poems, and maybe even improving a phrase or two in the translation—"

He was reading them and grinning broadly. "Never wrote them," he said.

"Who did, then?"

"Daniel Samper?" he suggested.

I laughed. "I want to see Daniel's face tomorrow when I tell him *that!*"

"What was the other thing you discovered?"

"That your way of looking at Colombia began with Luis Carlos López—you'll concede that?"

"Who knows what one's influences were or are?" he said. "A writer couldn't write if worried by such questions. Maybe he couldn't write if he even *knew*. But I will admit that I passionately devoured López's poetry at a very early age, including the 'Tropic Siesta' you quote:

> Sultry Sunday, noon
> of shimmering
> sun; a policeman
> as if embedded in the curb
> profoundly asleep. A dog's
> filth smeared on a fence. An abbot's
> indigestion, the muffled
> cacophany of a locust . . .
> Solitude of the grave, complete
> and sullen silence. But
> suddenly in the ugly town,
> the dominical hush is broken
> as a raving drunkard screams
> *Hurray for the Liberal Party!*

That's good! Especially the policeman embedded in the curb and that dominical hush! But perhaps 'devoured' is the wrong word for my reaction. I was there, and it was there, as tarnished and comical as life itself."

"Why is there no other big Colombian poet," I said, "in such a nation of little poets and poetry worshippers?"

He didn't know, but he agreed with me that it was so, and that Leon de Greiff was more interesting for his personality than for anything he wrote. I mentioned thinking that Neruda had his tongue in his cheek when he greeted the sixty-nine-year-old de Greiff at the Bogotá airport last year as "Colombia's youngest poet."

"Neruda," García Márquez observed, "is in a class by himself, probably the greatest poet in the world today."

"How familiar are you with American writing, Gabo?"

"Nothing since Faulkner and Hemingway," he said. "We read Poe and Whitman and Melville and Mark Twain in school, but with that my English language education stopped —lamentably. I've met Graves in Majorca, of course, but Graves is like a tourist monument walking his beach at Deja. They all come to see Majorca's Number One attraction."

"He talks to them?" I asked.

"He talks to himself. If they move in front of him perhaps they think he's talking to them. Miró, who still lives in Catalonia, is more untalkative—shy, perhaps."

"Do you think Picasso will ever return to Spain?"

"Never."

"Why do you live there?"

"I can't live here," he said. "I'm too—how you say?—notorious? I can't go out in the street without being molested. No—that's the wrong word; because it's really kindness and love they want to express. But I have no privacy. Yesterday I took a taxi and thought, 'Ah, at last! One man who doesn't recognize me!' So we drew up to the door and I started to pay the fare and the driver says, 'From you, *maestro*, nothing!' I can hardly wait for Carnival so I can go out in the streets in disguise . . . But to come back to Barcelona—I don't know, except that it's a small city, like this one, my kind of city. I could live just as well in Paris, for I speak French almost as well as Spanish, or in Rome—my Italian is much better than my English—but neither are small. Ideally, I'd live here in Barranquilla and travel to Paris by *train*. Planes frighten me, but long boat rides, like the one that brought me here, bore me. Perhaps one night of terror is better than fifteen days of boredom."

"Will you visit Aracataca this time, Gabo?"

"Probably not. It's like visiting a cemetery. Too many excruciating memories. They say I'll go there to 'research' *El Ocaso del Patriarca,* but that's nonsense."

"I've heard it's about a dictator a hundred years old, with a hundred women and five hundred children, who's lost his memory and doesn't know his own age: Juan Vicente Gómez?"

"In part. There are two good accounts of Gómez's life, both by *Norte Americanos.* Roark Bradford's *Gómez: Tyrant of the Andes* is especially good."

"Will it return to the more realistic style of *El Coronel* and *Mama Grande* or carry on in the fantasy-vein of *Cien Años?"*

"Neither. It will be extremely poetic, though. Like an epic poem almost—"

"You say 'will be'—you haven't written any of it yet?"

"It's finished. In two or three years the public will be able to read it—if the writing is legible!"

"I get the impression," I said, "that you 'write' while you're talking."

He smiled. "I like to live my characters before writing them. I spoke the lines of the people in *Cien Años* for years before writing the book. I got to know them that way. Now I'm doing it with *El Ocaso."*

"Then it's true, Señor Gómez, that your book has made you very rich?"

"Am I rich! I have homes in Monte Carlo and the Costa

Brava, apartment buildings in Paris, New York, and Curaçao, stock in the New York Stock Exchange, a *dacha* in the U.S.S.R., a duplex pagoda in Peking—"

"Not to mention all those oil wells in your native Venezuela—"

"Actually," he said, "I have twenty bucks. Or, let's say, *Cien Años* has enabled me to live and write."

"You're living pretty good, as Papa would say. Any hobbies?"

"I'm going to publish a review in Paris, with Vargas Llosa and Cortazar."

"What are you trying to be, some kind of alienated expatriate intellectual?"

He grimaced. "I'm actually a very timid person, though many are convinced that I'm the most detestable person who ever walked this earth."

I wasn't finding him either shy or detestable, but *muy simpatico*, with a sense of humor that complemented my own. He is a very short man—perhaps five feet five—and a little on the pudgy side, with very white skin. Clearly he doesn't get much exercise or sun. His black hair and moustache are thick and frizzly. He has a way of looking at you sideways when he's about to say something witty, the look of a small boy who delights to shock.

Politically one could say he is a liberal, with the usual Latin American intellectual's assumptions regarding American foreign policy, capitalism, Castro's Cuba, and so on. He admires Allende. But he is just as frank in his detestation for the Russian and Chinese brands of Communism. I tried to pin him down about the way the United States is "retrogressing politically" and "entering a phase of social decomposition that is deep and irreversible," with successive governments "more brutal and reactionary than their predecessors," as he'd put it to an interviewer of *El Espectador* the day he arrived in Barranquilla.

He backtracked. At least he conceded that the ferment taking place in the United States was "healthy" and might very well transform our society for the better. "But for the time being," he said, "your liberties will be more and more restricted. Vietnam has reached Manhattan. The United States recognizes that the year 1970 was the worst for it in Latin America. And 1971 will be worse. That is to say: better for Latin America. Chile has now joined Peru and Cuba as your problems. Let's stop kidding ourselves. Latin America has entered a period of profound change which nothing can stop."

"Then you're optimistic about Chile?" I said. "You have no fears that the Communist party or the MIR will take it down the totalitarian path?"

"It *can* be an example," he replied, "an example of a socialistic regime with liberty of press, of criticism, with many parties—in glaring contrast to the Soviet Union where the politicians lost confidence in themselves and became insecure. Insecure politicians become despots. The appetite for power is the result of the incapacity for love."

"Do you think the Solzhenitzyns will ever be listened to in a society like that?" I asked him.

"His situation is ignominious. It's part of a larger problem: freedom of expression and criticism which doesn't exist in a society like the U.S.S.R.'s Their system is *not* socialism because socialism without democracy is a contradiction. But since Stalin's time those at the bottom have been exerting more and more pressure on those at the top. Sooner or later, as with all regimes that listen only to those who fawn on them, there will be a revolution. In their case, a revolution within the revolution."

"And Colombia?"

"There's a joke going around Europe to the effect that Colombia will be the only country to stay exactly as it is, so that the Pope can have a place of refuge when the rest of the world goes socialist. It's a good joke, but you know that history doesn't have much sense of humor."

"In other words," I said, "Colombia will have to join the revolution?"

He answered obliquely. "I'm always for the students who

protest, the women oppressed by their husbands, and disobedient children—like mine! It was the same at the university when I was there as it is now. We had repressive government then too. Many. One of them killed four hundred and fifty thousand of its enemies. But even then they never dared violate the university sanctuary of protest by sending in the army, as Lleras did this year."

"You're talking about special Latin problems, Gabo. What about the ones we give you? Do you go along with the theory that American imperialism is the root of all evil around the world? Or that we got involved in Vietnam to protect our business interests?"

"I think you got involved under Kennedy, or maybe even earlier, by thinking you could or should police the world; and that you stay involved because the American economy would collapse without a foreign war to stoke it. It's a vicious circle."

"I agree. Though I don't think for a minute that our economy would have to collapse. But before I let you sleep, and depart for my airport bench, one question about your own relation to the leftists. Do you think such an organization as the Casa de la Cultura in Cuba would ever give a prize to a neutral or conservative writer?"

"I think they cover a wide spectrum and the juries are impartial, in an atmosphere of complete freedom."

"Then why do the radical writers always get the prizes?"

"Well, the conservative ones don't compete or participate."

"Can you imagine Fidel inviting them?"

"The best writers are leftists," he said. "Isn't it so with you?"

"Most of them are liberals, I suppose."

"Borges is the big exception," he said.

"He may never get the Nobel Prize," I said, "but I've heard you mentioned. Would you accept it?"

"I'd like to receive it after I've made enough money to refuse—without economic remorse. The Nobel Prize has become an international lizard hunt."

As I was leaving I complimented him on his frankness, especially answering questions about his politics.

"*Si uno no se mete con la politica,*" he said, "*la politica acaba metiendose con uno!*" ("If you don't deal with politics, politics will deal with you!")

Upper left: Octavio Paz in Mexico City, 1956. Upper right: At Harvard University in Cambridge, Massachusetts, 1971. Lower left: The poet's wife on the Boston-New York express. "Marie-José, always laughing, brings out the best in everyone." Lower right: With the author. " 'Our conversation should be great, Selden, . . . because we disagree so much!' "

Chapter Seven

OCTAVIO PAZ

"The idea of Love in my poems is a kind of leap to the other side of Reality, and Time."

1

My grandfather, drinking his coffee-O
Talked to me of Juárez and Porfirio.
I could see the Zouaves, and the Silver-Plated-Ones.
And the tablecloth smelled of their guns.

My father, sipping his tequila,
Described Zapata and Francisco Villa,
Soto y Gama, and the Brothers Magón.
And the tablecloth smelled like a gun.

Where, after that, could I walk?
Of whom can *I* talk?

I hadn't seen this delightful bit of autobiography when I met Octavio Paz in Mexico City, but he did tell me that his lawyer father had fought with Zapata in the South between 1912 and 1914. He and Carlos Fuentes—we had met in 1957 at the apartment of the latter's father—were showing me a collection of documents that included an hilarious account of the famous meeting between the two guerrilla chieftains in the Presidential Palace. Villa had said that he'd been fighting twenty-six years "for what these windbags *talk* about," and he had gone on to say that as soon as educated people rephrase the people's demands, those demands somehow lose their original meaning. Zapata had replied that he'd been fighting just as long without once finding it necessary to rest his head on a linen pillowcase.

I remarked that Villa and Zapata were genuine folk heroes, but wasn't it easy for them to be radical extremists, having no responsibilities to anyone but their local partisans? And wasn't it unfair to judge the martyred Madero—who felt a responsibility for Mexico as a whole—by the same standards?

Paz's answer, which didn't completely satisfy me, was that Zapata and Villa understood instinctively the need of abolishing the feudal exploitation of the Indians once and for all; and that the Revolution was to accomplish that abolition (more or less) in the next twenty-five years.

2

I had been working on a book about the effect of Mexico's history on its contemporary culture.[1] I was aware of Paz's eminence as a poet—he had just begun to emerge as a major surrealist and the intellectual leader of his literary generation—but I was more interested in his view of Mexican history. Especially since he had just published a brilliant essay on the Mexican soul [2] and I was struggling with a translation of the passages that interested me:

> The Mexican does not rise above his solitude but rather encircles himself in it. We inhabit our solitude like Philoctetes his island. Hopelessly, without wishing too much to return to the world. . . . We consume our solitude without reference to a future redeemer or a present creator. We oscillate between surrender and reserve, scream and silence, feast and dearth, without ever delivering ourselves. Our impassibility covers life with the mask of death. . . . Both in life and in death the Mexican shuts himself from the world.
>
> All our contradictions, the extraordinariness of our situation,

[1] *Mexican Journal: The Conquerors Conquered*, by Selden Rodman, (Old Greenwich, Conn., Devin-Adair, 1958). University of Southern Illinois paperback, 1965. These early conversations with Paz are taken from it.

[2] *El Laberinto de la Soledad*, by Octavio Paz, Mexico City, n.d. Translated by Lysander Kemp as *Labyrinth of Solitude* (New York, Grove, 1962).

can be found in the fact that we are not only enigmatic to strangers but to ourselves. . . . Our intimacy never flourishes naturally without the goads of fiesta, alcohol, death. Slaves, serfs, submissive races always present themselves covered with a mask, smiling or intractable. . . . Fear of the master, distrust of his equals. Each one of us observes the other, because each companion can turn out to be a traitor. . . . Only in solitude does one venture to be.

It's a somber view, oddly related in some of its implications to those two Mexican-haters D. H. Lawrence and Graham Greene, but given perspective in the affirmation of Paz's writings as a whole.

I had described the poet, who was then in his early forties, as "solidly built, boyish looking, handsome" (the description still holds). His clear intelligence shed light on everything we discussed. Under the control of his intellect, his personality was elusive.

I asked him first about his mentor, Alfonso Reyes. Reyes's scholarly classicism and subservience to the French poets was then being deplored by young artists of the Juan Rulfo–José Luis Cuevas persuasion, who saw in it a negation of everything "Mexican"—from Posada and Azuela to Rubén Romero and Orozco. "Is Reyes a stuffed shirt, Octavio," I asked him, "or a creative influence?"

"A creative influence," Paz answered without hesitation. "He was the first Mexican intellectual to release us from our uncreative, centuries-old absorption in our own culture. I mean, of course, absorption to the point of total ignorance of other cultures. We were smugly satisfied with our own. The release is by no means complete yet—as you yourself have remarked in commenting on the unhealthy domination of the fine arts by nationalists like Rivera and Siqueiros. But if contemporary literature is comparatively more free, it is because of Reyes's insistence that we grow up and accept the cultures of the English, the French, the Germans, the Orientals, and the Greeks as part of our common heritage."

We discussed all the dramatic crises of Mexico's history, culminating in the cataclysmic events of his childhood.

"The Revolution of 1910," he said, "began under the pure, principled, but landed proprietor idealism of Madero as an attempt to correct the political abuses of the Díaz dictatorship. But very soon it became, under Villa and Zapata, a fundamental attempt to restore to the Indian his stolen rights and lands—to which he still had legal title. This Revolution helped us to recognize ourselves, but not our place in the world. It destroyed the liberal tradition that had followed the Catholic tradition, but what it replaced them with was ambiguous.

"In an early book he now repudiates, *La Raza Cósmica,* José Vasconcelos attempted to supply us with a philosophy. His idea was to make Latin America the base for a universal culture which would combine the best elements of East and West. Instead, the painters, and most of the other intellectuals, turned to Marxism—and Vasconcelos, in disgust, to Catholicism. Latin America, unfortunately, has created nothing in political philosophy, though it has created much in art. And as for us, we continued having our Revolution without an ideology. The primitive Revolutionary leaders—like Villa, Zapata, even Carranza—would have nothing to do with the intellectuals (like the Revolutionary socialist Flores Magón, for instance). In consequence, *we were not able to organize our new institutions effectively.* Carranza's democratic constitution of 1917 was not suited to the realities of Mexican life. It decreed a federal republic where centralism not only existed but was bound to become stronger.

"There was an advantage in this lack of ideology, though. We were saved from totalitarianism. There might be a one-party system, but the party couldn't possibly be monolithic. There could be no rigid 'party line.' No witch-hunts. No terrorism against heresy."

The last time I saw Octavio Paz that year I told him of talks I'd been having with Vasconcelos—who had ridiculed the young intellectuals under Reyes for "talking about the masses but knowing nothing about them" and for "making a religion of *style*." I mentioned an American journalist who had told me that democracy was being realized in Mexico through the right, center, and left wings of the official party, the PRI. "Does that theory hold water, Octavio?"

"Only a little water," he said. "If the PRI controls the workers, the peasants, and vast segments of the white-collar workers by controlling the unions' bureaucracies, how is one to know what the will of the majority really is? But what is even more serious is this: we haven't learned to respect the opinion of the minority. This is the cause of most of the violence you still find in Mexico—and not only in Mexico, in all Latin America. Our countries are the inheritors of a double intolerance: the Islamic and the Catholic. Neither we nor Spain had a *real* Enlightenment, a tradition of criticism. Now, the influence of Marxism among the intellectuals and the young works in the same direction. We can't tolerate dissent. With us, the minority is either destroyed or ignored. Thus we create a desert in public life, and in cultural life too! There are no dialogues in Mexico—only monologues. Siqueiros makes a monologue. Vasconcelos makes a monologue. How typical, his denouncing the younger writers in one breath as 'formalistic and without content' and in the next admitting to you that he's never heard of Juan Rulfo or Montes de Oca! If he carried on such an irresponsible monologue as that in a country of dialogues, somebody would pick him up. But here, who cares? They call you a name and let it go at that. I used to be a 'Trotskyite.' Anything to avoid a genuine difference of opinion followed by a rational argument on the merits of the case. Instead: damn the dissenters, the minority!"

He laughed. "I haven't talked so much politics in years. In this society, at least, art is more important than politics. It provides an answer to life. Even a badly run society may produce a great art. In times of vulgarity, poets—Mallarmé is an example—preserve purity. They show by their work that it is still possible to make clean, uncompromising, honest things."

Five little abominations
seen, heard, done:
See how they run,
these feasting butchers too full to fly.
Nearby
a cliffhanging rheumatic eagle
waits for the leftovers of carrion.

The barrister from Nagpur fishes the foreigner
from the veranda of the "Dak" bungalow, offering
in sugary English, a drink,
prunes from his garden, a road map,
a lunch of curry, regional scuttle butt
on the balcony of a house with a "unique
view" . . . His wife, observing him obliquely,
mumbles insults in Hindustani.

O to take the fresh air and to surprise
this moment of armistice
where the half-moon is really white, and the sun is still
the sun! . . . The old couple goes
out, resurrecting
a ferocious passion of insects:
Battle of seeds in a pod,
the hour of recriminations.

In the patio of The Club six eucalypti
drown in a half-light like honey. Three
survivors of the British *Raj*
discuss the Sidney cricket match with a Sikh.
Three Indian dowagers play bridge. One outcast
eclipses himself as he cleans the floor.
A black star

flares in my forehead
like a pomegranate
(IN PARIS THEY'RE BURNING THE BOURSE,
CAPITALISM'S CATHEDRAL)
Pines unstitch the hillside with their shadows' weight.

Dust and the whines
of birds complete the burnt afternoon
as I write these infamous lines.

This uncharacteristic, quasi-Marxist poem which Paz calls "Himachal State" represents the kind of enraged reaction to human cussedness which the poet succumbs to from time to time and which preserves him from being the minor poet his intellectual aestheticism would otherwise condemn him to be. Octavio wouldn't agree, of course. And in fact we were about to begin three days of disagreement on this subject, in Cambridge, Massachusetts, the last month of 1971. It was the month of the war between India and Pakistan over Bangladesh's struggle for self-determination, and I felt I had scored the first point when I told him of Allen Ginsberg's love affair with Indian mysticism.

"Ginsberg is a real poet," he said. "His view of Indian tradition comes from Whitman's 'Passage to India' but it doesn't matter as long as good poetry results. Gary Snyder has also explored Oriental thought, mainly Chinese and Japanese Buddhism. My own interest in the East, especially in Buddhism, springs from another source—Mallarmé. For the poets in the Whitman tradition the core of the experience is the act, the *doing;* for those in Mallarmé's tradition it is in the *seeing.*"

The Mexican poet's second wife came in and he introduced her. Marie-José Tramini is a Corsican born in Paris whom he had met in India while he was serving as Ambassador there. She is young, blonde, infectiously vivacious ("I write poetry, too, but in secret"), a real swinger. Octavio's first marriage ended badly but his relationship with Marie-José has not only kept him from being embittered but preserved his youth. The love between them is wonderful to see.

"I don't know whether there are significant poets in India today," he said. "I have a friend, Swaminathan, who is a painter but I consider him a poet. And I love the poets of the eighteenth and nineteenth centuries, mystics who sang and danced as they recited, not unlike Ginsberg. Of course there was Tagore," he added, "but I prefer him as a painter. Have you seen his manuscripts? In some ways he anticipated concrete poetry."

"And the Bengalis fighting today—?"

"It's a terrible tragedy," he replied. "My sympathy, like yours, is with the Bengalis and the Indians. But if the former do achieve their independence it will be on India's terms, and in a few years they'll have to fight for their independence all over again. The great problem of India is how to preserve its unity, and at the same time its plurality. In the past India was not a nation but a civilization. The dispute between India and Pakistan must be seen as an *interior* problem within the same civilization."

Leaving our first brief Cambridge meeting, and walking through the Harvard Yard under a cloudless sky, I thought of the four lines Octavio calls "In the Lodi Gardens," lines which Allen Ginsberg would surely approve:

> Under the unanimous blue
> The domes of the funerary tombs,
> Black, compact, thoughtful,
> Explode with birds.

4

Next morning I wanted to begin by straightening out some biographical details that had eluded me in Mexico. Octavio had been reading my *South America of the Poets* and chose to straighten me out first.

"Your enthusiasm for Luis Carlos López," he began. "—This vein of prosaic irony didn't spring full blown from the walls of Cartagena. It originated with Laforgue and came to our world by way of Lugones, César Vallejo, and our López Velarde. There's even a touch of something similar in Rubén Darío's poem 'Augurios' with its eagle flying overhead which turns out to be a common housefly, and then death. But Lugones's *Los Crepusculos de Jardín* of 1907 was full of Laforguian overtones, and by the time the Argentine poet had published *Lunario Sentimental* two years later the influence was obvious. We call this movement—with reference back to Darío—'Post-Modernism,' the modern poet beginning to criticize himself."

"Can we go back earlier?" I said, "all the way to your birth?"

"Yes. But first one more word about where I stand in relation to the others in this book you're working on. You must remember that I'm not of the generation of Borges and Neruda. My poetry is much closer to the 'antipoems' of Nicanor Parra, which I admire greatly, or to the prose of Julio Cortazar. João Cabral de Melo Neto is also my kind of poet. And Bioy Cásares—"

"García Márquez—?" I suggested. "Am I wrong in detecting a resemblance to *Cien Años* in the 'Cabeza de Angel' section of your *Aguila o Sol?*"

"I wrote that in the Forties," Octavio said. "Now I've read *Cien Años,* of course, and it's a great work, but García Márquez doesn't change the language the way Neruda and Vallejo and Borges did. They started a new tradition, he comes at the end of an old one—"

"Which is—?"

"The rural, epic, and magic tradition of Guïraldes, Quiroga, José Eustácio Rivera—"

"Rómulo Gallegos—?"

"Yes. But those others treat it more freely and poetically."

"We've lost sight of your biography," I said.

"Well, I was born in Mexico City in 1914, but when I was

forty days old my family moved to the village of Mixcoac, now alas! an anonymous suburban district of the sprawling capital. They were escaping from the 'city turmoil' to my grandfather's patriarchal house with its arcades. It was a French house with a huge garden, typical of the upper middle class under Porfirio Díaz. My grandfather was a *mestizo* born in Guadalajara, though his family probably came from Mixcoacán. He was a liberal, anticlerical Jacobin who sided with Juárez during the wars of the Reform. He fought as a *guerrillero* against the French in Tepic, and later openly at the siege of Querétaro. In the West Coast mountains his chief was Rojas who learned from the French how to be ruthless and kill prisoners, and when my grandfather protested, Rojas wanted to kill *him*. He escaped to the jungle, was captured and jailed by the French, escaped again and made it to Querétaro. After Emperor Maxmilian's execution, when Juárez's followers split, my grandfather joined the latter along with Porfirio Díaz and eventually defeated Juárez's successor, Lerdo de Tejado. Remember that all bandits were then considered heroes! But my grandfather protested again, this time against Díaz's ruthless authoritarianism and Díaz said to him, 'I don't want any dissidents.' So he never became a Díaz crony, but it was only at the very end of the thirty-year tyranny that he joined the opposition—"

"Becoming a Maderista—?"

"No. He joined the faction of General Reyes that believed in criticizing the old *caudillo* from within the party—"

"And your father—?"

"He was a young radical lawyer who had broken with his family by now, so when Don Porfirio was overthrown in the Revolution of 1910 my father went south to fight with Zapata—leaving us in Mixcoacán. Long before Zapata was ambushed, father had grown a beard and under an assumed name slipped into the United States to raise funds and publicize his chief. He spent four years in Texas and California editing a Mexican-American newspaper, and finally, some time in 1918 when Zapata was dead, we all joined him in Los Angeles. I had my first fights in kindergarten with boys who couldn't understand my accent or laughed at Mexico. The city was small and pleasant then, with gardens and wooden houses—I was already beginning to be amazed at the way Americans abandon their houses: you're a country of nomads, walking, marching, selling, moving, never stationary in time!

"Well, we returned to Mixcoacán in 1920. Father was in politics, *mas o menos,* under Obregón and Calles. Grandfather had died and the old house was crumbling, but its library of three thousand volumes was still there. I was the only child. I read in the garden when I wasn't attending French and English private schools. Father was a Deputy until he died in 1934 from an accident, but in his last years our close relationship was badly damaged by his temper and drinking. Mother was Spanish, though born in Mexico of working-class immigrants. She was pure Andalusian, not an intellectual, a woman of great vitality. In 1938 she remarried, to an old childhood lover, and she is alive still.

"For a while," Octavio continued, "I became an activist. My father's defense of the peasants brought me in contact with them. Under Rodríguez I was jailed briefly for demonstrating in the streets against American imperialism and our government's co-operation with it. Protesting against the dictatorship of Calles that followed, I came close to the Communists. I read Marx—and Nietzsche at the same time! I was affected by the Marx who is a master of sarcasm at the expense of bourgeois society; and by Nietzsche's tragic laughter filtering through his various masks.

"These two we should keep," he continued, "the sarcasm and the laughter. The first is a recourse against a reality we cannot immediately change: the ugly face of the superficially 'beautiful' . . . I began to feel that poetry and revolution, as the surrealists were saying, are equivalents: both criticisms of life, to use Matthew Arnold's phrase. Marx, however, wanted to *change* society. I wanted my poetry to change life, too!"

"But Octavio," I interjected, "can poetry as difficult as yours reach much beyond other poets, most of whom are revolutionists to begin with—?"

"All good poets are difficult," he said, with some asperity. "Donne, for example. Or Eliot, whose 'The Wasteland' seemed more difficult when it was published in the Twenties than now—no?"

"It's accepted now," I said, "but that doesn't mean it's read by any except the poets and scholars. It's certainly not changing the world."

"But who are the simple poets? Is William Carlos Williams simple? Even in 'The Red Wheelbarrow'?"

"Maybe too simple!"

"The poem is very baffling," Octavio said, "because it seems to have no meaning, but perhaps the key is in the opening phrase, 'So much depends . . .' Anyway, I began to believe that poetry changes life by magic. I suppose I got the idea from the surrealists, who in turn took it from the Romantics—"

"The Romantics wrote sensually, as you do too, but they were not difficult."

"*Piedra del Sol* has been translated into English five times, and into other languages. Students all over the world were writing me—"

"Maybe they were asking for explanations! I'll admit that it's one of your clearer poems, Octavio, but I still have difficulty understanding it. Were your school poems difficult?"

He laughed. "In school my teacher didn't understand Spanish poetry. All I got was an erotic education by looking at her beautiful legs and big eyes. I learnt more at that time from the Revolutionaries—"

"Like—"

"António Díaz Soto y Gama."

"I described him in *The Mexico Traveler* [3] as a socialist

[3] New York. Hawthorn. 1969.

146

orator who overplayed his role of being a *pelado* in white pants and sombrero—thereby depriving *zapatismo* of some of its primitive authenticity."

"As a child," Octavio said, "he seemed to me a legendary figure, an oracle. And years later when I returned to Mexico from Spain I looked for him and finally found him. He was then in his eighties, living in a small house. Like Don Quixote, he was tall, thin, and choleric. He said to me: 'Octavio, how fine that you write poetry!' I asked him what he'd been doing. 'Preserving myself alone,' he said. 'How?' 'Like a man in a street full of mud puddles,' he said. 'When a rich man passes, I say: Don't splash me, please! I don't want to be dirtied.'"

"Meaning—by the scum who had inherited the Revolution?"

"Precisely."

"You mentioned Spain, Octavio. Why did you go? And is it true you fought for the Republic?"

"I was twenty-three and wanted to fight. I was at the front, in the South, but I did not fight actually. I'd been invited to the Congress of Writers assembling in Paris to go to Madrid. I was met at the Gare de Nord by Neruda. He was tall and thin then. He had just written his *Residencia en la Tierra*—those dark, deep, flashing most difficult of his poems, which must be why I like them best! He was looking for himself inside, and finding himself in that black book. Later on he *used* what he'd written, diluting it, repeating it, degrading it, sometimes surpassing it. I object to most of those later poems on moral as well as aesthetic grounds. A Stalinist *has* to write bad poems, yet all through the years that followed he wrote some good poems, so I'm ready to forget the bad ones.

"Vallejo was with Neruda that night, though Neruda—for literary-political reasons—wasn't close to Vallejo. An icy wind blew between those mountain peaks! (I knew their poems very well already, and Borges's too.) Vallejo was less possessive and towering than Neruda. Neruda was a great, inhuman force of nature that came slouching out of the depths with the monotony of all monsters. Vallejo was thin and frail, consumed by passion. Volcanic lava, you might say, in contrast to Neruda's engulfing flood of water. Neruda gave one a cosmic embrace. Vallejo's was that of a *mestizo:* secret, Indian, more akin to what I already knew and was, being Mexican.

"The next day we all set out by train. Malraux, already the professional revolutionist, was there. And Stephen Spender, tall, curly headed, always blushing. After the Congress I stayed in Spain. I had some friends among the Spanish poets and they were open and generous: Rafael Alberti, a wonderful poet, José Bergamin, Miguel Hernández, who died later in Franco's jail, Manuel Altolaguirre, Luis Cernuda, and a group of young writers associated with a fine magazine *Hora de España.* Some of them were Communists; others were near the Party but not infected by its bureaucratic spirit. Through one of them, Serrano Plaja, I met Antonio Machado, the great old poet who was living like a hermit—not in a cave but in a small house in a village near Valencia.

"It was ten years later that I met Robert Frost in a little cabin in Vermont and I recalled immediately my encounter with Machado. Two different versions, the American and Mediterranean, of the same wisdom. Poetry and irony. The snow and fog of New England, the dust and wind of Castilla . . . I discovered soon that my friends of *Hora de España* were having trouble with the authorities, especially with the Ministry of Education, controlled by the Stalinists. My friends were distrusted by the Party. Some of them, one night in a park where nobody could hear, asked me eagerly if I had met Trotsky, who was already exiled in Mexico. To them Trotsky was the 'Devil' but, as you know, writers and poets are fascinated by the Devil as the spirit of rebellion, freedom, criticism. A poet I loved, Leon Felipe, published in a small press a poem, *El Hacha,* that had anarchist leanings, and immediately he was called to order, harshly, by the SIM (*Servicio de Información Militar*) controlled by the Stalinists. Then I became acquainted with a group of radical intellectuals, all foreigners, who were investigating the suspicious circumstances surrounding the death of the Anarchist leader, Durruti. This got me into trouble with SIM, so I left Valencia and went to Barcelona. There something I'll never forget happened to me. I'd had a student friend in Mexico who came from Barcelona, José Bosh. A magnetic personality, he'd greatly influenced me and my friends; he was an Anarchist and through him we'd read Kropotkin and others. One day, in spite of our protests, the Mexican government expelled him. Then, during the first months of the Spanish Civil War, the news arrived that our friend had been killed on the Aragon front. I wrote a poem 'In Memoriam José Bosh.' And later in Barcelona, when invited to speak at a Latin American Friendship for Catalonia meeting, I thought that the best thing I could do would be to read that poem. But the night of the meeting, just as I was about to read it, there was my friend sitting in the front row! I read the poem anyway, omitting his name, and as the meeting ended and I was on the way out a man put a piece of paper in my hand and disappeared. It was from José Bosh, asking me to meet him. We met the next day in the place he'd suggested, a park, walking and talking for many hours. He was thin, depressed, with fits of exaltation, anger, and fear alternating. At times I had the impression he was slightly mad, and at other times he seemed perfectly lucid. He told me that he was hiding, having participated in the uprising of May 1937. But the extraordinary thing was that he was hidden in the house of the President of Catalonia, Luis Companys. The President was protecting him—and others—from the persecution of the Stalinists. Catalonian nationalists felt threatened by the Communists, as had the Anarchists and the POUM (*Partida Obrera de Unificación Marxista*) before them. A month later I left Spain. I don't know what happened to Bosh. He disappeared in 1939. I'm afraid he was killed—perhaps by the Fascists, perhaps by the Communists. So I left Spain confused, with many doubts, troubled by questions I couldn't answer. Nevertheless I didn't break relations with the Communists at this time but a little afterward—at the moment of the Hitler-Stalin Pact."

"How did you support yourself during that year in Spain?" I asked.

"I wrote poems and articles and lived off them. Intellectuals were well paid in Republican Spain, comparatively speaking. I lived with friends. Manuel Altolaguirre, poet and publisher, made a beautiful edition of my poems. Some political poems were among them, including one I still rather like, "Los Viejos." They were the last political poems I was to write until—"

" 'Olympics: 1968'?"

"Right. It was written in reaction to the government's massacre of the demonstrators. The first line, 'la limpideza,' means 'clean' in a moral sense—"

"Thanks, Octavio! You've started me off. I'm going to try to do justice to at least a few of your poems before our visit is over, including that blockbuster which Carlos Fuentes read to me in Caracas four years ago. I'll begin with it:

> "Washed-clean"
>   (It's worth it, perhaps,
> To write this on the white sheen
> Of this paper)
>   But it's un-clean
> And raging
>   (Yellow and black
> Accumulation of bile in Spanish
> Smearing this page.
>
> Why?
>   Shame is anger
> Turned inward:
>   If

A whole nation has it
A lion about to spring has it.
                    They're cleaning
(The government pays them to clean it)
The blood
From the walls of the *Plaza of Sacrifices*.

Look at each stain before ever repeating again
"Washed-clean."

5

"By the way, Octavio," I said, when we had returned to
his apartment after lunch, "how did *Ladera Este* ("Eastern
Slope") get translated *Configurations?*"

"J. Laughlin thought the literal translation sounded too
much like a certain ski resort in New Hampshire."

"I'll have to talk to J. about that," I said. "As a ski buff
he shouldn't be averse to enlarging New Directions's poetry
audience with some of the *aficionados* of New England. While
we're on the subject of poetry, I've always wanted to know
who your favorite poets are."

"Góngora and Mallarmé used to be," he said. "But now I'm
coming to prefer Dante. His poem is a world, not a segment.
This idea, with its play of mirrors, is clarified in the last
canto of the Paradiso. Mallarmé really had the same idea, except that every page in *his* book is floating, lacking a center—
the weakness of our time, not Mallarmé's. He said: 'The
universe has only one function, to disappear in a book.' And
that is the difference: for Dante the universe is a book—but
no book is the universe. You remember the sonnet beginning
'*Ses pures ongles . . .*' It has a line which is a punishment
for all translators: '*Aboli bibelot d'inanité sonore.*' I translated the poem and since the *bibelot* is a sea shell and the
shell is a spiral, I wrote: '*Espinal espirada de inanidad
sonora.*'"

"It's a pretty precious idea," I said, "a sort of bibliocentric interpretation of the universe—with Mallarmé's beautiful, uncommunicative verse at the center."

"Uncommunicative? The sea shell sings . . ."

We went out again, this time to pick up a copy of Arthur Waley's *The Real Tripitaka*. He thought I'd understand Mallarmé better if I read the part called "The Real Mrs. White," but the Fogg Museum across the street wouldn't release it. I asked him what it was about.

"I can't tell you. But Borges would love to have written it—if it weren't a bit obscene for him, perhaps."

We stopped to admire some of the Chinese and Indian sculptures. "If I could be reborn after my death," he mused, "it would be to read Sanskrit and Chinese fluently. Not to save the world!"

"And not to write the greatest poems?"

"There is no such thing. Poetry isn't competitive."

"Would you want to return centuries hence as Octavio Paz?"

"In another universe. Making other things—engravings perhaps, like Dürer's!"

Seeing papers on the stands with news of India's three-pronged thrust into East Pakistan, I asked him how he thought China's support of Pakistan's suppression of Bengali independence would affect Maoists in Latin America, like the Chilean MIR.

"Read Hume's *Dialogues on Natural Religion* to see why it won't affect them at all, any more than Neruda was affected by the enormity of Stalin's crimes. If they can swallow Mao's poetry, they can swallow anything! But don't get me wrong. I'm not against revolution. Except in the underdeveloped countries—there revolutions spawn bureaucratic and repressive regimes, as in Russia and China. Socialism was thought of and conceived *in* and *for* developed societies."

"Does that include Mexico?"

"Mexico is not a developed country yet, nor do we need

a revolution again. What is needed is a democratization of the PRI. So you see I'm detested by the Stalinists and Maoists, and the PRI!—though the PRI tried to seduce me to use my words for their game."

"I think you're becoming a political man, in spite of yourself, Octavio!"

"I am and always have been *openly* a political man. For this reason I have written a book of independent political speculation, *Posdata*—translated in English as *The Other Mexico: Critique of the Pyramid*.[4]

Back in his apartment, I asked Octavio whether what he'd been saying about reincarnation at the Fogg Museum implied that he believed in God.

"No. But it's presumptuous to say I do or I don't, isn't it? Here, in *this* life, we are vouchsafed glimpses of Eternity —like Blake or Whitman—or even of Nothingness, like Mallarmé. The idea of Love in my poems is a kind of leap to the other side of Reality, and Time. My poem 'Blanco' links two experiences: love in its most physical sense, love with my wife; and the idea of Not-being (nothingness). Ginsberg will tell you, I'm sure, that these two are identical. Neruda in his erotic poems, and even Borges in some of his poems, recognizes this implicitly. I don't have visions but I have illuminations, through my experience of reality, which I express in my poems. But the poems themselves are not important. They are only fragments of the great 'poem' that is being composed by all poets."

"And music? What role has music played—?"

"I was very late discovering it," he said. "In India, really, with the help of Marie-Jo. First Indian music, then jazz, finally Bach, Stravinsky, Webern. You've read my poem about Webern? It was translated by Charles Tomlinson, an English poet and painter I greatly admire."

"It's not one of my favorite Paz poems," I said. "I found

4 Translated by Lysander Kemp, and published in 1972 by Grove (New York).

it rather inhuman, like the music. I'd rather have seen you put Webern in the context of his life, which was heroic—and tragic—his accidental death at the hands of an American G.I. But back to poetry. Why do you consider Mexican poetry as distinct from the rest of Latin-American poetry?"

"Because we have the only *continuous* tradition of poetry in the language. Except for Spain's, of course."

"But the poets of the Mexican tradition have had no influence at all outside of Mexico, have they? Nothing like Neruda's for instance, which goes far beyond Chile. I've heard you talk about the greatness of López Velarde, but who reads him—except in Mexico?"

"Well . . . I *think* Neruda and Borges admire him. He's not a great poet, but a marvelous minor one. His originality was in speaking very colloquially."

"The trouble may be with his translators," I said, "and yours, too, Octavio; you haven't been lucky like Pablo in finding Reids and Belitts. And Samuel Beckett, who did that dreadful anthology they use in our schools—what a disaster to have Mexico's best presented by a man who can't make a poem in English out of one in Spanish! For example this nugget from Alfonso Reyes:

'They drink spirits of maize and peyotl
herbs of portents,
symphony of positive esthetics
whereby into colors forms are changed
and ample metaphysical ebriety . . .'

—or this, which is supposed to represent López Velarde:

'. . . life's convulsions seem a bridge
above an abyss, on which we tread together,
my kisses scour you devoutly serried
over a sacrilegious cloak of skulls
as over an erotic domino—' "

Octavio grimaced. "We have only one major poet," he said.

"You?"

He laughed. "Sor Juana. She's the only major poet in Spanish after Calderón. Until you get to José Martí, Rubén Darío, and Lugones—"

"And in Spain?—"

"Machado, Jiménez, Lorca, Guillén. Like Yeats, Jiménez was three poets in one. He begins as a minor sentimentalist, a follower of Darío. After his visit to the United States he began to write more nakedly and discovered popular Spanish verse. But even those were sentimental poems and he wrote too many of them. But they influenced Guillén, Lorca, Salinas, Alberti, all the younger poets—and Jiménez, like Yeats again, was in turn influenced by *them*. In his third period, exiled, he wrote only the long and very difficult poem 'Espácio.' The poem is not naked and pure like the earlier work, but very vulnerable, a confession of his life, past and present. In the second edition he eliminated the spaces between lines, thus disguising it as 'prose,' for there were left no pauses between the long and short lines for respiration."

"Was your own 'prose-poem' *Eagle or Sun* originally composed in verse?" I asked.

"No. It was written just as it is, in an effort of great concentration, like Williams's *Kora in Hell*."

I mentioned the resemblance of the one called "Head of an Angel" to García Márquez's *Cien Años de Soledad*. "Is the one you call 'Before Sleep' about your talent?" I asked.

"It's about my other side, and about death."

"What about 'A Poet'?"

"It's related to my disillusion with leftist politics."

"You were prophesying the Padilla case in Cuba twenty years before it occurred?"

"I suppose—you said it!"

"Octavio, do you feel that you'll 'survive' through your poems?"

"Survive? It's more impersonal than that. Something is being written *through* me—out of my memory, tribal experience, and so on. Who was Homer? Maybe not even a man. But the poetry survives."

"Our poetry is more personal than that today, though, isn't it? 'Confessional' as they say."

"I don't like Alvarez's phrase. Confession belongs to the world of psychoanalysis. It implies guilt—which I don't feel, and which is a concept I dislike. Or justice. These are Judaeo-Christian ideas. I'm with Blake, or Whitman. I believe we're originally innocent. When Sylvia Plath talks about 'Daddy' it's not personal, not really her father, is it? It's our civilization she hates. But I agree with you that Alvarez is a fine critic. I like the way he insists that the poet must respond to his life with his poems."

"Would you do it differently, Octavio, if you had your life to live over?"

"If I had to re-do it, I'd make the same or different mistakes. I'm not ashamed of my life. Success and failure are external. After things like Marie-Jo, and the beautiful friends I've had, and the books I've read—there's no end! and no beginning! If it goes on, I'm still alive. Not a 'career' but a series of instantaneous discoveries, with moments of depression, fear, vanity, love, joy. 'Under the leaves of this tree let's eat our salad, we are only men,' says Bashō. Is being a good carpenter less than being a good poet—or Napoleon? Bashō says it again:

> 'Admirable
> this one, who, seeing the lightning
> doesn't say "Life is short." '

That's my philosophy!"

6

We had dinner, the night before I left Cambridge, with

some Harvard students with whom I was staying. I knew the table talk would be political, but I had a chance before we sat down to ask Paz what he meant by defining poetry as "transcending history and language."

"What I mean is that the circumstances are dated almost as soon as they occur; but the poem transcends them. That's the 'history.' As for the language, if poetry were *only* language you could explain it in other words."

"I haven't read your latest nonpoetry, Octavio. What is *Posdata* about?"

"It's on several levels," he said. "One level is that of the youth rebellion taking place all over the world. Another is the Mexican level: what could happen only in Mexico. Why our government overreacted to the Olympic demonstrations; the socioeconomic forces behind this, and the forces of Mexican psychology and myth. My discussion of this was badly received in Mexico. The whole idea that there is a Mexican archetype was distasteful. I had pointed out that the *caudillo* —a Moorish import that reached us via the Conquest—blossomed later in such dissimilar figures as Bolívar, Perón, Castro, but all alike in being accepted as the exceptional man who makes the rules. This blended in Mexico with the Aztec archetype of the sacred king-priest—the symbol of anonymous power. Our conception of the President resulted. Porfirio Díaz was the Spanish-type *caudillo* incarnate, but the Presidents that followed him in the wake of the Revolution represented a more impersonal authority and father figure. Cárdenas alone tried to cut away the *caudillo* part. He wanted to be human, not one who reduces humanity to ciphers. But he failed. To get out of that sterile pattern we must understand ourselves. But *that* suggestion made my critics even madder!"

"When you visited Robert Frost in 1945," I said, "you talked about Mexican history, didn't you?"

"One of his earliest poems," Octavio said, "was about the *Noche Triste*. 'We're in Vermont,' Frost told me, 'where all good things came from before the Great Corruption. I'm proud that Vermont didn't participate in the Mexican War.'

I told him I was proud that Yucatán didn't participate in the defense!"

"How come, Octavio?"

"Because Santa Anna, as you showed so well in your *Mexico Traveler,* was corrupt to the core. I feel ambivalent about what happened, in other words. But I was proud of that one state that had the courage to oppose the federal government."

"Likewise when Santa Anna was trying to hold on to Texas—?"

"I berated Borges severely for writing a poem about the 'heroes' of the Alamo."

"Why, Octavio? They *were* heroes. Just as Winfield Scott in '48 was a hero—the Mexicans themselves recognized that or they would never have asked him to stay on in Mexico City and be their ruler. Are you so nationalistic you can't recognize the heroism of Travis, Crockett & Co. who were fighting for their homesteads against a totally corrupt Mexican administration that had no interest in Texas and California except to bleed them? I don't assume that Borges understands that, necessarily, though he may—I haven't read his poem—but even if he writes only in celebration of the *courage* of the little band of defenders: what's wrong with that? I could write a poem about your *Niños Heröes—*"

"I couldn't," Octavio said dryly. "They're a creation of official Mexican patriotism just as the heroes of the Alamo are the creation of your official propaganda. But I think Borges writes about the latter because he really *likes* American imperialism and detests its victims—"

"I agree with your point about creations of propaganda," I said, "but I wish you wouldn't use such awful clichés as 'American imperialism.' If I retaliated on that level I'd start talking about 'Mexican barbarism' or 'Hispanic incompetence.' Do you really think Borges detests the 'victims of American imperialism,' if we must call them that—?"

"Who knows?" Paz said. "Borges is a right-wing anarchist and I love him for his anarchism. He *could* be writing his

Alamo poem to shock self-righteous intellectuals—which would be amusing, and O.K. But actually he believes that the Americans represented Civilization, Morality, Goodness—and that the Mexicans were the bad ones—a Manichean way of seeing history. Manicheism appears also in Neruda. He was justly enraged at the spectacle of the destruction of the Spanish people by Fascism with the complicity of the Western democracies. But later he became the defender of Stalin, a tyrant no better than Hitler, and of a bureaucratic regime which is the negation of socialism."

The subject came up again at dinner after we'd had quite a few drinks and Octavio wasn't feeling quite so Olympian. He said: "Perhaps we should understand, not condemn. I like one side of Borges: he is a skeptic. In this sense he is a free man—skepticism and freedom live in neighboring houses. I like Borges, his anarchism and his skepticism, even if I disagree with his conservative politics. In the case of Neruda, I admire his poetical power but I dislike his *clericalism*. He has become a bishop of a church—a religion without gods but with an ecclesiastical bureaucracy. The great subject of our time is the religious instinct masked as revolutionary ideology. Religious passion is a ferocious passion (Baudelaire saw that very well) unless its natural savagery is tempered by a great ethic, as in Buddhism, and, sometimes, in Christianity. Political religions are not the opium of the people but a toxic, a bloody delirium."

I defended Neruda, citing the role of Milton's intolerant politics in fueling his poetry, and refused to agree that Neruda should not be compared with such a sovereign figure.

"Our 'conversation' should be great, Selden," Octavio said as we were breaking up, "because we disagree so much!"

7

Octavio was in a relaxed and wonderful mood when I picked him and his wife up at eight the next morning to make the train to New York. Marie-José, always laughing, brings out the best in everyone. My hangover vanished. "I'm so glad you talked us into taking this train," Octavio said. "Those buses with their blue glass are detestable. They want you to see a color photograph of reality." At breakfast in the dining car they both autographed my copy of *Ladera Este*, with jokes about my pen, which was making blue spots on the seats and getting all over their hands. Octavio called me 'The Octopus' and helped me translate the poems I have included here, including a favorite of his which he said had never been translated, "Sunday in Elephant Island":

(Curse)

At the base of the sublime sculptures
Disfigured by Moslems and Portuguese
The rabble leaves the remains of its picnic
Of garbage to the dogs.
I condemn them to be reborn a hundred times
In incinerators.
              As for those others,
For aeons in living flesh may they be carved anew
In whatever hell mutilated statues go to.

(Blessing)

Shiva and Parvati
              we adore you
Not as gods
            but as images
Of Man's divinity.
You are what Man makes and is not,
When he pays the debt of his doing.
Shiva:
         your four arms are mirrors,
Fountains:
         your whole being spouts
And in that pool bathes lovely Parvati,

Rocking like a trim skiff.
If
The sea palpitates under the sun
It is the lips of Shiva smiling. If
The sea is in conflagration
It is Parvati's footsteps bruising the water.
Shiva and Parvati:
                        The woman who's my woman
And I
        ask you no favors, nothing
From your world:
                        only
The light over the sea
Barefooted, and the land sleeping.

Upper left: Norman Mailer at Provincetown, Massachusetts, 1958. Upper right: With the author at Provincetown. Lower left: Sparring with his wife's son, David, at South Londonderry, Vermont, August 1971. Lower right: "'It's not a matter of happiness,' he said, 'but of survival.'"

Chapter Eight

NORMAN MAILER

". . . I choose, as Sartre puts it, to be heterosexual."

1

What is there to say about Norman Mailer that hasn't already been said? Nothing, possibly—except that the descriptions, the quoted words, even the accurately reported deeds, seem to have very little to do with the gentle friend I've known since 1946. I'm not denying that the public Mailer is a blusterer, an exhibitionist, a loser—I've seen him often enough on T.V. without recognizing him. And I suppose the private Mailer of the disastrous marriages is as violently sadistic, as consumed with *machismo,* and as ambivalent sexually as the various self-portraits-with-women in his own fiction and non-fiction; though with each of the three wives I've known, the relationship seemed to be loving.

It wasn't until the summer of 1971 that I managed to spend enough time with Mailer at his home to attempt to resolve these contradictions conversationally, so the bulk of this chapter is the record of those talks; but first a summary of earlier encounters may serve to establish the nature of our relationship.

2

From the beginning we disagreed about almost everything. In 1948 I was organizing the first exhibitions of Haitian primitive art in New York, and putting together *100 Modern Poems,* in which I wanted to make a distinction between "poetry" and "verse" by including poetic passages from novelists like Kafka, Joyce, Hemingway, Faulkner, Agee—and Norman Mailer, whose *The Naked and the Dead* had just been published. We disagreed about primitive painters, whom I saw as carriers of values being jettisoned by Western High Art, and whom he saw as regressive. If he were consistent, I told him, he should feel as attracted to their genuineness as his fellow exile from immigrant Brooklyn, Ben Shahn, whose biography I'd begun to plan.

We also disagreed about his novel, which he was beginning to hate, in part because of its instant success, but more because the traditional novel form seemed trite; and he was already wrestling with the semiconfessional open form that was to give him so much trouble in the books ahead. But most of all we disagreed about Henry Wallace, whose Progressive party he (like Shahn) was actively supporting and whom I regarded as lovable but naïve. "You were the only one at that time," Norman wrote me later, "who talked that way about Wallace without driving me up the wall. I respected your reasons though I couldn't agree with them."

When our paths crossed next in the summer of 1962, it was Norman who was accusing *me* of being politically naïve. For supporting President Kennedy. During a visit which he and his third wife, Jean, made to my home in Oakland, New Jersey, he said: "The New Frontier's interest in art is about as real as Dorothy Dix's interest in sex. When they ask Henry Miller to the White House instead of Robert Frost I'll take their culture seriously." It was much better, he added, for art to be ignored totally, as under Truman and Eisenhower, than for artists to be lulled into a false sense of security. "Kennedy's making hypocrites of the liberals with whom he surrounds himself. He'd like to emasculate the artists in the same way. He's trying to buy them off with social recognition."

"So you'd still prefer to see Jackie Robinson or Steve Allen or Archie Moore President?" I said.

"I said I preferred them to Eisenhower. But the point I was making still holds. People like that are hip. They're not pompous, not squares. They're the exact opposite of the types who are leading us to military, economic, moral, and aesthetic ruin—via total dishonesty." I remembered his telling Mike Wallace that writers suffer from bad livers because it's their business "to delve deeper than other people into material that normally belongs on a psychoanalyst's couch"—a good definition of his kind of writing.

We continued to disagree about painting. I had written a polemic contending that Picasso was a genius who painted trivia. Norman was writing a book entirely about Picasso (so he told me—whatever happened to it?) and wanted to see the works of art in my collection of figurative "humanists" like Orozco, Kearns, Cuevas, Birmelin, Leichman, and others. We'd been drinking tequila and I suggested he hold off on his third until he'd had a good look. "My eyesight's so bad," he replied, "I rarely read any more; I actually see better after several drinks, or pot." He warmed to the "compulsive imagery," as he put it, of Landuyt, Lebrun, and Francisco Icaza, but he didn't agree with me that the content of art was as important as the form.

Months before, I had written a review of his *Deaths for the Ladies and Other Disasters* for *The New York Times,* and he asked me whether, in view of the fact that the *Times* evidently wasn't printing it, his publisher could quote from it. I showed him the review:

This is a book [it began] that should be required reading for statesmen, editorial writers, ad men, doctors, lawyers, TV and Hollywood producers, moralists, ministers, professors and (especially) poets. None of them, or very few, will like it. And the poets—at least those who write what passes for poetry these days—will say that Mailer's verses have nothing in common with Shakespeare, T. S. Eliot or Wallace Stevens; and as far as the last two go, they will be right. Mailer himself makes the distinction: "So curious a man/this Eliot/exquisite forceful superb/but dimmed in his climax/No wonder he caught/the spirit of an age."

Shakespeare, however, has several qualities in common with Mailer, all of them qualities absent from the characteristic (academic) poetry of the postwar period. To name a few: forthrightness, savagery, humor, irreverence, familiarity with and delight in the vernacular, outrageous punning, obscenity. In all of these Mailer's verse is rich. And though in these un-Elysian Fields Allen Ginsberg, with less humor and more self-pity, is a worthy competitor, one has to go back to Cummings in his prime for a display as irresistible and pyrotechnic. Cummings, to be sure, matched these beat and off-beat qualities with a lyric strain and metric ingenuity that are not part of Mailer's equipment, but for fast footwork, low blows and a capacity to beat the reader to the punch the younger poet yields to none. . . .

I quote so much because the review pinpoints both our continuing ideological divergence and our congruence as nonconformists. In the wake of protests, by Dwight Macdonald among others, the *Times* finally printed the review; but the (then) editor penalized me severely for having shown the review to the author. The strengthening of the bond between us was compensation for the blanket of silence that now turned my public career as a writer into a virtually private one.

My own feeling about Mailer's achievement as a writer is that he "found" himself in this period of the early Sixties when he seemed to be floundering, "escaping" the big novel that the critics—and for a while he himself—expected would succeed *The Naked and the Dead.* He found himself in that highly personal, seminovelistic "reportage" that culminated in *The Armies of the Night* and *Of a Fire on the Moon.* When he leaned too far toward fiction (*Why Are We in Vietnam?, The American Dream*) he failed dismally. When he succumbed, at the other extreme, to outright sociological polemic (*The Prisoner of Sex*) he was out of his element. Perhaps the turning point was his brilliant essay in *Advertisements for Myself,* "The White Negro." But in our last two encounters in the early Sixties, he was still hesitating.

The converted brownstone in Brooklyn Heights, where I

had dinner with him during his last year with Jean, symbolized the contradictions not resolved. Visiting him there, I was disturbed by contradictions of my own. All my life I'd been avoiding Brooklyn Heights where my family, from which I'd been alienated in childhood, had lorded it for generations, before being "driven" across the river in the Nineties to Murray Hill by the "invasion" of the elder Mailers and Shahns from Eastern Europe's ghettos. I saw so many ghosts I passed Mailer's house twice before remembering what I was looking for. I suppose the restrained High Society *décor* of the Mailers' living room—18th-century antiques, Abstract Expressionist pictures, low circular glass tables loaded with expensive wines, liqueurs and sweetmeats—represented the taste of Lord Beaverbrook's daughter more than Norman's; yet the paradox of finding the Hipsters' Apostle in this setting, with butler, chambermaid, and Negro nurse moving unobtrusively in the background, did startle me.

I couldn't make Norman admit that evening that he underestimated women, nor could I get him to agree that our civilization's future depended on getting people out of cities. In fact I still have pages covered with his sketches illustrating his current enthusiasm: hanging prefabricated apartments in eccentric clusters from widely separated towers half a mile high, connected with bridges, and accessible by elevators and cable cars. "I've always wanted to be an engineer—secretly," he said. "Now I have to be!"

"Do you really think people will be happier living like regimented birds?" I asked.

"It's not a matter of happiness," he said, "but of survival."

3

The village in southern Vermont where Norman and his fifth wife, Carol Stevens Kay, a divorced jazz singer, had rented a rambling farmhouse in the summer of 1971, was a long day's drive from my New Jersey home. My nineteen-year-old daughter, Oriana, was with me, and when we arrived at sundown Carol Mailer, with three-month-old Maggie in the crook of her arm, came to the door and gave us a very hostile look. When we gave her our names, she was all smiles. Even this far from New York City, which Norman had tried to turn into the Fifty-first State two years ago, his fans besiege him. Like Jean and Beverly, the two other wives I'd known, Carol seemed to be wholly feminine, but less involved in his intellectual life—perhaps a good omen.

Norman greeted us and took us out back to see the stable full of horses and the artificial pond said to be full of trout. Until last week his eight children had been here. He'd taken the two boys on a camping trip to a remote lake, and he told us of their uneasiness in the blackness until the moon came up ever-so-slowly between two trees. He showed us a mounted 36" × 36" photo he'd just received: canons and craters and awesome frozen cataracts. He asked me what I thought it was.

"The moon," I guessed, "or an enlargement of detergent bubbles from a washing machine?"

"An enlargement of a hole on a moon rock the size of a pinhead."

We had gin-and-tonics with his mother and father, who had been reading a book called *Fasting Can Save Your Life*. Unpretentious lower-middle-class Brooklynites who seem to take their son's fame entirely in stride, they accept (no doubt with original outrage) Norman's uninhibited barracks talk; though if they weren't fond and proud of him I'm sure they wouldn't. Myrtle, their black cook from Honduras, was formally introduced and seated with us at the dinner table. She didn't say much, but neither did anyone else with Norman holding forth. I started him off on Mexico—his admiration of Cortez, "my favorite adventurer," and his distaste for the present totalitarian politics, crumbling *multifamiliars* and hazardous waste products. He recapped with great gusto his recent sparring bouts with José Torres, the former lightweight champion whose book *Sting Like a Bee* he'd sponsored, and his current obsession with "jogging" uphill for an hour or two every morning—"mental as well as physical relaxation" he called it.

With David, Carol's eighteen-year-old son, he settled down to a game of gō, a Japanese stone game that he prefers to chess "because it exercises both one's tactical and strategic talents." But he wasn't concentrating too hard to discuss with my daughter the plots of half a dozen old movies they had seen recently.

The film of *From Here to Eternity,* I interjected, was more sharply focused than the novel. "But at what a loss!" Norman demurred. "Like Jones's great insight in the line the dying bully Fatso delivers to Prewit—'What did you have to go and do *that* for?' showing Fatso never *knew* he'd been a bully. Left out of the movie entirely!"

He recalled later on living in the same Brooklyn rooming house with Arthur Miller after the war. "Unknown to me, he was writing his masterpiece while unknown to him I was slogging away at *The Naked and the Dead.* If anyone had told me that middle-class type was writing something as powerful as *Death of a Salesman* I wouldn't have believed it. Seeing him empty his garbage cans day after day, and exchanging small talk about nothing, I can remember thinking, 'Shit! That guy's never going *anywhere!*' "

I recall also Norman saying, after everyone else had gone to bed and I was congratulating him on Carol, "Those four marriages . . . In the nineteenth century one of them would have lasted my lifetime. We have less toleration for misery."

4

After breakfast the next morning I "jogged" part way uphill with Norman and David, and then watched the two of them spar on the front lawn and punch the elaborate bags in the barn. It took Norman a long time to tape his hands.

He uses a regulation rubber mouthpiece, and he offered David a padded leather sparring helmet. I wondered whether David politely refused for fear it woud give Norman leeway to land some big punches. But he was rather miffed when Norman (who is surprisingly quick and skillful) didn't hit him solidly at all. "O.K., David," Norman said, "tomorrow I'll let you have a few to the mid-section."

The worried look returned to David's face.

"Look, David, what kind of a teacher would I be if I slapped and banged you all over the place, or decked you with a right cross? You've got to start anything slowly, and build your confidence along with your skill. You've got talent. You move exceptionally well and you use your hands instinctively. So let's progress little by little, O.K.?"

David went inside the house and I sat on the lawn with Norman while he peeled the tape from his hands. A daddy longlegs was coming down the lightning-rod ground. "Isn't it amazing," Norman said, pointing to it, "that creature has no function, makes no sense in our world. Look at the awkwardness of its locomotion. It's not from our universe!"

"Can you prove that, Norman?"

"Of course not. Can you prove a poem? On a scale of one hundred, poetry's answers, or better its successes, are one hundred to zero compared with science's. Science's answers to the basic questions it's supposed to deal with are anemic. It's a record of total failure."

"Like what basic questions?" I asked.

"The nature of gravity, of electricity, of light, time, life—what do they offer? Nothing really. Take time. The possibility is never considered that a second here may not be a second twenty galaxies away. And I'm not talking about Einstein's relativity. Scientists know *less* about the atom the more they delve into it."

"What you're saying is that Lucretius had all the answers. When they invented the microscope and the telescope those answers looked absurd."

"No, I mean take the latest attempt to explain what holds

those protons together: the scientists' postulation of 'nuclear force' is far less precise and far more mysterious than the earlier postulations—"

"Another way of saying we know more and more about less and less?"

"There's a cluttering of philosophies and concepts that would be intolerable in the making of a poem—"

"A poem by Frost maybe, but what about one by Wallace Stevens?"

"Can't read him. In medicine it becomes a comedy!"

"Medicine?"

"Yes. There's a self-regulating system in the universe—"

"There is? What is it?"

"That only the unloved die. We violate it! Don't be taken in by the statistic that life expectancy has increased from thirty-nine in 1850 to seventy today. The expectancy would have been sixty-nine in 1850 if they could have duplicated our rate of survival for babies under a year old. In other words, all medicine has accomplished is to save most of the weaker, sicklier infants."

"Are you advocating something like Swift's *A Modest Proposal* to get rid of them?" I asked.

He laughed. "I'm not advocating anything. I'm just objecting to the adenoidal tone of the liberal who says, 'It's a human life. We must save it.' That's a totalitarian idea—"

"Why?"

"Because it assumes that one state in itself is good, that life is an absolute, regardless of quality. I say that only human life transcending itself is a good state—"

"And if it doesn't it's bad? And by implication should be eliminated?"

"You're going to accuse me of Hitlerism?"

"I'm going to warn you of a philosophy under which the Hitlers will make the decisions! But carry on—"

"O.K. Medicine says, 'Give us money so we can save life.' There are three crocks of shit in that request. One: at least three quarters of the money they get won't go for research at all but to the medical bureaucracy. Two: the premise of their request—that medicine is something *good*—isn't true. Three: human life, untested and without achievements, is not necessarily desirable."

"You sound like a latter-day Nietzsche," I said, "but speak on, Zarathustra."

"Medicine's antibiotic successes in our time may turn out to be the horror story of the Seventies and Eighties. The failure of cancer research is symbolic of medicine's lack of inspiration. They simply refuse to recognize the possibility—probability, I'd say—that cancer's in everybody, but takes over only when the body's balance is tipped in favor of psychic anxiety, when the personality becomes a technological robot out of touch with primitive forces and emotions, on a collision course with environmental poisons—"

"Speaking of poisons," I said, "I see you're all reading this book on health by way of fasting. Is that a way of eliminating them from the body?"

"One way. Dieting is for the birds, but fasting—I fasted for two weeks recently, nothing but water—"

"Weren't you in an agony of hunger the first few days, until you got too weak to care?"

"Not at all. By the fourth day you lose your appetite entirely. The only problem is that you begin to smell bad and get constipated—"

"On *nothing*?" I asked with surprise.

"You're burning your excess body fats for fuel. All your poisons are coming out as sweat. The body is an efficient self-perpetuating factory. I began to get actually *calm!* No temper, no fighting any more. My mind became extraordinarily *clear.* I recommend it especially for schizophrenics—"

"I'm a hungry schizophrenic," I said, "let's eat!"

5

We walked out to the trout pond after lunch and made some casts with the spinning rod. Though August 1, it was much too cold to swim and I'd been wearing Norman's ski jacket ever since we arrived. Across the valley were the green ski trails of Magic Mountain, and in the meadow between we could see Bobbie and Oriana riding the Apalusas. I asked Norman whether he was thinking of buying the farm.

"I've thought about it. But there are 470 acres and that would bring the price to half a million. I don't have that kind of money, or when I do I spend it on my movie ventures. Even before those three losers I went broke keeping the play of *The Deer Park* going for weeks when it should have folded. Just because the company was so enthusiastic and I kept telling myself it would catch on."

I reminded him of my play about King Christophe which ANTA was about to produce when we first met.

"I wonder why I liked you from the start when we disagreed so violently about Wallace," he mused.

"You sensed I was a fellow antiliberal."

"It must have been that."

"And what I liked about you, apart from your novel, was that you had the courage and integrity to break with Wallace when you realized that he was being manipulated by the Stalinists . . . Wasn't there ever a time in the beginning of Vietnam, Norman, when you said to yourself as I did, 'This will go down as an honorable intervention in behalf of a weak country threatened by totalitarianism, if we don't make the mistakes of Korea, and win it quickly?' Wasn't Goldwater the one to warn that those who fight a war halfheartedly lose, and that unless we quit giving the enemy sanctuaries we'd wind up crippling ourselves with guilt and self-loathing?"

"Goldwater wanted to win the war by defoliating the trees and making Southeast Asia a wasteland," he said. "How could I be for him?"

"You're using a liberal's arguments against war. War is always ugly," I said.

"I've never been either a liberal or a pacifist," he said. "I've been against the Vietnam War for two reasons. One: the rich boy shouldn't kill the poor boy just because he has the marbles—that is, weapons. It's bad for the rich boy's moral fiber. And Two: just from the point of view of our own system's survival, we should have strengthened North Vietnam and encouraged them to organize Southeast Asia as a counterweight to totalitarian China, their traditional enemy."

"Letting the two fight it out, in true Machiavellian fashion?"

"Sort of. At least leaving us free to face our own domestic evils, and not allied with corruptionists like Diem, Thieu, and Ky."

We took two chairs out of the kitchen and set them facing the pastoral scene.

"God, I'm glad you don't use a tape recorder!" he said.

"No chance. Even if I wanted to, I'd put it out of order or be electrocuted. But you're more scientifically oriented, judging by *Of a Fire on the Moon,* my favorite—"

"Not really," he said, "certainly not philosophically. You saw me in the only time I wished I'd been an engineer."

"Were there engineers in your family?"

"My dad used to be an accountant. He was a British subject from Johannesburg, South Africa, coming here after World War I. But his family was from Lithuania."

"Where would we be without Lithuania?" I laughed. "Ben Shahn, Stanley Kunitz, you—and your mother?"

"She was born in Long Branch, New Jersey, where I was born. We moved to Brooklyn when I was four."

"Seeing you with them I have to assume that your childhood was happy."

"It was happy," he said. "Very pleasant, very middle class."

"So what gave you your drive?"

"The transplant from Brooklyn to Harvard when I was sixteen. I can't say that I was put down for being Jewish, or that I raged in isolation. It was more a case of cultural shock, finding the world of Harvard so unlike Brooklyn. Even the fact that I was part of the majority, discriminated against by the minority of Hasty Pudding . . . Well, it was irritating, but not exactly *painful*. I don't know . . . I suppose if I'd gone to C.C.N.Y. I'd have grown up an engineer."

We took a couple of more futile casts in the fading light and exchanged yarns about our Supermen five-year-olds. "When José Torres caught a bullfrog in the pond last week," Norman said, "Steve said to the former lightweight champion of the world, 'If that frog dies I'm gonna make ya *eat* it!' "

"Would he like to be an astronaut?" I asked.

"I wouldn't encourage him," Norman said. "I couldn't get through to those astronauts at all. I wrote Neil Armstrong a long letter, asking him for an interview. 'You wouldn't have let even a *good* airlines pilot take the LEM down from the Command Module, would you?' I wrote. 'So why not let a writer who is recognized to be one of the best in his field . . .?' But all Armstrong replied was, 'Your argument is most convincing but I'm afraid the answer has to be No.' They didn't really trust me. Except perhaps Aldrin, and by the time he got around to considering it it was too late. A friend of mine on *Life* who tried to talk Collins into it with 'What have you got to lose?' says he got the answer, 'What have I got to gain?' " He gave me a lugubrious look.

"'A man alone ain't got no fuckin' chance,' " I said, "to quote your hero—or do you have ambivalent feelings about Hemingway, Norman?"

"They were a lot more ambivalent before he died," he said. "His death took all the envy out of me. I'd sent him *The Deer Park* once, expecting some response. 'Why doesn't he recognize me?' I used to think."

I never remembered to carry that question further, for we were called in for gin-and-tonics, and after dinner there were bouts of chess, and long after I'd gone to bed the horses broke out of the stable, and Norman and Oriana spent a good part of the night rounding them up while the rest of us slept blissfully.

6

" 'Existential' is your favorite word," I said to Norman next morning after breakfast, "how do you define it?"

"Like when you don't know how something will turn out," he said. "Like David not knowing whether he could trust me when we sparred yesterday."

"I've never understood Kierkegaard very well," I said.

"I'm afraid I've gotten most of Kierkegaard secondhand from my friend Jean Malaquais," he said.

"You say somewhere that magic, dread, and the perception of death are the roots of all motivation—"

"For some people. For the protagonist of *An American Dream*, for instance."

"You wouldn't deny that you have something in common with those writers like Pound, Eliot, Lawrence, Yeats, Campbell, who were attracted to fascism in some degree—?"

"No, I wouldn't deny it."

"What did they see in it that seemed so necessary to them —and to you?"

"A return, a necessary return, to primitive and traditional values, as the rest of the world raced into undifferentiated technology. That's as far as I accompany them. The irony was that they thought fascism would protect them from totalitarianism! But you go along with me on that, don't you?"

"Yes. Where I differ with you most," I said, "is in placing the sex drive ahead of all other motivations in the creative life—and the masculine sex drive exclusively. And about the way you seem to treat women as objects, to be pursued, violated, conquered, tossed aside. I have to agree with many of Kate Millet's indictments in that regard, though I'm no proponent of Women's Lib and like to see women as sharply differentiated from men as possible—physically but not neces-

176

sarily economically. It seems to warp your social thinking, too, as when you say 'we'll be able to reduce the birthrate only when we stop trying contraception.' How, Norman, how—?"

"Women have the power of *natural* contraception in their physiologies—"

"You've got to be kidding!"

"Wait. But now, like men, they're becoming technological beasts. It goes back to what I was saying about medicine. We've got to give less care to preserving babies at all costs. In a country like India fornication becomes a serious act; it has consequences—"

"The only consequence I can see is that they breed like rabbits and the children die of malnutrition."

"It may be too late to resist technology," he replied vaguely, "to develop within oneself the power to exercise natural contraception."

"I've lost you there," I said. "Let me take another tack. Why is it that so many of your characters—Croft, Cummings, Rojak, O'Shaughnessy—are latent homosexuals, or suffer the dread of being such. Do you have such a dread yourself—?"

He smiled. "Don't we all?"

"Why," I asked him, "does the male protagonist of 'The Time of Her Time' say 'She was a hero fit for me' at the end, after he's buggered her and she's told him that his whole life has been a running away from homosexuality?"

"It's his ironic recognition! Buggering a girl doesn't make one *ipso facto* a homosexual. It can be out of a liking for shit, or cruelty, or any number of other things. Can't I have sophistication enough to create a character a little above or below me? My answer to my Women's Lib critics is: '*Of course* I'm a latent homosexual. But I choose, as Sartre puts it, to be heterosexual.'"

"Carole—my Carole, not yours—says, 'People should sleep with their friends, not their enemies. Allen Ginsberg is at peace with his hangup and so he wants a peaceful world.' Your hangup, Norman, if I can call it that—?"

177

"Go right ahead!"

"Well, look at it this way. Many of the greatest creators—Beethoven, Whitman, Keats, Borges, to mention four—seem to have had no sex life at all, no matter how much they wanted it—"

"True. But not relevant. You can be a great artist either way. The great creators survive with huge powers, deficiencies, imbalances, because their *wit* enables them to achieve balance, as in O'Shaughnessy's line at the end of 'The Time of Her Time'—he likes a fighting woman! (I happen not to, by the way: deliver me from scrappy women! I'm not that pugnacious. You heard Carol at lunch yesterday telling how I rushed upstairs to get my gun to shoot that raccoon, and then couldn't shoot—I, the great *macho!*)"

"Germaine Greer says—"

"I refuse to immortalize Greer by counterpunching her. She quotes as sloppily as Millett. The only difference is that Greer *knows* what she's doing."

"Why don't you stop writing novels about all these scruffy perverts, Norman, and write one about the arch-hipster-revolutionary?"

"Don't you think 'D. J.' is on the edge?"

"Give him a shove . . . No. I think you'll have to start fresh in the next one. D. J. is too self-oriented. Incidentally, do you still think the social decision is between the nihilism of the hip-revolutionary, and those squares like me who want to improve society as it is, make democracy work, and so on?"

"No. I don't have the confidence that I had in the Sixties (my decade). I find the Seventies confusing. I now lean toward the idea of participatory democracy, as in my New York mayoral campaign. You know: old people in one community, pot smokers in another, Catholics in a third, hippies in a fourth, and so on. Then, and only then, will we be able to find out which works and prospers. Polemics, battles over ideologies, are no longer productive. The political instruments we have are rudimentary, compared with our political desires. Example: the Women's Day Care Centers advocated by Women's Lib can only be tested in a commune. I'm all for that testing—as long as I don't have to send *my* children."

"You say somewhere that 'orgasm is the therapy and purpose of life.' You still believe that?"

"Orgasm is only a guide, the inescapable existential moment—that word again!—of finding out what you are," he said.

"I'm afraid I have to go along with Millett," I said, "when she says that for Henry Miller and the like, orgasm is only a guide to finding out how many women he can lay in a given time, and how ridiculous he can make them look while he's doing it."

"Miller's genius," Norman replied, "was to make cock the center of the universe, as it is for many if not most men anyway, and to do this unashamedly and with great gusto. My answer to Millett is that I'd be even *more* grateful for the first novel by a woman to make cunt the beginning and end of everything. I'd have more to learn from it!"

"What you'd learn wouldn't be much use to you!" I said. "I agree about the gusto, and I enjoy *talking* with Henry as much as with anybody I can think of. It's the obsession with the subject—*any* obsession with *any* subject, whether its cookery or crockery or buggery—that is boring: and sexually deflating—if I wanted to be turned off sex, well, I can think of few writers except maybe Philip Roth that manage to make it more repulsive. But let's return to that book of yours about the moon that does turn me on. Is it your conclusion (rage or outrage) that the Wasps did it while the Hips were dropping out?"

"Not my major conclusion," he said. "You'd agree, I'm sure, that any good book is opposed to the succinct, that it can't be summed up. One thing I was trying to do was give the literary reader some idea of what it is like to pass through a technological experience. If our future is technological—to what degree is that tolerable? Will the sensitive man, the creative spirit, the individualist, be obliged to drop out? Do you think I succeeded in that intention?"

"Definitely. The beginning and end are wonderful. You lost me in the 'Psychology of the Machine' chapter. Weren't you worried about having written too much, produced a book that might be a formidable table-talk object or book end, like *Science for the Citizen*—or *Giles Goat Boy?* You admit yourself you read only half of *Ulysses* and scraps of *Finnegans Wake.*"

"Yes, I worried. It's too long—or maybe too short. The middle part may be intolerably tedious. 'A Day in Space and Another Day' might have been cut. But 'Psychology of the Machine' never. So I'd have lost you anyway!"

"In *Cannibals and Christians* you lump together all beatniks and Bolsheviks and do-gooders from LBJ to Mao. And when you ask, 'Is the curse on the world or on oneself?' you imply that the blood-loving cannibals are narcissists—"

"I don't identify with either. Whenever an artist condemns a whole slice of society, isn't the curse on him? This was the fate of D. H. Lawrence at his worst (*Kangaroo*) when he anathematized every tribe and race he didn't like. Or Henry Miller, consigning all America to his *Air-Conditioned Nightmare.*"

"Why do you quote so little poetry and mention so few poets?"

"I came to poetry late. In the last five or ten years. Before my own book of poems, which you treated so generously, I never even *read* poetry. As it is, *Death to the Ladies* . . . is really a movie in words. And movies, my three anyway, are a way of getting away from the half-resolved plots we're used to. But to come back to the 'intentions' of the book you like: the *right* approach to the moon, I was trying to say, is to probe its psychic properties. NASA was trying to take the moon away from us. They were afraid of 'bad publicity,' like Mailer interviewing the astronauts and asking embarrassing questions. Mattingly's experiment with extrasensory properties on the last Apollo shot was the right approach."

As we were breaking up, Norman said: "I've been thinking of two questions we touched on. One: fasting. The cave men had to work or endure for weeks between kills. So our bodies were designed to go long periods unsatisfied. There's a primitive need to recognize our physical resources: a tonic for the psyche. And two. More on that favorite word of mine, 'existential.' I love it because you can't define it and because it only reveals itself in new contexts. Technologists live to get life into the now existential state of pulling a controlled switch. When people's lives have *no* existential content, like retired businessmen, they *die*. It was the dangers, or hazards, of business that kept them alive—an obvious remark, but the only good thing to be said for business is that it once was existential!"

Top left: Allen Ginsberg at his family's home in Paterson, New Jersey, 1970. Top right: With his father, the poet Louis Ginsberg, and the author's daughter Oriana. Bottom: In 1972, after returning from India. " 'We're recovering what's been lost in the West since the Middle Ages.' "

Chapter Nine

ALLEN GINSBERG

"Isn't Beethoven saying, 'Respect the Whale'?"

1

It was eight years into our friendship before we had the climactic conversation about the whale; but from the beginning Allen was working toward it.

We met in July of 1964, the "long hot summer" of the Harlem race riots and the Republican convention that nominated Barry Goldwater. Just back from India, Allen had secured a "pad" in the East Village, and I had gone to it to arrange an interview with him for a program Channel 13 had asked me to do on "Artists of New Jersey." George Siegel, Lee Gatch, and Roy Lichtenstein had already appeared and were saying predictable things. I figured that Ginsberg and LeRoi Jones would make it more controversial—and they did. But what impressed me first about Allen was not the exhibitionism that so shocked the public in that far-gone time of shockability—undressing occasionally in public, acknowledging his homosexuality matter-of-factly, glorying in the drug culture and gleefully sprinkling common four-letter words through his manuscripts—but his gentleness, his honesty, his sense of humor.

As it turned out to be with so many of the others, my 1947 anthology provided the key. "It was a seminal book in my development as a poet," Ginsberg told me on the phone before I'd met him, "my introduction to poets like Neruda, Mayakovsky, Apollinaire. Bill Williams has talked to me about you too, but you've probably seen him much more recently. How is he bearing up under the stroke?"

"Very badly," I said, "it's heartbreaking to see him with this sense of total defeat for what he calls a 'wasted life'—his of all people!"

"Maybe the stroke made him feel that he'd put all his eggs in one basket," Ginsberg said, "—the basket of the body, 'no ideas but in things,'—and that he had no other resources to fall back on."

"Like what?" I asked in surprise.

"I wouldn't have put it like that before I went to India," he said. "But since talking to their wise men and the Tibetan monks and all, I've revised my thinking. Here and now doesn't matter so much. I'm still the victim of my anxieties, but I'm aware that it's my own hell I'm manufacturing."

He and Peter Orlovsky were living in a dumbell-tenement on East 5th Street at the time. A white-haired Rumanian was on the stoop complaining of the mess the kids were making with an open hydrant. Allen came to the door and took in the scene at a glance. "Where else have they got to play?" he said, putting his hand on her shoulder. She retreated down the corridor grumbling "Yeah, yeah . . ." Allen unlocked the door and I stumbled over a mattress and two rumpled pillows. He introduced me to Gregory Corso, who was sitting by the blaring radio in flannel pajamas, apparently writing poetry. "That poem of Jacques Prévert you translated really turned me on," Corso said, shaking his shaggy locks and grinning at me fiercely, "thanks, pal!" He had to shout to make himself heard above the din in the Cow Palace. "Those dirty fuckers," he added, pointing to the loudspeaker, "they're digging their graves, and ours too—not that it matters *who* they nominate!"

Allen gave me the grand tour of his Tibetan paintings and tapestries, explaining the intricate symbolism of each diagrammatic picture in great detail. While he did, Corso handed him bits of steak from a frying pan and he seemed to swallow them without chewing. He poured some tomato juice from a can into three glasses. "You knew Hart Crane, didn't you?" he said.

I said I hadn't known him, but that we corresponded when I was at Yale.

"He was the best of his generation," Allen said. "What drove him to suicide was that bunch of poet-critics who wanted him to suppress his homosexuality and be another Eliot."

The phone rang. He answered briefly and laughed. "That's the third call I've had this afternoon beginning 'Hey, Allen, come up to Harlem, they're having another great riot!' Can you imagine treating it like a ball game? How can you get any work done? Not that I'm working! Let's go over to the Metro."

Corso was staying in the hot flat with his poem and the noisy convention. We walked over to the coffeehouse 'Le Metro' where a poetry free-for-all was in progress. The poem being read was long, dull, and scatalogical. "It's by a heroin addict who has just been slammed by the pigs," Allen explained. "He was picked up by two other junkies. They're passing the breadbaskets for a collection to spring him."

An hour passed. A dozen poets read their poems. Only one, by Diane Wakoski, impressed me. But I was impressed by the group, their naturalness, their devotion to poetry. It was my introduction to what came to be called "the counter-culture." Without any feeling of self-consciousness or back-slapping, an extraordinary atmosphere of friendliness and dedication was generated. On the surface this was a collection of freaks—they use the word proudly to combat its pejorative use by journalists: long-haired, dirty, frowsy; homosexuals and Lesbians, barflies and misfits, dope addicts, Negroes and Negrophiles, ordinary people as well as Conscientious Objectors and conscientious pornographers. Ed Sanders handed me a free copy (everything is free here) of his publication, *Fuck You/A Magazine of the Arts,* with its slogan "Fucking, Fertility, Freaking, Freedom!" and its lead article a clinical dialogue by Allen and Peter Orlovsky describing their relationship. Sanders also passed out "The Complete Works of Thales, with a Foreword by Aristotle," a mimeographed page of Greek followed by a blank page. But this gathering of perhaps a hundred young people sipping their tea or lemonade, never raised their voices in an argument or treated anyone with disrespect or contempt.

"Does anyone screen the poems?" I asked Allen.

"No. Everyone is free to read and be heard. If there was screening there'd be dictation, cliquishness, bad feeling, competition, hate—inevitably."

"Come again," said Peter from under his floppy, knitted wool beret, as we were leaving, "and read a poem if you'd like to."

"Next Monday," added Allen as he waved good-by to me, "when we'll *all* get into the act."

2

We all did, and I wrote a poem especially for the occasion, but there was little opportunity to talk. The next time we met was after the first of his "twin bill" performances with his father, Louis. Allen had let his hair and beard grow until his face was hard to find. We met in the Ginsberg house in Paterson, so like the house of William Carlos Williams a few miles away in Rutherford that I half expected the latter (who had died since our last meeting) to make a ghostly appearance and put an end to our wilder assertions with his nasal country doctor's authority.

I kidded Allen about staring through me at the performance.

"I just don't see very well," he said. "And maybe I'm a little scared in front of that sea of faces. But I wasn't in a trance . . . I *did* have a mystical experience, though, just now before you rang the bell. *From drinking a glass of soda water!* It landed on my palate and stayed there for a split second, transporting me into a world of effervescent visions!"

"I think you've solved the drug problem, Allen," I said, "and saved the addicts millions."

He laughed, and I asked him whether he'd had any bad trips from LSD.

"Never," he said, "unless I was feeling rotten to begin with, and then I deserved what I got. If you take it to expand your consciousness or heighten your awareness, it does just that."

"And is never addictive—?"

"Never—and unlike heroin, which I'm always warning

against. There's an army medical report on LSD which bears me out. Washington refuses to release it."

Allen is (or was) very hung up on the Federal government, which he spoke of as if it consisted of a series of interlocking evil conspiracies designed to hoodwink the public. He refuses to believe that stupidity or passivity are responsible for any of our mistakes in foreign policy—or that any of Washington's decisions are motivated by good intentions. "AID," he said at one point, "devotes its resources to supporting military dictatorships and training their police forces in the use of torture—as in Brazil and Uruguay. Dan Mitrione was a typical AID operative."

I had just returned from both countries, staying with friends in AID in Montevideo and Porto Alegre. "Look, Allen," I said, "I never met Mitrione, whose assignment, before the Tupamaros murdered him was certainly to help train Montevideo's police, at the request of the Uruguayan government, but I can assure you that Uruguay is no military dictatorship—it has by far the most democratic government in South America. *Most* AID employes are engaged in providing loans for roads, irrigation canals, and other good works."

"It's a cover," he said.

"The roads?"

"—to facilitate the movement of military vehicles?"

"I'm reassured to hear you laugh when you say that!" I said.

He asked Louis to show me a clipping he'd asked him to save, an 'admission' that Che Guevara had been hunted down by CIA agents. He berated his father good-naturedly for having removed the source and date of the news item—thus rendering it useless as evidence.

"Clearly," I said, "because Louis is in the pay of the CIA!"

"The CIA trapped Che," he said, "with the use of infrared sensors used to detect guerrillas in foliated areas by the body heat they give off."

"Maybe so," I said, "but if they were there it was Barrientos who had asked for their help, and Barrientos had the Bolivian peasants behind him—that was the real reason Che got nowhere . . . But tell me about Bob Dylan, Allen, is he a peasant or an intellectual? I've been trying to reach him for a month to unscramble the texts of two of those lyrics I want to include in the revised *100 American Poems*. Why is he so elusive? And do you dig him as a poet?"

"You heard me on the phone for ten minutes just after you came in?" said Allen by way of explanation. "It was some kid in Haledon who just wanted to 'discuss poetry' with me for a few minutes—which he did, even though I told him I was busy with an old friend. If Dylan had a telephone where he could be reached, tried to answer his enormous mail, kept files, or even had secretaries to make his life 'efficient,' he'd have no time to lead a normal life with his two children and his new wife's three—much less create any more music. Do you answer letters, Selden?"

"Yes. Unless they're from bona fide cranks—"

"Aha! You see? You make exceptions too. But I admire your industry and wish I were as well organized. But to come back to Dylan—Creeley and I once made a line-by-line count of the lyrics to see how much of it could be called poetry. One line of genius out of four—"

"Pretty good batting average for *any* poet."

He agreed. And he asked me why I wasn't including Olson, Duncan, and Creeley in the revised edition. Or Corso or Kerouac.

I told him I was including Olson and Corso. "But they don't really send me, and the others not at all. By the way, are you still friends with LeRoi Jones?"

"He won't speak to me any more."

"How come?"

"I'm white. But maybe now that his friend Kenneth Gibson has made it in Newark he won't be so uptight." He showed me two little pictures he and his father had bought in Haiti, asking me how recently I'd been there, and why our government "keeps Papa Doc in power."

"We haven't given Haiti a penny in five years or more," I said.

"I've heard that Port-au-Prince is crawling with CIA agents

whose only occupation is exposing dissident Haitians to Papa Doc."

"You mean the Creole-speaking department of CIA—?"

He laughed. "Why not?"

"The danger for Latin America," I said, "is that this preoccupation with foreign conspirators gives them another excuse for not putting their own houses in order. It's a cop-out."

"I was saying to Allen at breakfast that suicide is a cop-out," Louis said.

"And I was disagreeing, and continue to disagree," Allen said. "It's becoming a more and more effective means of protest—and a legitimate one. Ten years from now—if the world is still here—there will be hundreds of suicides, like that of the friend we were talking about, maybe enough to paralyze the country!"

3

It was hardly a year later, in the fall of 1971, that I returned to Paterson to find Allen a changed man. I don't suppose he would have disavowed any of the opinions expressed the year before, but he wasn't talking on that level and his perceptions seemed to have deepened.

Once again there had been a public performance with Louis —this one in Teaneck. I sat down in the packed high school auditorium a few minutes late. Louis was warming them up, as he puts it, with his puns. Red China had been admitted into the United Nations the day before and he had one for that occasion: " 'What do you think of Red China, Mrs. Goldberg?' " the pollster asks, and Mrs. Goldberg replies, " 'Not bad on a blue tablecloth.' " Then there was the time he had gone to an agricultural college to read his poetry and the teacher said, "I know all about poultry . . ." "In this world of proton, neutron and electron," the lighthearted sage of Paterson concluded, "it's worst to be a moron . . . In this world of wars and death camps where all men are cremated equal . . ."

I was dozing but that one made my eyes pop open. Louis

must have noticed the five hundred students and their parents cringe, too, for he picked up his book. "I will now read 'Morning in Spring'—spring being the favorite season of poets . . ." I looked at Allen, slumped in his chair on the other side of the lectern; he was looking at his father with the same benign expression. Louis proceeded to read the poem, and then paused. "Is life worth living? It depends on the feelings. But I always think of Marvell's marvelous lines,

> 'But at my back I always hear
> Time's wingéd chariot drawing [*sic*] near' . . ."

Now it is Allen's turn to hold the stage . . . He begins with some deep-breathing exercises—Om—Ah—Hum—intoned with deep vibrations into the microphone above chords on the little pink harmonium held close to his ear, his left hand pumping the bellows. He describes the bodily equivalents of these sounds, the regions of the body they reach—"Head—Heart—Belly—Cock-or-Cunt." He invites "the adventurous" to chant with him. "For those of you who are trying, it's best to have a straight, completely straight, spine." The little organ groans now, his intoning of the mantra gets more guttural, almost ecstatic in the treble. "The sounds are Sanskrit," he says, "but I dedicate these mantric syllables of the body to those of you who still pay your taxes to the government:

> WHOM—BOMB? YOU—BOMB—YOU . . .
> WHAT DO WE DO?
> WE DO—YOU
> WE BOMB—WE BOMB THEM!
> WHOM BOMB
> YOU BOMB—YOU BOMB YOU!

He reads some recent haikus next, very Rexrothian, about "tiny brachiapods, skeletons of the Cambrian"; then some longer, recent poems, "mostly published in the underground press. 'Pine branches hang in rain . . . Grey streaks my beard . . . Rheumatism twinges my knees when I walk . . .

Well, I still must be Buddha here—if not, who am I?' "
Then a long Rexrothian-Hopkinsesque string of nature
images, some seemingly disjointed à la Kerouac, "pissed out by
the forest's bladdery" something or other, and ending, "Grandmother ocean shirt silver hair ear to ear." He'd been with
John Lennon and Yoko in Syracuse the week before, he told
me later, "learning their way of singing and teaching them
mine," and there was a poem in their style, ending ". . . to die
happy." And an autumn poem about driving from Boston to
Hanover that reminded me sadly of late Whitman when the
cataloguing had become perfunctory, a kind of "Howl"-gone-
travelogue. And an elegy to Che, with some of the fine vintage
rage directed at imperialists and other bourgeois: "One—
face driven mad with the rifle, confronting the electric net-
works . . ." And a moon shot poem with an announcer shout-
ing, " 'Man Lands on *Sun!* ' " And finally the Blake *Songs of
Experience,* given a moving new dimension by the Gins-
bergian plain song with organ accompaniment.

The question period that followed was as interesting.

(To Louis from one of the few adults in the audience):
"Did you encourage him to write poetry as a child?"

"Well," said Louis, "when he and Eugene lay on the floor
screaming—their mother was in the asylum—I quoted Keats
and Shelley as I paced between them."

(To Allen): "What do you see happening to the 'best minds'
of your generation now?"

(Answer): "I see the world, threatened or cracking when I
wrote that, coming to an end. You saw Jacques Cousteau
quoted in the *Times* this morning about the oceans being
dead twenty-five years from now? The living standards being
enjoyed by our generation of middle-class Americans can no
longer be permitted if the world is to survive. I feel, in other
words, far more certain of Moloch than when I was your age,
writing "Howl." Our greed now threatens to destroy the rest
of the planet. I hesitate to write poems any more, to talk into
this electric-powered mike, to travel in a jet. We must become
ascetics and stop consuming. Or is it too late? I'm confused at
the enormity of it, confused to be living in such a world! Yet

the liberals, like the *New York Post* yesterday with its headline 'War Casualties Diminish,' might as well be living on another planet. Whose casualties? I was in India two weeks ago, invited to see the Bengali refugees. The Bengali genocide is like Hitler's gas chambers—and we're providing Pakistan with the arms to massacre the helpless ones who thought they could win their freedom by voting! No. I see nothing but doom ahead and have nothing to offer but 'Ring down the Curtain.' "

A woman got up to protest these apocalyptic observations. "I wouldn't take Allen too seriously," Louis answered her. "It's good for all of us to have him flagellate the world but he doesn't see the whole picture."

(From a younger voice): "Do you?"

"It's a picture we're all making together," Allen interjected.

"Who are the great poets today, Mr. Ginsberg?"

"Corso, Robert Duncan, Philip Lamantia, Gary Snyder, Kerouac—" Kerouac, he added, was a victim of Momism [Philip Wylie had died the day before] who never unlocked to confront his true sexual nature.

"Isn't all this tragedy and war and injustice *good* for poetry, Mr. Ginsberg?"

"No. We'd have a greater poetry if this was a time of tranquillity. We'd have a poetry of expanding human consciousness, through meditation on technological breakthroughs, and transcendence in the cosmos."

The last questioner asked him to explain his chanting.

"By placing vibrations in different parts of the body you awaken the various neural centers—heart, brain, genitals, etc. A rhythmic tingling from the nose bone goes to the base of the brain and then down the spine. From me to you, hopefully! The satisfaction of exhaling is like the peace that follows orgasm—a familiar sensation with all of you, I hope!"

4

We had agreed after the performance to meet at Louis' house in Paterson for lunch next day. When I arrived Allen was on the telephone. When he got off I told him I was sorry I hadn't been able to visit him at his Cherry Valley chicken farm last summer.

"Just as well," he said, "I had to give it up to Peter Orlovsky. Peter has several girls going now, you know—a good thing for Peter, who's always been ambivalent about his homosexuality."

"Could you go that way, Allen?"

"No. I couldn't. But I'm glad for Peter that he can."

I asked him whether he'd read Karl Shapiro's sensational description of his visit to the Nebraska campus in *Edsel*. He hadn't and was glad I'd brought the novel with me. He read the chapter while I ate some soup and chicken-rice he'd warmed up for me. "Well?"

"It's fiction, of course," Allen said, "which puts it out of range in a sense. But if you ask: Was I there? and: Was that the way it was? I'd have to say I was, and that wasn't the way it was. Peter didn't have his face smashed. There was no violence, no fire, no police—though our party was certainly under surveillance and they breathed more easily when we moved on. But I'm surprised at the vehemence of Karl's distaste. He didn't show it then—though he didn't come to our meeting, preferring to hear a tape of it next day at his house—nor has he shown it since, most recently in Davis, California, a few weeks ago when we discussed only poetry. When he wrote *Essay on Rime* in 1946 he was defending the strict constructionists, but later he came over to Whitman's long line, to my way of writing I thought, in that loose thing he wrote, giving up rhyme and metrics entirely—so why is he so uptight, I wonder?"

"Speaking of strict constructionists," I said, "how do you feel about Stanley Kunitz's poetry?"

"I know he does what he does well, and I respect him, of course; but I can't really read that kind of traditional verse any more. It doesn't turn me on."

I reminded him of the passage in his *Indian Journals* where he says: "Generally rhymed verse sounds self-conscious—except where some Genius has opened up and the Self Consciousness is lost in a burst of sincerity or passion or amazement or ecstasy or comedy—as in Hart Crane." "—Or Stanley Kunitz," I added, "or any good poet. A little of that artificial restraint or containment wouldn't hurt your verse at all, Allen!"

"Maybe," he said with a smile, "and maybe not!"

What I wanted him to talk about was the relationship of his nonviolent Indian religion to his political activism, as manifested in his analysis of Che last night for instance. "Isn't India," I said, "more a symbol of social injustice, maldistribution of wealth, disease, and pollution than we are?"

"In India," he replied, "it's true that more people suffer poverty, but the earth is still funky, still relatively unpolluted. You throw the tea from your earthenware cup on the ground when you've finished drinking—not an indestructible plastic teacup."

"I was interested in what you said about ecology last night, Allen; your remark about the near-extinction of the whale—"

"The whale has a larger brain than we have, you know," he said.

I laughed. "I'm for saving the whale," I said, "because I like the idea of such a huge and harmless mammal lording it over the seas, and perhaps also because its existence there contributes to keeping the ocean clean and alive. But brains? What does the whale create, except other whales?"

His eyes flashed. "That's like saying 'Niggers are dumber than whites,' when it's the white chauvinist with his conceptual slide rule (which doesn't include music, for instance) making the comparison. Whales may not have written epic poems or invented computers. We don't know enough about their music-making yet to say whether it's superior or inferior to ours. But why is it necessary to have any reason at all to preserve the whale? Remember the passage in Job about the glory of Leviathan? Isn't it *maniacal* of us to have to *apologize* for the whale! Besides—what have *we* created?"

"The Ninth Symphony?" I suggested.

"All right. The Ninth. But what is the Ninth with its 'Hymn to Joy' but a manifestation of awe and respect for the universe and all its creatures? Like St. Francis's 'Canticle to the Creatures'? Or these lines from Wordsworth's "Tintern Abbey":

> '. . . For I have learned
> To look on nature, not as in the hour
> Of thoughtless youth; but hearing oftentimes
> The still, sad music of humanity,
> Nor harsh, nor grating, tho' of ample power
> To chasten or subdue . . . A sense sublime
> Of something far more deeply interfused
> Whose dwelling is the light of setting suns,
> And the round ocean and the living air
> And the blue sky, and in the mind of man
> A motion and a spirit that impells
> All thinking things, all objects of all thought,
> And rolls through all things . . .'

Isn't Beethoven saying, 'Respect the Whale'?"

"In a sense. You could interpret it that way."

"Isn't St. Francis saying 'God-consciousness and union with nature are one'?"

"Clearly."

"Isn't even old what's-his-name saying that the living don't need the production of works of art to justify them:

> 'Poems are made by fools like me
> But only God can make a tree . . .' "

I laughed. "Maybe you and Joyce Kilmer and Wordsworth in his long-winded dotage are saying it, but Beethoven—I have to doubt whether he'd have felt any such sense of creative inferiority, even vis-à-vis God."

"—Or take Dante," said Allen, who wasn't listening. "He says it in the thirty-third canto of the Paradiso, the passage about recognizing something superior to his consciousness as an artist, when he cries out 'Words fail me!' or something like that.

[O quanto e corto'l dire, e come fioco
Al mio concetto! e questo a quel, ch'io vidi
E tanto, che no basta a dicer poco . . .]

"Anyway," Allen continued, "my point is: to say that the criterion for what will survive is the production of works of art reflecting the human spirit is to say the opposite of what the artworks themselves say: 'I AM THAT I AM'—"

"The Hebrew motto Beethoven kept over his piano," I said, "but Beethoven put it there long after his deafness isolated him from the humanity he was so eager to reach. While he was still trying, by the evidence of his own letters, to lead a 'normal' life, wasn't he as sure that his 'Eroica' was a key to immortality as Shakespeare proclaiming that his 'powerful rhyme' would outlive 'marble and the gilded monuments of princes'? The motto—"

"The Hindu version of it," Allen said, "is 'Thou art that which is.' . . . But to come back to the whale; if men have to have *reasons* for saving the whale, the battle is already lost—"

"Why?"

"Blake's *Urizon* (You Reason) is an evil figure, trying to willfully control things, isn't he? Or Jehovah in the Garden of Eden—Jehovah is a supremely evil figure in Blake's cosmogony. Or Newton—trying to reduce the universe to numbers—more than enough to make Blake hate him as the Arch Mental Bureaucrat! Once you have to argue and find reasons, you're already lost. You've lost the organic relationship, the capacity for adoration, the inflowing-outflowing . . . I was doing it myself when I pointed out that the whale has a bigger braincase than man. It's a specious argument. I was building bridges.

"Look!" he continued. "The whole of Nature is a machine, a machine more complex than any we can conceive, so any rational step we take only removes a few of the moving parts of that machine—a machine so complex that it appears to be an organism. You know about the artists' (or scientists') attempt to square the circle. Well, Nature has already squared the circle!"

"And this Nature, or Machine," I said, "has it a soul?"

"Yes. It has a soul, a consciousness of its own. And it doesn't need us at all! So if we're so egotistical or anthropocentric as to measure the whale in terms of its 'usefulness' to us—well, that's like a cancer making judgments about the organism it feeds on, or Hitler thinking of the Slavs only in terms of a labor supply for the Aryans—and destroying the Jews who alone (as it turned out) could have saved him by giving him the atomic bomb . . . The human problem is to live up to the criteria of the universe as a whole. The rest is ego-talk."

5

We went out in the backyard and took some photographs of each other (he'd just gotten a new small camera that he wanted to try out). When we were in the kitchen again, I tried to steer the conversation back to the conflict between his political activism and the Indian religious passivity. "The idea of nirvana, for instance—?"

"Nirvana is a Western conception," he said, "a honky interpretation of Buddhism. How many Western 'activists' burned themselves up to illuminate their conviction as the Buddhist monks did in Saigon?"

"But isn't there any connection between the Indian religions of self-scrutiny and even self-immolation (as with those monks) and the Indian inability to feed and clothe its own people?" I asked.

"Indian philosophies and religions didn't cause the famine," he replied, "or the malnutrition or overpopulation, until the Mohammedans came, followed by the British. It was then that the forests were cut down and the deserts created and the pestilence first appeared. In the sixteenth and seventeenth centuries they destroyed the old agriculture, creating big estates in land and parceling them out in return for political control.

"One must distinguish Buddhism from Hinduism," he went on. "Buddhism began as a revolt against Hinduism with its caste system. I myself am initiated as a Shivaite—one who practices *kundalini yoga*—and I am a formal practitioner of the Buddhist mantras (prayers) and meditations."

"How much time do you devote to this?"

"I sing Padma Sambhava mantras ten or twelve hours a week. I'm commissioned (instructed) by three different teacher-schools to teach and spread the primary mantra of each: the Shivaite prayer of the Hindus; the Vaishnav (Harekrishna) chants of the Hindus; and the Nyingmapa of the Tibetan Buddhists who sing the Padma Sambhava mantras like the ones you heard me sing last night."

"Do you think you made any converts?" I asked.

"Maybe one—a good batting average! But perhaps twenty or thirty others were intrigued enough to look into it further. At least they enjoyed the vibrations . . . I began the Hare-krishna mantra back in 1963 after my first visit to India. Now George Harrison's recording of it is Number One on the jukeboxes! I told you about John and Yoko—"

"Is Bob Dylan's mysticism related?"

"Very remotely. He's getting into Hassidic studies, I hear. The mantras aren't 'mystical' in an otherworldly sense since they are very precise breathing exercises."

"And how is all this related to poetry?"

"We're recovering what's been lost in the West since the Middle Ages. The invention of the printing press transferred vocalization to the silent eye-studies, as McLuhan puts it. Of course the Hebrew Gnostic tradition of vocalization survived into the twelfth century in Spain, and was preserved there in hermetic studies. By various channels—astrology, witchcraft, alchemy, Rosicrucian cults, drugs, Pythagorean numbers—it was passed on from Paracelsus and Jakob Boehme and Swedenborg to Spenser and Bacon, Blake, De Quincey, Coleridge, Shelley, and through Bronson Alcott to Emerson's Transcendentalists and Herman Melville.

"Or, tracing it backward," he continued, "modern Western yoga relates to the Gnostic tradition, and from there to the *cabala* and the whole Hassidic culture. The Hebrews, in turn, got it out of the Zoroastrian ideas infiltrating the Middle East. Zoroaster himself took it from the *Indian* religions that seeped into Mesopotamia and Persia in the wake of Alexander the Great's push to the Indus River. The *Zohar* was written in twelfth-century Spain. Blake's illustrations for his *Book of Job* are based on Hebrew lettering in the cabalistic tradition. And so on.

"The point is, Selden, that this was *always* the unofficial Western tradition. Gary Snyder, more than me, is trying to bring it back, linking it with our own North American Indian practices. I'm trying to link it with Buddhism—another integration of Natural Consciousness. The 'Oversoul' Emerson talks about becomes in the East the Ultimate Emptiness, or better, a vast Ocean of Being. What the Zen philosophers call 'No Mind' may be equated with what Jung calls 'The Collective Unconscious'—"

"Henry Vaughan's 'great ring of pure and endless light'—?"

"Exactly! The Gnostics' Abyss of Light. Or St. John's 'In the beginning was the Word . . .' Or Prospero's speech in Act V, after he's abandoned magic, talks of returning to the rational, humdrum life of Naples or Milan, and says, 'Every third thought shall be my grave'—"

"Even more so in the Epilogue," I said, "where he says:

> 'Now my charms are all o'erthrown
> And what strength I have's my own;
> *Which is more faint* . . . Now I want
> Spirits to enforce, art to enchant;
> And my enemy is despair,
> Unless I be reliev'd by prayer,
> Which pierces so that it assaults
> Mercy itself and frees all faults . . .' "

"Have you read Pound's recent Cantos?" Allen asked me. "You must read the fragment of Canto 115, I think it is, where he says something like, 'The scientists are in terror and the European mind stops.' That's another way of saying what I've been trying to say. The poets are not in terror."

Top left: Vinícius de Moraes with his wife, Gessy Gesse, at Itapoán, Brazil, 1972. Top right: With the author's son, Van Nostrand, on the beach north of Salvador do Bahia. Bottom: " 'The style of Brazilians is wholly antithetical to authoritarianism or any form of repression.' "

Chapter Ten

VINÍCIUS DE MORAES

"I want to write the Black Mass of the candomblé. . . *."*

1

That girl who flings herself so cold
And wanton to my arms, who aims
Her breasts and kisses at me, stammering bold
Verses, and vows of love, and ugly names;

That girl, that flower of melancholy, who
Laughs at my colorless suspicions (two)
She, only, who would never have to shun
Caresses lavished on another one;

That woman who to every love proclaims
The misery and greatness of her aims,
Proud of the signature my teeth inbled,

That woman is a world!—a bitch, a trull
Perhaps . . . but for the impression in a bed
Never was any quite so beautiful!

"You must see Vinícius," Pablo Neruda said to me when I told him I was going to Brazil, and gave me a letter to him which I still have, a purple scrawl on green paper. I still have the letter because that year the ageless troubadour had just taken off on a grand tour with a young girl who wanted to see Italy. So I settled for translating the characteristic sonnet above, with the help of a young Brazilian diplomat-poet to whom Elizabeth Bishop had given me an introduction. I was no luckier the following year when I came back, armed this time with a commission from *Look* to write a profile of the guitar-playing poet in his Copacabana *boîte*. I came directly from Mar del Plata, the Argentine resort where I'd been careful to avoid the night clubs in anticipation of long sessions in Rio with Vinícius. "Alas," said Dona Lígia when I called to find out where her brother might be entertaining, "he's in Mar del Plata and will still be there when you've left Brazil for your home."

It was better the following year that I came with no introduction and no commission (for *Look* had since folded). This time the author of the famous scenario for *Black Orpheus* was in a little fishing village near Salvador do Bahia, rehearsing his troupe, though he would soon be back in Rio, his sister assured me. I took no chances and flew to Salvador at once. And in a matter of hours I was knocking on the gate of the beachhouse in Itapoán. "He'll see you this once," said Bob Sanden, the American Consul who had made the contact for me and driven me out, "but he's way out here to escape his fans and he may never see you again." "I'll take care of that," I said, as the corpulent poet in his bathing trunks and red bathrobe approached up the path to let us in.

Days later when I had gotten to know him well, Vinícius asked me what my first impression of him had been. "Petronius!" I said. "Perhaps from the toga-effect, and perhaps because I'd expected a tall, romantic type, slightly blasé from the *réclame* of café society—which you certainly are not." Nor is there anything at all cynical or debauched in the poet, who gives on the contrary an impression of complete dedication to his calling, of natural simplicity and warmth in his relations with everyone. He wears heavy black-rimmed glasses, but the Roman impression was perhaps enhanced by Vinícius' physical characteristics—he is very short, with a pendulous paunch, and his iron-grey hair is tied in back in a sort of pony tail—and by the setting: all those lovely singers and handsome young musicians with long hair reclining on deck chairs listening to bossa nova from the Master's tape recorder.

My passport was *South America of the Poets,* containing the translation of the sonnet, which Vinícius liked. I asked him where he'd acquired English good enough to appreciate it. I knew that English has superseded French as the second language of the Brazilian aristocracy, but still I was surprised by Vinícius' fluency. "I acquired it during my five years as Consul in Los Angeles," he said. "Before that in the company of Waldo Frank; and still earlier at Oxford. But tell me about yourself. How long will you be in Bahia and where have you come from?"

"Four more days—"

"Good. Then you will hear at least the rehearsals of our poetry show in Salvador next week end, and you can come out here and talk every day, if you like, after I get up—"

"Which is—?"

"About three in the afternoon, or maybe," he added apologetically, "about two."

"I was in Belo Horizonte yesterday," I said, "and met a friend of yours, Lúcia Machado de Almeida, who told me a lot about the poet Cecelia Mereiles, whom she knew very well, and about her husband's younger brother, the late Guilherme de Almeida, who was once elected 'Prince of Poets' by all the Brazilian poets, she said. Were you in on that coronation?"

Vinícius laughed. "Comic opera, isn't it? But true. We decided in advance that he *needed* it. So Drummond and I and the others gave him our votes. Cecelia Mereiles *was* a poet—"

"I struggled over two of her poems in the plane," I said, "trying to translate them. Am I wrong in sensing that she's a little academic?"

"A little," he said, "but quite wonderfully accomplished in the classical forms."

"No Emily Dickinson—?"

"Heavens, no. Not on that scale of greatness at all, but still very good."

"Speaking of greatness," I said, "how did you find Pablo in Paris last month? I mean, how does the Nobel Prize sit with him? He's happier now that he's got it at last?"

"I don't think so," Vinícius said. "He'd expected it for so many years, it came as no fulfillment. And I don't think that diplomacy is Pablo's style any more—if it ever was. He was fretting and cursing the day I saw him—about the crew of a Chilean destroyer that had just arrived. He was going to have to entertain them. Can you imagine?"

2

Our second afternoon was as short: rehearsal problems. We sat out back on the patio, where little wooden tables and chairs are set in the sand, under cover, just short of the beach. There are huge black rocks in the shallow water and a view around the curving sand of the fishing village. Vinícius, who has the reputation of being a heavy drinker, placed a bottle of Scotch between us, but hardly touched it. His young wife, a beautiful mulatto from Bahia, Brazil's most "African" state, joined us for a few minutes. She speaks no English. I asked Vinícius about Waldo Frank.

"He was the biggest influence in my youth," Vinícius said. "Not his novels, but his personality and his social idealism. We traveled together in '45, all over Brazil, which otherwise I might never have seen. He'd been badly beaten up by Argentine fascists, for he was fearless, and I was detached from my diplomatic training to be his bodyguard lest they follow him to Brazil. I carried a revolver because the *favelas* were then hotbeds of crime. The Day of St. George (Shango by syncretism) is very important in Rio, and we spent it in the street of the fiercest prostitutes. I saw crime and sexual degradation and poverty for the first time. It was also the gestation of one of my best-known poems, 'Balada do Mangue.' Within thirty days I was no longer a boy, no longer a citizen of the Upper Middle Class prepared by their priesthood to be a good rightist. I swung full circle. My vision was never the same again."

"You're still a leftist, Vinícius?"

"I still believe in democracy and social justice for the little man, if that's the definition," he replied, "and I oppose authoritarian censorship as best I can. At our International Festival of Music last year I was one of the fifteen composers who refused to accept the censorship. Up to then, they were finding a double meaning in the most harmless lyrics. We won out, and had the censorship lifted—in part, they say, because the decision went all the way up to President Médici, and he was annoyed by the censors' stupidity. The songs of the most influential young composer-poet, Chico Buarque de Holanda, weren't really that radical. (You must meet him, by the way.) But they express a very strong feeling, a feeling that democracy will return, perhaps. Médici himself, compared with his predecessors, would like to relax the repressive measures; at least that's my impression. He *could* be more than just a brilliant administrator who was smart enough to put Delfim Neto in charge of our production."

"How active are the hippies?" I asked.

"Very active. And their movement is growing. All the educated youth smoke marijuana, and LSD trips are not uncommon. But the hippies here are only for love and peace, and maybe LSD. The political ones in the schools have been picked up long ago."

"Does racial integration work both ways in Brazil? I mean, white men are attracted to black women as always; but do white girls have affairs with black men?"

"Only in this state of Bahia," Vinícius said. "In Rio or São Paulo the *machismo* of the white élite is too strong, as in the Spanish-speaking countries. They're too underdeveloped, culturally, to permit it. Bahia is more telluric, more in harmony with deep ancestral roots."

I told him about the great experience I'd had here three years ago, participating in the rites of Yemanja, the sea goddess, and how surprised I had been to find the dancing, the drumming, and the symbolism of the transplanted African deities virtually identical with Haitian *vaudun*. (They call the rites *candomblé* here, *makumba* or *umbanda* in the regions of Rio and São Paulo.) I asked Vinícius whether there'd be any ceremonies to see before we had to fly back Saturday, and he said I should check it out with Jorge Amado or Carybé. "They're believers, like me, but they know this region better. Ask them to put you in touch with Olga do Ala-Ketu—that's her African name."

"You've been possessed, Vinícius?"

"No. I haven't had that privilege yet. If you don't have either the Catholic or African background it's hard to be totally involved. But I think that possession is less crucial than in Haitian *vaudun*—from what you tell me. The purest believer I know is my priestess, Menininha do Gautois. She's eighty years old and has never been possessed. She never had to be. She had the powers from birth!"

"Since I met her," he went on, "my life has changed. For example, I was on the first Air France flight to Brazil years ago. We crashed in Uruguay and I saw one of my closest friends cut in half by the flying propeller, so that I was bathed in his blood. I went on flying, reluctantly; but five years ago the fear began to get me. (Oscar Niemeyer and Jorge Amado will never fly, you know.) Then one day Gessy Gesse, a believer, and now my wife, took me to Menininha, and I lost all my fears. 'My son,' she said, 'the hand of your Father, Oxala, will hold you!' (Oxala is the supreme god, and my particular deity, but not hers.) My songs, my poetry, got stronger too. I'll give you an example." (He sang, and then translated.)

Voce que sabe demais
Meu Pai mandou lle dizer
Que o tempo tendo desfaz
Que a morte nunca estudou
E a vida nat sabe ler.

O you who know too much,
My Father asked me to tell you
That time corrodes everything,
That death has never studied
And life doesn't know how to read.

I came to a point, Selden, where human relationships meant more to me than temporal ambitions or intellectual things. I want to write the Black Mass of the *candomblé*, and those lines I just sang you would be a part of it. Simple people sense one's sincerity. We believers don't take any step without consultation. I call my black Mother, Menininha, from Rio on the telephone, and she never fails me. It's a religion that makes one responsible for oneself. You're not guilty for being born, but only for not responding to the normal obligations of a human being. Menininha calls me 'Father' because my god, Oxala, is more powerful than hers, Oxossi, the hunter."

"What made Oxala your god, Vinícius?"

"The shells, the sea shells, which are fanned out on the table and interpreted, as in Africa—where they once served as money, too. They tell which god-saint is yours. When you are inhabited by bad spirits, your priestess 'washes' you symbolically with herbs, sacrificed doves and goats, and so on, and your innocence, your self-confidence, returns."

3

Vinícius had borrowed the typescript of the anthology of British poetry I was working on, and asked me when I came out to Itapoán for the third time whether he might keep it another day. "I was up reading it until seven A.M. but still have the last quarter to go. I'm still stunned by Chaucer's 'Prologue' to *The Canterbury Tales,* which I'd forgotten, and by your translation of Langland, a poet I didn't know at all. Poetry is the most humble and humbling of the arts, isn't it?"

"In what sense?"

"Because it's life. Everyone can do it."

"But most don't."

He laughed. "True. But how unfortunate that they don't. For them. And for all of us. Of course, sometimes a tragic experience helps. As with Miguel Hernández, who became a great poet only after Franco put him in the prison where he died."

"You knew him?"

"No. But Pablo did. And Alberti, who was his best friend, I think."

"You were starting to tell me the other day about *Black Orpheus*—*Orfeu da Conceiçao* was the original title, right?"

"Right. 'Orpheus Jones,' you might say in English. The racial romanticism came later. I was sitting in my room in Rio, in Niteroi to be exact, and somewhere in the distance the Batucada drums were beating their samba rhythms. I was reading a French anthology of classical myths. Suddenly—*boing!*—the two ideas connected. You have to bear in mind that the *favelas* were romantic places back in 1954, with almost the only crimes committed crimes of passion. I finished Act I as the dawn was breaking. Then—it was my first play—I got stuck."

"I had no idea you'd written others—"

"Two. All three set in *favelas: A Rose in the Darkness*—after Mallarmé's line—and *The Beasts*, about a family incest-fight, a girl seduced by her uncle who had promised to protect her when her family of migratory construction workers arrived from the Northeast—the Graciliano Ramos country."

"Our friend Flavio de Macedo called Graciliano Ramos the most underestimated Brazilian novelist. You think he was one of the great ones?"

"Perhaps the greatest—"

"Greater than Guimarães Rosa?"

"I like Guimarães's early novels very much; not so much the later ones where he's trying too self-consciously to write the Brazilian *Ulysses*. I knew him very well in the Foreign Office. He'd been a—how you say?—midwife doctor to women in labor in the back country, always carrying his stethoscope with him on horseback, and examining *everything* with that magnifying glass of his—everything but the human beings, as time went on, and it became an obsession. Once I came to his office and found him poring over cattle-disease bulletins from Australia, and asked him why. 'Because I want to know everything there is to know about the subject,' he said."

"I can understand that," I said. "Don't you get hopelessly

absorbed sometimes in *any* subject, Vinícius? For instance when you open an encyclopedia or a dictionary?"

"My God, yes. In fact, I'm writing, from time to time, a book called 'Word for Word.' It started one day when I opened the dictionary to 'avocado' and associated back to my Bahian father—born a hundred kilometers from here—and how he used to eat them. Then I remembered back to age two when I watched my sister's birth through a keyhole! And it was *true* because I checked with my mother years later and she said I'd taken the footstool and she had to remove it for fear I'd fall."

"We've come a long way from Orpheus, Vinícius!"

"What's that saying you have? 'It's a brand new ball game'? I must have picked that up in Los Angeles. That was where Act II came to me. I was trying to avoid a literal descent into Hades and I remembered the *carioca* Carnival. In Rio there are Negro dance halls they call *gafieras* and one of them took the name 'Hell's Angels.' There, among the masked ones, my Orpheus would seek his Eurydice! . . . So I wrote the third act in L.A. too, but lost it in the uproar of separating from Tatti (Beatríz), my first wife. Temporarily I gave up. But then one day in São Paulo, João Cabral de Melo Neto, with his infectious enthusiasm, insisted that I rewrite it to enter the play in the city's centennial drama competition. I hate competitions, but I agreed and typed it on the rocking train, finishing it just an hour before the entries closed. I shared first prize. Oscar Niemeyer did his first (and last) décor for it, and that helped. But as for the movie version, well, you've seen it. It won an Oscar and the Palme d'Or at Cannes, but Marcel Camus really spoiled it with his exoticism, what the French call *bon sauvage*, and it turned out to be just a good commercial film. I worked on it myself, of course, that winter of 1955, adapting it for Sacha Gordine. He was too broke to produce it, so we went to Rio to enlist our millionaires, and when that failed we picked up 'natural actors' in the *favelas*, which gave it authenticity. So now they talk of making an opera of it in New York—"

"Who?"

"Somebody named 'Padulla' who has 'Bye-Bye Birdie' on his letterhead. It's crazy the way that play keeps popping in and out of my life! So now this man says, 'Not Broadway. It's dated!' And another man says, 'Not off-Broadway. That's dated!' So it will have to be 'off-off-Broadway' I guess."

A plane flew over Itapoán and Vinícius said: "That's Toquiño, who will play the guitar in our fiesta Saturday night."

"You won't play, yourself?"

"I'm an amateur," Vinícius said. "I wouldn't play in Toquiño's presence. He and Baden-Powell are our two best when it comes to bossa nova. —Which reminds me, I should have mentioned it: bossa nova originated in the *Orpheus*."

"How come?"

"Very complicated. Antonio Carlos Jobim played the piano and guitar in it. It gave him the opportunity to develop his musical ideas for the first time. He discovered the 'new beat,' short-circuiting the immense contrapuntal complexities of the old Brazilian-African samba style."

"How did samba itself start?"

"After slavery was abolished in Brazil in 1888. Before that the blacks used only percussion. The waltz, polka, fox trot, and so on, created a syncretism that was samba."

"And their language? How much of the African survived in that?"

"Ketu survives to this day, in the god-talk that goes on while the shells are being shuffled. Ketu is the language of Portuguese Angola still."

4

Fourth visit with Vinícius. I took Carole and the children along to his hide-out this time, so a part of the afternoon was spent swimming with them in the shallow water, and taking pictures. I told Vinícius we were going to see the *capoeira* gymnasts at the Teatro Castro Álves tonight. He told me the dance originated among the escaped slaves who formed the short-lived Republic of Palmares near here in the seventeenth century. The slaves held out against the Portuguese soldiers for almost sixty years. "Their two great leaders," Vinícius continued, "were Zumbi and his son Ganga Zumba. Often lacking firearms, they used the one-string *berimbau* to warn of approaching danger, *and their feet to fight with!—*"

"Hence *capoeira?—*"

"Yes. They learned how to capsize a pursuer with their feet, disarming the pursuer once he'd been thrown to the ground and seizing what guns and other weapons they could for future use. As at Canudos later on, they fought to the last man, and, legend has it, jumped from the cliffs to their death rather than surrender at the final stage."

Vinícius was born, he told me, on October 19, 1913 at Gavea in Rio. (His present home is in that district of the former capital). "My poet father," he said, "was my first great influence. At six I was reading the anthologies and writing pastiches of our famous poets. Father was a Latinist. And since I was born the year *Quo Vadis* appeared, they named me after its hero, Marcus Vinicius, and my sister, Lýgia, after the heroine."

I reminded him of my first impression of him, and he laughed. "Very apt! Petronius was a character in Sienkiewicz's novel too!"

"Tell me something about your poetic roots, Vinícius," I said. "How good, actually, are the Portuguese poets, by world standards? And the Brazilians before your generation?"

"There are two major Portuguese poets," he said. "Camões's *Luziadas* is one of the great epics, and Camões's sonnets are also first rate. The second major Portuguese poet was Fernando Pessoa, who died in the late Thirties, a poet of Lorca's stature or Machado's. As for Brazil, well, we have certainly *more* very good poets than Portugal. Carlos Drummond and João Cabral are probably the most original, but Mario Andrade who died in 1945 was almost as good. He, and his brother, Oswaldo, and Manuel Bandeira, were our pioneer modernists. The so-called 'Week of Modern Art' that São

Paulo staged in 1922 signaled the revolt (simultaneously) against Parnassian symbolism, and the bourgeois-academic ways of thinking and writing. Overnight Brazilian literature —and art—became very nationalistic, very conscious of regions, native fruits, flowers, and trees, the Brazilian landscape, the exotic quality of our life."

"How did your own somewhat younger generation react to that already-accomplished revolution?"

"We returned more to poetry's so-called eternal themes. My first book appeared in 1933. Drummond's perhaps four years earlier. João Cabral's a decade later. That first book of mine was mystical, esoteric, metaphysical, very personal. The anguish it expressed was the residue of my false education. —Not that my family weren't lovable people, and idealistic, and intelligent; but that they were unaware of the prejudices of their class: Catholic, bourgeois, rightist. The critics who loved my first book (I already hated it) praised it for returning to the classical verities. My second book—*Forma e Exegese,* what a title!—won the Felipe d'Oliveira prize in 1935, just nosing out Jorge Amado's second novel. It was deeply influenced by Rimbaud—the aesthetics of seeing what no one else dares see, as expressed in the famous letter he wrote to his teacher when he was nineteen. All the *poètes maudits* were my heroes, along with Pascal, Nietzsche, Baudelaire, and Kierkegaard.

"Manuel Bandeira," he continued, "wrote a very important article (it made me furious at the time) urging me to pay more attention to craftsmanship, to take poetry more seriously. We became very good friends, and I came down to earth—with Waldo Frank's help, as I told you the other day. From the first person singular I moved more toward the third person, but I still have a long way to go. That poem I sang and translated for you yesterday is the way I *want* to write . . . But to go back. At Oxford I started my *Five Elegies* (the fifth is partly in English). The influence of the English poets was crucial in making my verse clearer, more communicative—at least I hope it's become so! My guiding stars from that time on were the ultimate simplicities of such poets as Blake, St. Teresa, John of the Cross, Garsillaso de la Vega—troubadours, those last, who preceded Góngora, a poet who, great though he was in his way, twisted words for the sake of verbal, decorative conceits—greatly, I'll grant you, but less profoundly than John Donne."

5

Vinícius was rehearsing his troupe when I arrived at Itapoán for my fifth and last visit with him. The song they were singing was an adaptation of the post-Gesualdo composer, Albinoni. Vinícius was sitting in an armchair at the head of the long dining room table, as always with his typewriter in front of him, his long-haired, bearded musician-disciples in their bathing trunks, dashikis, or whatever, ranged on either side with their various instruments. He got up as soon as I entered and offered me the armchair. I refused to take it, of course, but he insisted. This went on while everyone laughed until I finally complied to avoid a wrestling match. Vinícius pulled up a chair beside me and continued the song, chanting the words in monotone against the crescendos and decrescendos of the various tambourine and percussion instruments. The three drummers, I learned later, call themselves the Trio Moquoto and are well known. But the stars are Toquiño, who took care of the guitar, and the singer, Mária Creuza, who sat at the foot of the table. Décor was provided by a large color photo which Vinícius had found in the house and liked so well he'd put it in an appropriate bridal frame: a fat lady leaning demurely on a baroque twisted column while coyly holding her ermine stole just off the ground with her other hand. When he'd finished rehearsing the song, Vinícius suggested we move to the patio to talk. I agreed on condition he'd return and sing my favorite (among those I'd heard on records), "The Apprentice Poet."

When we were seated outside and had kicked off our sandals, the better to enjoy the feeling of the sand between our toes, I asked him what differentiates Brazilian poetry from Spanish—"other than the language, of course."

"The roots are the same," Vinícius answered. "It's our racial mixture that accounts for our real identity. Gregório de Matos, a great black poet of the seventeenth century, was the first to curse and use bad words. Then came Castro Alvez, a white Bahian of the time of the Emancipation who died at the age of twenty-four. You must read Amado's *The ABC of Castro Alvez*. This poet, by the way, is my relation—a first cousin of the mother of my great-grandfather. He wrote splendid poems about the liberation of the slaves. (By the way, Selden, the first line of that poem I gave you the other day translates better, 'You who are much too learned'—that is, too intellectual.)"

"What do you conceive poetry's function to be, Vinícius?" I said. "I mean, should it communicate primarily, or be a self-contained work of art?"

"Both," he replied. "Poetry is in the air, but only a few have the capacity to give it form. Nonpoets have a great nostalgia to be poets, don't you think?"

I agreed, citing the cases of Hemingway and Mailer, whose poems were certainly not comparable to their prose. He didn't know their poems, but he had met Mailer in Los Angeles.

"In the beginning," Vinícius went on, "I wrote *l'art pour l'art* or thought I did. Now I feel the world needs poetry so badly I *must* communicate—and in the simplest (but not simplified) terms. The process of creation is like a reverse abyss: the idea is to see how much you can reveal as you make the plunge down through it—or up!"

"And your own function—?"

"Also. *But,* you have to have inner feelings, things you can only know and reveal through yourself, but things that are important to other people if the poetry is to mean anything to nonpoets."

"What's your vision of Brazil's future?"

"The fact that we're a country of such vast resources—and,

now, industrial development—is a real danger to our retaining our special character, and becoming civilized. For we are a sensual, pleasure-loving people, and (the *carioca* of Rio especially) with a great sense of humor about ourselves. Just consider all the good cartoonists we've produced in my lifetime! Brazil is *bound* to re-democratize itself. The style of Brazilians is wholly antithetical to authoritarianism or any form of repression. But then, one would have to admit that our style has been antithetical to the methods of *any* Brazilian government, except perhaps Kubitschek's."

I told him that I was having lunch with the "cassated" former President on Monday.

"Give him an *abraço* from me," Vinícius said. "For all his bad hangers-on—and he was surrounded by them at times—Kubitschek turned Brazil upside down in his administration, and let our inner resources out. Brasilia—"

"You don't really think people should live in machines, do you, Vinícius?"

"Not for myself, certainly! But don't forget that it was Dom Helder and the Left who talked us into rehousing the poor in skyscrapers!"

"Do you see values in the world in general becoming more ephemeral, Vinícius?"

"They certainly are becoming more ephemeral, but the revolution of youth is bringing the world's attention back to what is *rough,* hand-made, nonviolent, lasting. Nevertheless I always tell my young friends, 'It's easy to be a revolutionary at your age. It's natural to youth: all youth is a state of revolt. But the hard thing is to be a revolutionary ten years later when you're in a position of some responsibility. Never drop out, or join a commune, is my advice. That's self-indulgence. Teach others how to be truly revolutionary in their thinking, their living, their loving.' "

"You foresee a religious revival, Vinícius?"

"Not in the old sense, world-wide or organized. Love and understanding must be achieved between people. I'm all for local religions, regional ones at most. *Candomblé,* for example, helps integrate and fulfill Brazilians because its beauty and magic are part of our genius."

The time had come to leave. The time had come to hear Vinícius sing "The Apprentice Poet." We walked back to the long table where Toquiño and the others were waiting. Vinícius, to their accompaniment, chanted, the big toe of his right foot keeping time as his fingers drummed his bare knee below the typewriter:

> He was a boy
> Goatlike and bold
> With the natural joy
> Of a healthy climber:
> Ten years old
> With wings for socks,
> You could track his orbit
> By the plic-plocs
> Of his slingshot gunning.
> Eyes clear green
> As lightning, stunning
> Here a tangerine,
> There a ball.
> His dark body
> Was always running.
> He'd jump a high wall
> With never a fall
> By night. His swan dive
> Would slice the water
> Noiselessly. Rocking
> By day his football
> (a bulging stocking)
> He'd dribble or groove
> From wing to wing.
> What he loved was to love.
> He loved the princeling
> Of his brown kingdom;
> The servants whose brooms

Made dusty swirls
On the steps; the girls
Of the streets, doing nothing;
Or in empty rooms
His cousins, sometimes
To whom he'd throw kisses
Or clever rhymes.
His aunts he'd greet:
They smelled so sweet.
He loved the queens
Of the silver screens,
The tart, the belle:
He loved all women
Extremely well,
And to each his morsel
Of poetry fell;
And everything written
Seemed beautiful
And tinged with sadness.
If he suffered as they,
Acting out what they dreamed upon,
Couldn't he some day
(Why not?) be one.

Top left: João Cabral de Melo Neto at the Brazilian embassy, Asunción, Paraguay, 1971. Top right: In Asunción, 1972. " 'All *nordestinos*,' he has written, 'look alike, the size of the head so difficult to balance—' " Bottom: " 'They elected me to the Brazilian Academy. They call us the Forty Immortals. Can you think of anything more ridiculous?' "

Chapter Eleven

JOÃO CABRAL DE MELO NETO

". . . I'd like to write a poem that couldn't *be read aloud!"*

1

The city is pierced by the river
as a street
by a mongrel,
a fruit
by a sword . . .

Man,
because he lives
collides with what is living . . .

. . . the way a bird
fights every second
to conquer flight . . .

When I showed João Cabral in Paraguay the five-line poem
Vinícius had given me in Bahia nineteen days before,[1] he
smiled and said: "It is addressed to me, subconsciously perhaps. It's a dialogue Vinícius and I have been having all our
lives. He thinks I am in danger of capsizing from too much
intellect; I secretly envy the way he abandons himself to the
senses. Maybe it's good for both of us to feel that way."

2

The two Brazilian poets are as unlike in others ways: in
appearance, in the way they live, in reflecting so profoundly
the antithetical regions that gave them birth. Cabral is a

[1] See above, Chapter Ten, pp. 201–17.

small, almost emaciated man with taut features, deep-set, shadow-lined eyes, wiry black hair peppered with white, the fleshy nose too large for the face and disfigured with a cross-shaped pockmark at the tip. "All *nordestinos*," he has written, "look alike, the size of the head so difficult to balance—" and on his short body, it could be a description of his own, were it not that the typical man of the desert has features uninformed by such acute and humorous self-awareness. For although the poverty-stricken Northeast is, as he says, "like a *gitano's* song sung without music, the sound of the human voice with no frills, like a knife, or the sun on a shadeless noonday," such a grandeur of dryness, like any other grandeur, is invisible until a poet sees it.

Even here in Paraguay—separated from his arid *sertão* by a thousand miles of tropical jungle and all the transplanted sensualities of Africa and Italy, not to mention the cultural baggage the poet has accumulated wherever diplomatic missions during twenty years of "exile" permitted him to pursue his restless search for spiritual brethren—the Minister's décor reflects his roots. The "modern" home, spotless white walls outside and in, is properly astringent. The tiny pictures selected with exquisite taste—abstractions by Juan Gris, Picasso, Miró, Marcoussis, Sonia Delauney, and their Brazilian exponents—are tight lipped. The glass coffee table contains nothing but a silver cigarette box, a disembodied polished marble statuette by Archipenko and a single diminutive cactus. Not a book is in evidence anywhere in the room, not a speck of dust anywhere on the immaculate floor across which the sun slanted through sliding glass from the patio with its motionless pool. Not a trace here of Vinícius' Bohemian beachhouse tracked with sand and littered with books, records, bottles, plates of stewing fish, and itinerant musicians!

I had come here the year before, on the way back from my second visit with Borges, and since I was Rio-bound where I had expected to meet Vinícius and Carlos Drummond, I asked João Cabral to give me a summary education in their ambiance. I discovered at once something about the Brazilian literary scene that must make it unique. Drummond, his friends had already told me, regards João Cabral and Vinícius as Brazil's outstanding poets. Vinícius expressed the same conviction about Drummond and João Cabral. And now the uncompromising hermeticist from Recife, who shares nothing of the *mineiro's* old flirtation with leftist politics or the *carioca's* worship of African gods and rhythms, casually endorsed *their* primacy. I asked Cabral whether Drummond's life-style resembled his own, or Vinícius'.

"Neither," he said. "Carlos Drummond is very hard to talk to, even to meet. He writes a regular essay column, a *crónica* we call it, for a newspaper. Oddly enough, it is not at all poetical, or even lyrical, like Rubem Braga's, for instance, who is not a poet at all but a novelist and the man who publishes all of us. I can't say that I care for that sort of journalism, or for the poems in that manner which seem to be Carlos Drummond's latest, but even if he wrote nothing he would have to be excused. He is, after all, our greatest poet."

"Dating from—?"

"Just before my generation. He inherited the pioneering breakthrough of the generation of Mário de Andrade—more or less contemporaneous with the Pound-Eliot-Joyce generation in your world—so that all the hard work had been done. Drummond, however, was unique in steadily changing and advancing in his art. His first period was nonpolitical, perhaps imitative of the generation before. In his second, when he met Luis Carlos Prestes and other Communist party members, he wrote very political poetry. In his present (third) period he is very personal again, confessional, maybe you could say mystical. But oddly enough, in his political poems Carlos Drummond *never* writes about the farmers of Minas Gerais where he grew up and whom he must know very well. He writes about Balts and Czechs and Basques and such!"

"How would you characterize his originality as a poet?" I asked.

"Almost impossible. All one can say is that his versatility has made him popular with people who admire one style and despise the others. Up to 1945 he wrote a little like Neruda. Then he broke with the Left—"

"Why?"

"It's difficult for him to work with *anyone*. He is a lonely man, jealous sometimes. Up to that year, or 1942 perhaps, he wrote very little but with great density—"

"Your way of writing?"

"I suppose. But I was born in 1920 and my generation, unlike his, tended to be social rather than political. I write about Pernambuco only because I happen to come from there. I never use the pronoun 'I' because I feel that the obligation of the poet is not to introduce himself in his poems. I agree with Suzanne Langer that art must be a 'presentation of reality,' not the reality itself, or the artist's ego, or—"

"But surely you wouldn't say," I interrupted, "that the opposite stance isn't just as capable of generating poetry— or would you?"

"No. You're right. It's only my personal way. I can't generalize beyond what I feel is right for me. But it influences *what* I like. Borges, for instance; Neruda not at all; and so on. Carlos Drummond's confessional kind of poetry I can at least understand, but Neruda's exhortative rhetoric I find very distasteful. Poetry, for me, is for the eyes; to be read to oneself, not aloud—least of all in an auditorium before a cheering mob that doesn't know the difference between a pentameter and a pitchfork."

By coincidence João Cabral was living on the only street the Paraguayans ever named after a citizen of the nation that defeated them—Avenida Kubitschek. When I came back to Asunción to see him again the next year he was still there. But he was preparing to leave for his next post, Senegal, to which the Brazilian government had just appointed him Ambassador. I was staying with an American friend who ran the Binational Center in Asunción and I hoped to do my friend a favor by prevailing on the poet to speak there or read his poetry. I'd completely forgotten his remark about the cheering mob in the auditorium.

"The Paraguayans have been trying to get me to lecture or read for years," he said, shaking his head sadly. "I can't face an audience. My mouth refuses to obey orders!"

"Won't you be sorry to be leaving Paraguay, João? I mean, won't you feel even more isolated in Dakar?"

"Not at all," he said. "In a way it will be much *closer* to Brazil."

"I've never heard a Brazilian say anything complimentary about Paraguay, or about any other country in Latin America, for that matter!"

He laughed. "You have a point. Brazilians feel closer to Americans, or to the Italians, or the French. Maybe that's why I expect to feel happier in Dakar. Latin America is a creation of the American mind. At any rate they are different from us. The Spanish American, for example, feels he must be recognized in Europe. We Brazilians couldn't care less. Vinícius and Carlos Drummond are indifferent to being translated, and so am I. It always surprises us that anyone would bother. A Spanish writer translated my whole last book and sent me the manuscript. I held it a year, and then I lost it. Unintentionally, of course. But I never did read it."

"Rubem Braga told me," I said, "that he's had a fantastic success with the Portuguese edition of García Márquez's *Cien Años de Soledad*. Couldn't that be a sign that the indifference of your country for the rest of the continent is breaking down? What do you think of *Cien Años*, by the way?"

"As a work of literature, I enjoyed it and admired it. But I think it's bound to have a bad influence on this continent. Underdeveloped countries must learn to *face* reality, not lose themselves in a world of fantasy where failing to face up to one's problems is applauded as a virtue. Maybe fantasy is what *you* need in the developed countries! How do you feel about *Cien Años*, by the way?"

"As ambivalently as you, but for different reasons. I preferred the more realistic *El Coronél No Tiene Quien Le Escriba*. Perhaps it's the pragmatic American in me that is disturbed by the lack of motivation in the characters of the longer novel. I feel the same way about some of Borges's stories."

"Motivation is not a value," he said. "Are Shakespeare's characters motivated? Not rationally—look at Othello or Lear. García Márquez is writing about primitives—and that's not a criticism in these countries of ours. The primitive doesn't act rationally in our terms. But when I criticize the effect of García Márquez's fantasy I'm making an ideological not a literary criticism. A work of art must be judged for its aesthetic quality, not for what it represents. The conduct of many criminals, for example, is inexplicable, as Truman Capote shows us. The artist writes always about exceptions, not about what is typical. García Márquez's *Cien Años* appeals to intellectuals, like me, not to students or the poor who have their own fantasies to absorb them. The Welsh novelist Gwynne Thomas, by the way, is as great a fantasist, but he's been forgotten. So you may be right—in the long run!"

3

I had moved with my family to a pension not far from the poet-diplomat's home, and one day he dropped in while I was having breakfast. I read him something in *Time* about the ecological disaster threatening the world and asked him whether he was concerned about the smog that now envelops cities like São Paulo and Rio in the wake of the rapid industrialization his government is pushing.

"Pollution?" he said, with some asperity. "Pauperism is the worst form of pollution. Perhaps the underdeveloped world is not paradise. Yet many Westerners would like to keep it the way it is."

"Is Brazil thinking in terms of continental hegemony, as many of your neighbors charge?"

"We are certainly not working toward any such goal," he replied.

I told him I would be visiting his native city, Recife, next month and that I expected to have a second talk with Archbishop Helder Cámara, the only outspoken critic of the military government who remains in Brazil. "I know that his views can't be mentioned publicly," I said, "but do you think he is still an influential figure?"

He preferred not to speak about Dom Helder for publication.

João had asked us to spend the afternoon at his pool, where our seven-year-old sons had already begun to emulate each other in the more daring somersaults. Since I knew Cabral wouldn't go near the water himself, it was a chance to corner him for the kind of dialogue that takes time. It began philologically, when I told him an American friend wanted to know how to pronounce 'João' and whether the poet should be addressed "Senhor Cabral" or "Senhor Neto."

" 'Cabral' or 'Cabral de Melo,' " he said. " 'Senhor Neto' would be like saying 'Mr. Third' or 'Mr. Junior.' We're very casual about names in Brazil. There are no real rules." The closest I can come to approximating his pronunciation of his first name is "Shoo-ownnw." I asked him the same question I'd asked Vinícius about the differences in Brazilian and Portuguese poetry.

"There's a greater difference than between British and American. You might call ours the tropical difference. It began when we had to find names for nameless things. The Indians' bread was 'manioca' and you've undoubtedly noticed the Indian place-names all over Brazil—Niteroi, Goiás, Cuiabá, Paraíba, Pernambuco, Curitiba, Pará, and so on. Then came the Africans with *their* words. 'Banguê' is the word for a primitive sugar mill in northeast Brazil, and it comes from the name of the skin used to carry off the bagasse—"

"What about 'mangué'?"

"No. That word for swamp was brought from East India, whence came the mango and, perhaps, the mangrove that grew in tidal swamps . . . But the Portuguese itself changed. When you export a language it becomes more conservative. So

Brazilian today sounds more the way Portuguese sounded to Camões. The first line of his *Luciad* reads:

As armas e os barões assinalados

But we would pronounce it:

As armas e os b'rões assinalados."

"It sounds like the opening of Virgil's *Aeneid*," I said.

"It is. A plagiarism, 'Of arms and the famous barons—' "

" 'I sing'?—"

"Yes—but twelve lines later! . . . But to come back to the Brazilian, all primitive languages are monosyllabic; so to communicate with the Indians and Africans, we learned to speak slowly, in a kind of singsong. Maybe the climate had something to do with slowing us down too!"

"The way you pronounce 'Vinícius' intrigues me—"

" 'Viníshiush,' " he said.

"And the Spanish—?"

"They are very vocal. The Portuguese don't *talk* so easily, and neither do we. Therefore our poems tend to be more *intimiste* than the Spanish, more subjective. But the Brazilian is not *quite* as subjective as the Portuguese. He doesn't have quite so much time to concern himself with himself. (Of course there are exceptions, like Rosalia Castro, the Galician poet—Galicia being on Portugal's northern border; or among the Spanish poets, Juan Ramón Jiménez, who is definitely not an orator—"

"Or Octavio Paz—"

"I don't know Paz's poetry."

"Well, your own—"

"As you know, I can't make speeches! That goes for my poems, too. Ideally, I'd like to write a poem that *couldn't* be read aloud! Neruda's poems *gain* by being read aloud. When we read a poem, we use our eyes—and so observe all the details, an impossibility when listening."

"Speaking of which," I said, "you promised to play me the

new record of Chico Buarque de Holanda singing his '*Construçao.*'"

"O.K.," he said, and while his wife came out of the pool long enough to find the record and hook up their hi-fi, I kidded him about detesting popular and folk music when it had been the production of his own verse-play *Morte e Vida Severina* in 1964 that touched off the whole bossa nova 'protest lyric' that peaked under Marshal Costa e Silva's unpopular but comparatively permissive regime. One of the songs on the record, '*Deos lhe pague,*' has a refrain that goes 'May God pay you back . . . for all the noise and smoke we have to breathe . . . for all the falls off buildings . . . for all the work we don't get . . .' In the title song, which I translated later in Rio, with an assist from Chico himself, the protest is less explicit:

He made love that time as if it were the last;
as if it were the last time, kissed his wife
and each son as if he were the only one.
Crossing the street, he began to climb
the building-shell still in construction.
Like a machine, he gave it form:
four thick walls, and then a platform
brick by brick (by magical intent?)
Each eye covered by a tear of cement.

Pausing to rest (was he the architect?)
Eating rice and beans as if he were a prince,
He ate and danced as if shipwrecked:
dancing, laughing, he tripped on the air.
Like a drunk, or a bird, he floated there;
then hit the ground like a loaded sack
and lay on the sidewalk on his back
in a one-way street, blocking the traffic . . .

Crossing the street, his footsteps reeling,
He had mounted that building as if for flight,

Built four walls without floor or ceiling,
and come to rest by a king's own right.

Now a popular idol with a reputation (and income) comparable to that of Bob Dylan in the United States, Chico Buarque became known for the incidental music he had written to accompany the 1964 production of João's play. As the son of one of Brazil's most distinguished historians his education and upbringing had been strictly élitist. "Because he was a popular singer-composer who happened to have a culture deeply rooted in his family," João mused, "his lyrics can be taken seriously as poetry. But Vinícius' songs written especially to be sung are better, and those songs of Vinícius are almost always inferior to his poems without musical intention.

"The black Cuban poet Nicolas Guillén, who doesn't write songs at all," he continued, "is unique for writing poetry actually based on folk rhythms. But Vinícius, a cultured *carioca,* writes songs quite uninfluenced by samba—at least until 1953, when he wrote sambas of his own, deliberately. He claims to have transformed samba into bossa nova by introducing certain jazz rhythms into the former for the first time. I wouldn't know."

I asked him who his favorite Brazilian prose stylist was.

"Graciliano Ramos."

"You're saying that as a loyal citizen of Pernambuco?"

He smiled. "I wrote a poem in homage to Graciliano Ramos. He wasn't of my generation, but of Jorge Amado's, though never rivaling Amado's Erskine-Caldwell-like popularity. His style grew out of José Americo de Almeidas, whose style in turn could never have developed without the breakthrough a few years before him of the poets Manuel Bandeira, Mário de Andrade, and the whole São Paulo modern art movement."

"Tell me about *Morte e Vida Severina,*" I said, "and how it was received."

"It's a sort of medieval pageant play, about what the poor man from the *sertão* finds on his trip to Recife. It made me known as my poems never could have, from the time when students first put it on in São Paulo to the time when it took the prize in the festival in Nancy in 1966 and was produced at the Odéon in Paris. It has sold sixty thousand copies here. It's been translated into Japanese and put on there, as well as in Peru, Spain, and Yugoslavia."

"You consider it your best work?"

"No. I prefer to write a poetry more dense and intellectual than one used for the stage. It's not as good as Vinícius' *Orfeu da Conceição*—I gave him that title, by the way—though it's less rhetorical. His play, unlike mine, was never a success on the stage. Perhaps it was too wordy. We're all well known for irrelevant reasons: I for my play, Vinícius for his singing, Carlos Drummond for his column."

The music was turned off and our families were back in the pool by this time. He closed the sliding glass doors and we settled down in a corner with iced lemon sodas.

"What is the function of poetry as you see it, João?"

"Poets write for two reasons," he said. "Some write to let out blood—you know, the way doctors used to bleed one? To get one's equilibrium. This is the way of Neruda, or of Vinícius. The other motivation, mine, is the crutch. The poem is a crutch that I make to complete myself. The first group writes because it is too rich, the second because it is not rich enough. Marianne Moore and Elizabeth Bishop use poetry as a crutch. You might call us con-structive poets, not at all like Paul Claudel or Walt Whitman. Auden once wrote with a crutch, but now it's a bloodletting—about anything and everything with no discrimination. Ginsberg is a blood-letter. Richard Wilbur, or Eliot, or George Herbert are the parsimonious kind."

"How would you describe the kind of poetry you write, more specifically."

"Well, the social aspect of it is that my factual datum happens to be the northeast of Brazil. But I don't teach or preach about it, as Neruda would, or the pre-1945 Drummond. I present it as Goya presents war, or Picasso in the "Guernica," as a brutal fact of life. That is why I prefer Lorca to Neruda.

Paul Eluard has a book about painters entitled *Donner à Voir*—'to make-see'—which could be the epigraph of all my books. My poems are descriptions, but in the act of describing I release my *Weltanschauung*, my vision of reality. As a young man I took Eliot's 'objective correlative' very seriously. I don't like to write a poem of ideas, but one that describes a thing factually, and then—"

He took me into his book-lined study where the only picture hanging was a large photograph of Marianne Moore, and took down an anthology by Herbert Read. "Here's a poem by Andrew Young called 'The Dead Crab.' Read it . . . It's in my manner. In my book I never use the word 'I'—"

"Vinícius said the same thing about his latest!"

He smiled. "I've been influenced by Donne, but I don't care for Donne's ego, his way of describing his experiences directly. I'd like to write a completely objective poem, but for the sake of description as description."

"What are you writing now?"

"Very little. I've lost interest. I write only on command."

"Help me translate one that's typical—and short!"

He got out his *Obras Completas* and we made a first draft of "Education Through Stone" which I worked over later as follows:

> For an education through stone, these courses:
> To learn from it, live with it; then
> To tune in on any of its subtle voices
> Listen impersonally, and begin again.
> It teaches morality by its resistance
> To whatever flows or tries to shape it;
> Instructs poetically by being dense;
> Outside to in unfolds its mute terrain
> For him who subjects himself with persistence.
>
> Elsewhere (for instance in the backland bush)
> Its way's reversed: to outside from within.
> The stone's too old to be didactic; push

However hard, it will not teach a thing.
Ask it no questions on that barren earth,
Its soul entrailed, that was a stone from birth.

I asked João what his rhyme scheme was.

"Assonantal," he said, "as before Camões. Only Cecilia Mereiles uses it in Brazil."

"How good is Cecilia Mereiles, João?"

"Our best woman poet."

"Meaning—?"

"Not as good as Marianne Moore. Perhaps as good as Louise Bogan?"

"To come back to your motivation," I said, "are you driven in any degree by the desire for immortality?"

"No. I'm indifferent to that. What does it mean? Does Shakespeare get any satisfaction out of what he now represents to humanity? Maybe a hundred years from now I'll be forgotten. Then, conceivably, a century later rediscovered. How could it affect me? It's a game. They elected me to the Brazilian Academy. They call us the Forty Immortals. Can you think of anything more ridiculous?"

"Poetry aside," I said, "do you believe in any kind of survival?"

"I was brought up a Catholic, but I lost faith at thirteen or fourteen. Now I don't believe in Heaven. But in my unconscious I still believe in Hell! I suppose because the fathers in school frightened me enough with their threats. I guess I'm the only such believer—a masochist!"

"What started you writing?"

"In my family I was the smallest and the ugliest. My brother got all the attention. I needed to affirm myself and couldn't through sports, so I became a good pupil. And an intellectual poet—there it is again! Poetry became my crutch!

"I don't believe deeply in the value of my poetry," he concluded. "I still am not sure of myself, still have doubts—and I hope to die that way."

Top left: Derek Walcott at Port of Spain, Trinidad, 1966, demonstrating the correct stance with a cricket bat. Top right: With his wife, Margaret, and the author, at Oakland, N.J., 1971. Bottom: " 'Existentialism is just another efflorescence of the Myth of the Noble Savage. . . .' "

Chapter Twelve

DEREK WALCOTT

"Most black writers cripple themselves by their separatism.
You can't be a poet and believe in the division of man."

1

I remember a road, brown as a snake
sometimes breaking its back in the fog
sometimes shining like the cry of a flute
and a mist full of diamonds.
I remember the metal screeching of parrots
and the earth exhaling the fume, the engine of morning
and the kettle of sunlight, boiling with vapour
when I set my foot down on the changing earth . . .

It's curious that my friendship with Derek Walcott began in
Trinidad in 1966 while I was copying down these lines from a
projected play, *The Dream on Monkey Mountain.* Curious
because our friendship almost foundered five years later over
what I thought the New York producers had done to convert
the play—by then a hit on the "off-Broadways" of several
continents—into a vehicle of racist propaganda. But the rift
between us healed irrevocably when subsequent talks with
the poet revealed depths of understanding which a white
"tourist" in this terrain like myself could never approach.

I suppose Walcott rejected these particular eight lines when
he came to prepare the play for book publication because
they no longer measured up to his deepening conception of
language as the ultimate rejuvenator of nation and race. But
at the time I copied them down, their springtime freshness
seemed to have the same bloom I had marveled at in the
paintings of Haiti's self-taught artists. Haiti, with whose artists I had been working for years, remained innocent because

isolated from the world. But Trinidad was in perhaps the last glow of its unself-consciousness. Carnival had not quite been taken over by the hucksters, nor Calypso by the hipsters, nor had the chilling wind of Black Power begun to blow over the urban desolation White Power had just evacuated. And the Walcotts' address—Duke of Edinburgh, Petit Valley, Diego Martin—seemed to symbolize all the historical catalysts in this most mixed-up brew of an island, all but the two basic ingredients: African and Oriental.

The union of Derek, part African, and his wife Margaret, part Oriental, already blessed with two children, might be part of a cosmic process (I then thought) reconciling these contentious racial strains and a harbinger of the ultimate salvation of Trinidad. But even to suggest any such conscious intention on the part of the poet and his wife would have been to strip them of all the natural beauty, spontaneous humor, and uncomplicated ease that was theirs and to reduce the creative process to a biological rut.

Derek was born in St. Lucia in 1930 and went to Jamaica's University of the West Indies on a scholarship in 1950. "I was almost tossed out," he told me, "for writing a paper answering silly questions with silly answers. Like, for instance, 'What is the difference between a ruler and a philosopher?' which I answered, 'A ruler is a foot long but a philosopher will go to any length.' But I got a degree, finally; married a Jamaican girl; and in 1954 I was back in Castries teaching English at St. Mary's College. Then I came here, and in 1960 I married Margaret Maillard—"

"As in duck," said Margaret.

"It sounds teddibly English," I said.

"People used to evade their non-Caucasian backgrounds," she said, "by saying 'My grandfather was Dutch' or 'My great-grandfather was Spanish.' We're all mixtures here. I have an East Indian grandmother, along with an African one. Derek has English and Dutch."

"Negro is the only thing we have in common," said Derek.

"I'm low-caste Indian," said Margaret. "The Negroes lowered the caste."

We were laughing in a way that would be unusual among Americans of different complexions.

The talk shifted to hair styles, Carnival, architecture, painting, politics, and mutual friends like Frank Collymore, John Hearne, and Robert Lowell. Derek's son, Peter, was in the street batting a ball around with neighborhood kids. Derek showed me the proper stance with a cricket bat and how to throw curves underhand. On the way to Maracas Beach he asked me if I knew the painter Roland Dorcély in Haiti: "I always like this line, 'You have in your eyes a Sunday in black.' Whatever happened to him?"

"Dorcély went to Paris and hasn't been heard of since," I said.

"Well, if he's disappeared," Derek said, "I suppose I can take the line."

At the beach Margaret was joined by several other beautiful African-East Indian women who looked especially stunning against the sand.

"I've discovered at last the advantage of white sand over black," I said.

"The white sand can vote," said Derek.

It sounds as if we were preoccupied with the racial question. We weren't. If the subject evoked a lot of joking, it was because it seemed the natural way to express our ease with one another. No doubt there was, too, the unconscious recognition that race *is* the single most unsettling, divisive, and explosive question in Trinidad, and that to avoid it entirely is to evade it.

It all began between 1833 and 1917, when Britain imported one hundred forty-five thousand East Indians to work the sugar fields to which the emancipated Negroes refused to return. V. S. Naipaul, the brilliant Trinidadian novelist, goes so far as to maintain that Trinidad "teeters on the brink of racial war" because the Negro and the East Indian, lacking any real respect for their own races, take out the frustrations of their particular rootlessness on each other. The greatest damage done to the Negro by slavery was to teach him self-contempt. "Twenty million Africans made the middle passage, and scarcely an African name remains in the New World."

Until recently news films of African tribesmen on the screen evoked hoots of laughter. Ads in Port-of-Spain still show men and women with exaggeratedly Caucasian features—slightly tinted bronze. The Indian, for his part, despises the Negro for not being Indian. He has "taken over all the white prejudices against the Negro and, with the convert's zeal, regards as Negro everyone who has a tincture of Negro blood." Indians who have visited their homeland have returned to Trinidad "disgusted by the poverty and convinced of their own superiority." Nor did political independence, mostly the work of the Negro majority, help much; the politician "soon to be rewarded by great wealth, bared his pale chest and shouted, 'I is a nigger too.' " [1]

A friend at the hotel where I was staying, Martin James, suggested we spend our last night in Trinidad [2] taking in the notorious Miramar. Derek agreed to go along. "You realize it's sinful," he said jokingly, "but what the hell." (Margaret had a headache from taking the children to see Santa Claus at the Hilton the night before.) Driving in Derek's car through the dark, deserted streets, I conjured up a *Walpurgisnacht*. To break the spell I asked the poet whether he thought Naipaul's harsh criticisms of Trinidad were exaggerations arising from an expatriate's guilt.

"For instance?"

"You know. That Trinidad is an 'uncreative society,' that on the highways you drive without dipping your lights 'to make your opponent swerve,' that everyone in Trinidad knows that to run over an Indian in an Indian village and to stop is to ask for trouble and so on. True or false?"

"You saw my column in the *Guardian* yesterday," Derek said, "the one on Walt Disney's death? I have a less critical temper. Maybe I'm soft."

I'd seen the column. "He was not a great artist. He lacked savagery, his satire was saccharin, inoffensive. He could sweeten

---

[1] V.S. Naipaul, *The Middle Passage*, London, Deutsch, 1962.

[2] The whole visit, from which these first talks are taken, is in my book *The Caribbean*, New York, Hawthorn, 1968.

all the savagery out of nature. But . . . he educated a century in the appreciation of the living line. . . . His morality was Franciscan, because it imbued every creature with reverence. . . . The world he made for us was real as that in the fable of the creation. Tenderness, after all, looks like an easy kill, but it is natural and indestructible.

"Isn't it too easy," I persisted, "when you have as much sensitivity, honesty, and talent as Naipaul, to pack up and live abroad, leaving this dirty little world with its hypocrisies and provincial pretensions behind? Could you leave Trinidad?"

"I could once," he said, "but never again. This is where I belong. This is where my roots are. All the criticisms he makes of Trinidad are true—true but irrelevant."

The electric sign on the Miramar read "Six Hours of Continuous Entertainment" but the only thing that was continuous was the efforts of the slinky black whores to lure us to their adjoining "hotel." They danced with us, sat on our laps, drank our rums, fondled every part of our torsos they could reach without sawing the seats out from under us.

"I salute your detachment," I said to Derek, who finally managed to get a bench to himself.

"I can't do it, man. Soft again! It makes me feel too guilty the day after."

"There goes another broken prejudice," I laughed. "I'd always thought we whites had a corner on the guilt market."

"Look at Martin," Derek said pointing to our white companion, knotted with the most African of queens. "He has no qualms about his Countess Dracula!"

But we finally managed to untangle ourselves, reel down the street, and say a reluctant farewell to our friend. Back in the hotel Martin wanted to hear one of the poems. There was nothing soft in the appropriate one I read him from the book Derek had given me:

> Night, our black summer, simplifies her smells
> into a village; she assumes the impenetrable
>
> musk of the Negro, grows secret as sweat,
> her alleys odorous with shucked oyster shells,

coals of gold oranges, braziers of melon.
Commerce and tambourines increase her heat.

Hellfire or the whorehouse: crossing Park Street,
a surf of sailors' faces crests, is gone

with the sea's phosphorescence; the boîtes de nuit
twinkle like fireflies in her thick hair.

Blinded by headlamps, deaf to taxi klaxons,
she lifts her face from the cheap, pitch-oil flare

towards white stars, like cities, flashing neon,
burning to be the bitch she will become.

As daylight breaks the Indian turns his tumbril
of hacked, beheaded cocoanuts towards home.[3]

2

I came back to Trinidad five years later with my family,
eager to talk with Walcott about *Dream on Monkey Mountain*. I had just reviewed the published version [4] (which con-
tained three earlier plays and a truly Shavian preface) for
The New York Times, and expected to see the off-Broadway
production in a few weeks.

The play is about a charcoal burner, Makak (Monkey),
a primitive natural man who is discovered to be a miraculous
healer, and his crippled side-kick, Moustique (Mosquito), who
tries to cash in on Makak's selfless aura and make a paying
religion of it. Moustique is killed by Corporal Lestrade, a
mulatto in the pay of the Establishment, and Makak,
taking the "converted" corporal's advice, "beheads" the white
woman who was his vision of God and returns to his primor-
dial home on the Mountain. There are overtones of Christ-

[4] New York, Farrar, Straus & Giroux, 1971.
[3] "Nights in the Gardens of Port-of-Spain," in *The Castaway and
Other Poems* by Derek Walcott, London, Cape, 1965.

Paul and of Quixote-Sancho Panza in the relationship of Makak and his disciple. The black peasants and fishermen in all four of the plays in the book are seen as carriers, albeit unconsciously, of a regenerative counterculture, but off their guard at the mercy of their leaders who succumb to power and religious intolerance as easily as the old white masters.

The preface is a wonderfully poetic exploration of the Caribbean black artist's "malarial enervation, his reflective and mannered inner language . . . as far above its subjects as that sun which would never set until its twilight became a metaphor for the withdrawal of the Empire and the beginning of our doubt."

Twenty years ago, in his "schizophrenic boyhood," the poet says, there was boundless hope. "One could lead two lives: the interior life of poetry, and the outward life of action and dialect. Twenty years later with nothing essentially changed came the realization that to record the anguish of one's race one must "make the journey back from man to ape. . . . The children of slaves must sear their memory with a torch. . . ." Not only in "nostalgia for innocence, but the enactment of remorse for the genocides of civilization, a search for the wellspring of tragic joy in ritual, a confession of aboriginal calamity for their wars, their concentration camps, their millions of displaced souls" who have "degraded and shucked the body as food for the machines. . . . The colonial begins with this knowledge but it has taken one twenty years to accept it."

The trap is, Walcott's preface goes on, that the folk arts— "the old colonial grimace of the laughing nigger, steelbandsman, carnival masker, calypsian and limbo dancer have become symbols of a carefree, accommodating culture, an adjunct to tourism, since the State is impatient with anything it cannot trade." The "pathetic romanticism" of a return to Africa by way of voodoo ritual offers no answer to ex-Christians. "We had lost both gods and only blasphemy was left. . . . The New World black had tried to prove that he was as good as his master, when he should have proven not his equality but his difference. . . . Our poems remained laments, our novels propaganda tracts, as if one general apology on behalf of the past would supplant imagination, would spare us the necessity of great art. Pastorialists of the African revival should know that what is needed is not new names for old things, but the faith of using the old names anew, so that mongrel as I am, something prickles in me when I see the word Ashanti as with the word Warwickshire, both separately intimating my grandfathers' roots, both baptising this neither proud nor ashamed bastard, this hybrid, this West Indian. . . ."

For the West Indian Negro, he concluded, "was as avaricious and banal as those who had enslaved him. What would deliver him from servitude was the forging of a language that went beyond mimicry." And it must go beyond the tragicomic and the farcical too, because "the tragicomic was another form of self-contempt. . . . *The future of West Indian militancy lies in art.*"

3

I asked Derek, when he took us to the beachhouse he had found for us up-island, whether he thought West Indian culture could have any ennobling sociopolitical aim other than racial pride.

"Our mistake," he answered, "has been to try to align our real power, a human thing, with the hallucination of *sharing* it, either with Africa or America. Going back to Africa is assuming an inferiority. We must look *inside*. West India exists but we must find it. It's a mosaic, you might say. My character has assumed part of it since I came here by the fact of being here. I'd been brought up in the Matthew Arnold tradition: you know, Sweetness and Light, and let's integrate reasonably, and all that: a tradition that is what it always was, politically powerless. So what was left? Art—what we have made here—"

"Like Carnival? But you have some pretty scornful things to say about that in your preface. You call it 'a manual for stasis' on the part of intellectuals who 'apotheosize the folk forms, insist that calypsos are poems' and so on, no?"

"I'm not knocking Carnival," he replied, "or the steel bands either, but those who *use* them, like the government. Kitchener, this year's calypso winner, says it in one of his songs:

> 'This is not the way we used to play
> 'Mas in Trinidad:
> It's a one-way 'Mas to the Savannah . . .'

In other words it's become a directed thing, lacking spontaneity, tourist-oriented."

"And the solution—?"

"To find out what the people want."

"But suppose they only want revenge—revenge for having been the underdogs? You say that 'revenge is a kind of vision.' Revenge against whom? For what? Is the vision of all races working together corny?"

"One of the generating forces in any spiritual revolution is the rejection and dismantling of the old order. No, I'm not against the vision of all races working together and loving one another. It's not a corny vision but a good one, the only real one. But the ideal is betrayed by those who preach it. Like the rows of white faces in the expensive seats at black affairs, jumping up in the Turf Club's reserved section. It's those who feel threatened by Black Power, and rightfully so. And the most infuriating thing about them is that they're the same people who accept revolutionary attitudes and talk the jargon and see no contradiction in remaining the privileged ones!"

"I agree. But your plays aren't directed against them—or written for them. They're written for the masses—at least you'd like the masses to respond to them, right? So why do you give them a play that's so militantly antiwhite as *Dream* . . . that can be interpreted that way, anyway? Especially here where you're a member of a black society that has already rejected rule by whites?"

"That's not what it's about, Selden, really. You have to have a purgatory, or a purgation, before there's a reconciliation—"

'I know, I know. But let me press my point, however

wrong. Makak's vision of God is a white woman. Mine might be a black woman, but I wouldn't want to kill her. He does—"

"Any vision of God a black charcoal burner had would have to be white. But by the time Makak beheads her he's become a political figure. As soon as he commits that spurious act—he goes back to being a woodcutter."

"Is that the solution?" I asked.

"No. But in the context of the West Indian situation . . . the point is, whether he's doing his work in our society. That's his redemption: no longer to be tormented by being either a black man or a woodcutter. The *beginning* of a solution!"

"You say in the preface, 'We recognized illiteracy for what it was, a defect, not the attribute it is now considered to be by the revolutionaries—' "

"I'm disagreeing with the revolutionaries, of course. The idea that illiteracy is an advantage is the currency of the intellectual fascists."

"Why do you speak of 'the *apparent* conservatism of West Indian fiction—'?"

"All our stories have a beginning, a middle, and an end. The *avant-garde* idea of destroying the form is alien to us."

"Lamming—?"

"Even Lamming. He only edits the old forms. And so with the other good ones: Naipaul, Wilson Harris, Mais. And it's our advantage! What could be more ephemeral than the *avant-garde* novel? Our subject matter is too real to be trifled with—"

"Have you thought of the murderous African-Indian confrontation here in Trinidad as a subject?"

"I couldn't. It's unreal. I mean only the politicians could make it happen. There was a time when Granger had his people say they were going into the fields to help the Indians cut cane. The Indians were supposed to have replied, 'If you come with cutlasses, watch out!' but in fact it was the late Bhadase Maraj, the Indian boss, who said that. When they came, nothing happened . . . You don't want to be reminded,

242

either, that your melting pot's still melting. I had an American friend who was offended when reminded of his Irish accent. Even you and Cal Lowell have accents—the same accent. You're both New Englanders?"

"He is, but I'm a New Yorker. I suppose it's the aristocratic background, if that word has any meaning in the United States: same schools, colleges, churches. We could disguise our accents, I suppose!"

"You'd be trying to 'meet the people.' You wouldn't."

"Right . . . Tell me, Derek, does the feeling still persist that Trinidad is being exploited by imperialism?"

He snorted. "It's not a feeling. It's the truth. Burnham just took over the bauxite and gas companies in Guyana, with compensation. We should do the same. Not that we'd get the oil out more efficiently, but for our own self-respect. I'm neither a Marxist nor a fascist—and I don't deny there's an element of fascism in the way Fidel runs Cuba—but I wouldn't mind it at all if my son, Peter, was forced to work the land a couple of years here. I wouldn't even mind being forced to do it myself—if it helped make the Trinidadians feel this was truly *their* land, their responsibility to make it productive. We have no such sense yet. The Indians may have, but only for their personal gain; the blacks hardly at all.

"We're victims of our prejudices," he continued. "The African sees the Indian as a hoarder and a skinflint. The Indian sees the African as a lazy son-of-a-bitch who lives to fuck. The Chinese is the victim of the worst prejudice of all, since Africans and Indians alike consider him utterly materialistic and ruthless. Because he's smart enough to control business and run it efficiently. Yet he's peaceful and gentle, and probably contributes more to the arts than the others, in terms of his small number."

"Is he compassionate toward the majority races though—?"

"Probably not. Maybe only toward his own. But we've forced him into that protective stance. Just as you've forced your minorities into exaggerated attitudes. There's nothing

243

whiter than an American black, for instance, once he has money and puts on Bermuda shorts . . . Race? It's money, man, money, that's the root of all evil. Not race!"

4

Dream on Monkey Mountain opened in New York March 10, 1971, brilliantly acted and staged. My disgust with the way the play was *interpreted* at the Negro Neighborhood Playhouse and the momentary rupture of my friendship with the poet, would be of no interest to the reader except that they touched off Derek Walcott's visit to my home later in 1971, and our most interesting talk.

Everything about the play's production seemed to belie its deeper meaning (religious), the tolerant humanity of the playwright vis-à-vis the fanatical rhetoric in which some of his characters express themselves. Advertisements in the New York papers showed the clenched fist the black militants have taken over from the Communists, and the single line: "THEMES OF BLACK POWER." The stage production climaxed with Makak's slaying of his white goddess; if the audience took note of the epilogue in which the execution is interpreted as a dream, there was no sign of it. Reviewers responded predictably. "Makak slays the Moon Lady," *The New York Times* critic wrote, "—and with her, presumably, dies the evil of White colonial oppression. . . . The thesis is that the West cannot—nor should it—exist forever, given its deplorable record of racist exploitation and butchery throughout the world."

"What turns me off in New York," said Margaret, who had come up for the opening, "is that people keep calling us up to congratulate us on the reviews; nobody congratulates Derek for the *play*. Derek, you should give them hell!—"

"Maybe they don't mention the play," I said, "because it's disappeared in the production they made for the reviewers."

"Can I give you hell, Derek," said my wife, Carole, "for giving them the chance to distort your meaning by the way you ended the play?"

"I won't agree with you," Derek laughed, "but go right ahead!"

"The end of *Dream* is a great tragedy," Carole said. "Makak, for political reasons is forced to behead his god—merely because its color is white. But not in the play we just saw on the stage. To satisfy their black constituents, they substituted a political morality for a religious tragedy. The play as written is just ambiguous enough at the end to allow either interpretation. When you wrote it, were you clear in your own mind whether you were writing as an English poet who happened to be black, or a black who might have to give up being an English poet lest he betray his race?"

Guests came in at this point, and it wasn't until months later that Derek answered her question. Talk about the play continued in a more general way, but Derek did say that the attitude of the Negro Ensemble disturbed him. "In a way, their one idea was *not* to have a success on their hands, to screw the foundations and their other affluent sponsors even if it meant not getting a single white to attend and the seats went unsold. The attitude of the Black Establishment when it actually has power, as in this production, is the same as their incompetence running Trinidad. They won't take any white help or ideas even from their friends—on principle." And he went on to deplore the current tendency to make "art" out of "such catastrophic human failures as Buchenwald and Watts and Mylai. The artist has become a pornographer and a thief," he added, shaking his head. "It's as though Vietnam is something they invented to make T.V.-viewers feel guilty."

Derek and I took part in a seminar at Columbia University the following week, at which Borges and former President Fernando Belaúnde of Peru also spoke. Derek described his homeland's hangups as typical of the once-colonial Caribbean. "We try so hard to make the best of both worlds," he said, "we Afro-Saxons—white niggers, if you prefer," and went on eloquently to deplore the psychologies of revenge on the part of blacks and remorse on the part of whites. "Neither are good for writers or artists or anyone else trying to make a new world," he said. "It will always be the Caribbeans' fate to be squeezed. Soon the Colossus of the North will be replaced by the Colossus of the South—when South America recognizes its potential and unites. Our role must be to mediate between North and South, black and white, preserving the myths and the language, preserving whatever is truly creative."

After the seminar there was a dinner for the speakers at the Center for Inter-American Relations. Borges read several of his greatest poems and received a standing ovation. Derek was asked to read some of his but declined, in a graceful speech, to "compete with so great a poet as Borges." A young man with a mop of curls who had attached himself to Derek insisted. He recited a short poem, "Codicil." The guests left their tables and the serious drinking began. Derek and Borges sank into a sofa and talked for an hour about the derivation of their names. Long past midnight we set out for my home, where Derek had promised to spend the night, but he wanted to stop on the West Side to pick up his pajamas. He'd been staying with Michael Schultz, the director of *Dream*. We waited for fifteen minutes and finally Schultz came down to our car to tell us that Derek wouldn't be coming with us: "He didn't have the heart to tell you himself, but he has too much to do tomorrow with the play. He'll phone you in the morning."

Carole burst into tears. We drove home in silence. Derek never phoned. We concluded sadly—wrongly as it turned out, and perhaps paranoiacally—that Derek had capitulated to those who wanted to use him in their war for racial confrontation, and that in the circumstances his white friends were liabilities who must be sacrificed.

5

Derek came back to New York eight months later and phoned me from the airport. I met him at the Chelsea a few hours later and we spent the afternoon with Stanley Kunitz, before driving out to New Jersey. It was good to warm up with poetry. Derek and Stanley were old friends, and Derek wanted to hear about Robert Lowell's recent visit to him and what Stanley thought about the effect óf England—and separation from his wife—on the New Englander's poetry. Stanley scolded me good-naturedly about leaving "that great 'Lyke-wake Dirge' " out of my British anthology. "Too bad. You should have—shouldn't he, Derek?"

"I like it," Derek said. "But I wouldn't say he should have. I do think you should include George Darley's—or is it Carew's?—'Ask me no more . . .' " And he quoted it from memory.

"That one does send me, Derek," I said. "Especially

'. . . . in her sweet dividing throat
She winters, and keeps warm her note.' "

"I've always suspected the magic of 'dividing,' " Derek said. "It's magical all right, but probably had a commonplace connotation at the time."

Stanley asked us if we were coming to Voznesensky's reading next week, at which he would be officiating. Derek asked him if he really liked that poet's latest "concrete" poems.

"Not really—"

"And Yevtushenko's political ones?"

"Very bad," Stanley said, shaking his head. " 'Babi Yar' is especially bad. You can't write poems about collective or natural disasters. All you get is honest indignation."

"You don't apply that to Wilfred Owen, do you, Stanley?" I said.

"No. Yeats missed the point about Owen. It wasn't passive suffering. 'Strange Meeting' has grandeur, elevation, transcendence."

"You think the two Russians are overrated?" I asked.

"I think they're box-office," said Stanley with a smile, "as we can't be. The public isn't interested in their poetry, of course, but in their 'courage' as nonconformists rebelling against the 'enemy' dictatorship. Yevtushenko has asked for Lincoln Center to read in—and he will very likely fill it.

Which isn't bad for poetry, either, whether you think he's become corrupt, as I do, or not."

"And American younger poets?" Derek asked.

"In this country everybody is a nihilist," Stanley said. "The young admire only their contemporaries. The problem is to pass from this idolatry of one's peers to respect for the tradition of one's art—in which one's peers may not even have the stature to move."

"You don't go for the formless poem, do you?" Derek said. "Like me, you can't read, or remember poems without quotable lines. Like 'Howl' for instance—?"

"I've always liked 'Howl,'" Stanley said. "It has enough energy to carry its formlessness. But it's the end of a very short tradition. Nothing follows."

6

"Well, Derek," I said, when we'd reached Oakland, had dinner, and settled down with a bottle of Haitian rum between us, "let's get down to the nitty-gritty."

"Meaning *Dream on Monkey Mountain?*"

"Right on."

"Shoot."

"Philosophically which solution is preferable: the liberal ideal of integration and racelessness, or the one Carole says her Waspish, know-nothing parents espouse—black and white worlds untouchable—which seems to be the goal of the Black Panthers too."

"It's an American phenomenon," Derek answered, "this equation of segregation or total integration. *Both* parties are admitting the tragic failure of any possibility of reconciliation, of living together while glorying in their differences. Neither camp accepts the American idea—the idea of America! But interbreeding isn't going to bother the young; and only the Muslims still talk seriously of that chimera, a separate black state within a state."

"When we talked about it in Trinidad, you called Makak's

murder of his white goddess 'a spurious act.' Why spurious?"

"At that moment he has more abstract power, but less power as a human being. He even gets rid of Moustique. He becomes a political figure accustomed to giving orders."

"You speak of his 'redemption' when he returns to cutting cane. Isn't that just going primitive, being Rousseau's Noble Savage, escaping back to the womb?"

"Now I'm going to have to answer Carole's question, the one she asked me the last time I was here," he said. "Black critics of the play in New York were just as turned off by the ending. They called it a cop-out just as she did. And it *would* be, if Makak avoided action. But since he goes through the whole cycle from woodcutter to king and back, how can they argue that he's avoiding experience? Getting rid of his overwhelming awe of everything white is the first step every colonial must take. The error is that when you translate this into *political* terms it leads—wrongly, disastrously—into acts of murder, and eventually genocide. Makak realizes this when he wakes from the dream that had become a nightmare. The black intellectual critics overlooked Makak's trip back to Africa where he found the tribes slaughtering each other (the Ibos were being slaughtered by their Nigerian brothers while I wrote the play: a familiar human tragedy, of course, for civil wars are going on all over the world). Makak recognizes that human cruelty is raceless. So he becomes a working hermit—with a raceless god."

He leaned forward with a glint in his eye. "Look, Selden, I believe just as firmly that there's no such thing as black or white poetry. I get the same joy out of reading Aimé Césaire and Saint-John Perse when they write about the same French islands—one of them a black working class poet, the other a white colonial aristocrat:

> I want to hear a song in which the rainbow breaks
> and the curlew alights along forgotten shores.
> I want the liana creeping on the palm tree
> (On the trunk of the present 'tis our stubborn future)

> I want the Conquistador with unsealed armor
> lying in death among the perfumed flowers,
> the foam censing that sword gone rusty
> in the pure blue flight of slow wild cactuses . . .

or

> Wandering, what did we know of our ancestral bed, all
> blazoned though it were, in that speckled wood of the Islands?
> . . . There was no name for us in the ancient bronze gong of
> the old family house. There was no name for us in our mother's
> oratory (jacaranda wood or cedar) nor in the golden antennae
> quivering in the headdresses of our guardians, women of color;
> we were not in the lute-maker's wood, the spinnet or the harp;
> not . . .

I forget the rest. Which is which? What does it matter? Like
Borges, Perse can transport us from the mythology of the past
to the present without breaking step—just as Césaire can, or
Whitman. There is the same elemental praise of winds, seas,
and rain in Perse as in Whitman. They don't venerate them
but celebrate them as perennial carriers of freedom. They are
the poet-wanderers, all four poets; carrying culture in their
heads as they move among the ruins—"

"Like the Romantics—"

"Except that for Perse history isn't chronology. It's a
habitable element. Timeless."

"And Borges—?"

"When you read Borges for the first time you think of the
secretive genius, immured from life—"

"Can I interrupt your *raptus*," I said, "to ask whether you
discovered Borges and Neruda after I gave you *South America
of the Poets?* I don't recall your mentioning them five years
ago in Port-of-Spain."

"I knew their work, but only vaguely. You forced me to
read them."

"You were saying—"

"That however refined Borges seems to be on first reading, he too is really celebrating the New World—violent, vulgar, abrupt, the life of the *pampas* and the Buenos Aires slums. All of these are given a kind of instant archaism by Borges's hieratic style. You've noticed, haven't you, that all the action, however crude, is felt *not chronologically* but with the simultaneity of its *presence*. The death of a Gaucho repeats, or *is,* the death of Caesar. Fact evaporates into myth. It's not a jaded cynicism that sees nothing new under the sun, but a refined *elation,* a mystery which sees everything *renewed*, not merely repeated."

"The 'revolutionary' poets who think Borges is a reactionary don't see that," I said. "Neruda doesn't see it."

"Neruda may not see it with his conscious revolutionary mind, but the poet is doing exactly that. The citric taste of Neruda's poems corresponds to Perse's taste of sea-apples, or Césaire's—"

"What is it that gives those two French Caribs what they have in common?"

"Being 'colonials' maybe? I can only speak for myself. The colonial writer, unlike the revolutionary one, knows that by openly fighting the tradition he merely perpetuates it. He knows that revolutionary literature is a filial impulse. The secret of maturity is to assimilate (subtly) the features of one's ancestors! We know, too, that dead writers are presences, never out of date. The bravest, most hermetic writers can go even further. They can *reject* the pragmatic, rational idea of history as time for the aboriginal concept of history as fable and myth—"

"I'm thinking of Mandelstam," I said.

"I wrote a poem invoking Mandelstam in a dark moment just before I left. Want to hear it?"

"Naturally!"

"It's called 'Preparing for Exile':

Why do I imagine the death of Mandelstam
among the yellowing cocoanuts,
why does my gift already look over its shoulder

251

for a shadow to fill the door,
and pass this very page into eclipse?
Why does the moon increase into an arc lamp
and the inkstain on my hand prepare to press thumb
    downward
before a shrugging sergeant?
What is this new odor in the air,
that was once salt, that smelt like lime at daybreak,
and my cat, I know I imagine it, leap from my path,
and my children's eyes already seem like horizons,
and all my poems, even this one, wish to hide?"

"That's one of the great ones, Derek. Can I add it to the
four I'm already including in *100 British Poets?*"

"You're including too many already. Why don't you include
one of Larkin's instead? For instance the one that begins,
'There is an evening coming across the fields . . .' "

"I'll look at it. But I don't really go for Larkin. Hughes
is the only young English poet whose poems are not willed,
who says something that has to be said . . . But you were
talking about history as fable or myth. Go on."

"—Like our belief in the immortality of literature, say. It's
a belief in the immortality of something greater than we are.
Like the idea of God, or of the Earth as a living thing, or the
faith that Man isn't doomed just because civilizations decay,
but is renewed—that if man's 'flesh is grass' it will spring up
again in the most unexpected places."

"Wouldn't most black poets today paraphrase Marx and call
this philosophy the opium of the White Establishment?"

"Most black writers," he replied, "cripple themselves by
their separatism. *You can't be a poet and believe in the
division of man.* In a society that believed in that there was
no place for Mandelstam; they *had* to kill him . . . Why are
most battle poems so bad? Because the sentiments are tawdry."

He poured himself another drink, had a cheese sandwich,
and lit the cigar I'd given him. "I remember as a child,"
he said, "singing *Brittania Rules the Waves.* I sang it just as
fervently as a million other black children. Including the

line 'Britons never, never shall be slaves.' Amazing, isn't it, that we didn't feel any contradiction there! Of course it was wartime, and Churchill was defending all of us against the greater tyranny of Hitler—yet we sang it just as fervently *before* Churchill's crusade. Hallucination though it was, we saw ourselves as Britons, not blacks. We saw ourselves, you might say, as parts of something bigger, more universal than mere race—the ideal Britain—the England of Shakespeare."

He leaned back and laughed. "What else did I say in my post-hallucination period?"

"You said you'd accept the Revolution if it made Trinidadians more responsible to the land, making it productive. You said, 'We have no such sense yet. The Indians may have, but only for their personal gain; the blacks hardly at all.'"

"I take that back now," Derek said. "It was an irresponsible statement. You'd have to be an Indian peasant to know what he really feels. Maybe he works more for his family in India than for Trinidad, but anyone who works that hard *must* love the land. Remember, the black has an inborn contempt for the Indian cane-cutter . . . The whole sequence of ownership in the West Indies is absurd, man!"

"You said that you couldn't write a play that would contribute to making prejudice surface, but doesn't *Dream on Monkey Mountain* contribute to an exaggerated pride in being black, to the 'get Whitey' syndrome?"

"Only in the context of its production in New York," Derek answered. "The context of the United States in a virtual civil-war situation. In Trinidad no one could make such an interpretation, or be sane if he did. There are no whites to 'get.' In Trinidad the crisis of the play is a *spiritual* one, as I intended it to be."

He paused, and I thought he was going to explain how. Instead he said:

"You remember our agreement about Naipaul's deracinated stance, the cop-out of his exile? Well, I've been rereading him, and I begin to realize it isn't total despair and withdrawal he's offering us in those wonderful novels, but a kind of *withdrawal-to-contemplate* . . . Like the Buddhists, Makak returns to nature in the end of the play—to nature as a regenerative force. *Not* out of superstition."

I reminded him that he'd said in Trinidad, "We colonials can't exercise power, but we can exert spiritual strength through our culture and religions." "Are you doing it as a people, Derek?"

"Hell, no!" he said. "We're teaching in our schools the pursuit of material power, as everywhere else in the West. The same philosophy that is crippling the world."

"It doesn't matter," I reassured him. "Your philosophy, as I'm beginning to understand it, can be stronger than all the Eric Williamses in the world, if even a handful of dedicated people believe in it. But how much of the time do you believe in it?"

"What do you mean?"

I told him of our disillusionment last March, both with him—for letting Schultz's political maneuvers take precedence over our friendship—and with the play as interpreted by the Negro Ensemble with his blessing.

He denied firmly that Schultz had made him act as he had. "I was exhausted. I had an exhausting day ahead of me, and I knew that if I came down to the car you'd talk me into going, against my better judgment. You can be awfully persistent and persuasive, you know."

"But why didn't you phone the next morning, as Schultz said you would?"

"That was unforgivable. But that's weakness, like my inability to write letters. I shun confrontations so much I actually forget them. But friendships—yours especially—mean more to me than any political, or theatrical, or social, or financial success. Like E. M. Forster, I'd betray my country but I'd never betray my friends. Honestly!"

"I believe you. But the ambiguity in the play—the aspect of it that made Carole feel you weren't sure of your identity—was writing the part of Makak in such a way that he could so easily be taken as the vengeful Black Messiah of a new racism. Which is the real Makak? Isn't the dream-conclusion less convincing than his kingship? Isn't the dream almost an afterthought that can be ignored—as the New York audience and critics did indeed ignore it?"

"No," he said. "Makak's incarnation as a Black Power Messiah was more than a dream; it was a nightmare. The goodness of the West Indian personality is in that speech in which he praises God. What I was saying was that a society that loses its faith in any outside force (God) is lost."

"You really believe in God, Derek?"

"My faith in God has never wavered—which doesn't mean I have any use for the Mafialike churches!"

"How do you manifest it?"

"I pray. I give thanks. I don't ask God for things—that's childish . . . Even Neruda reveals faith in God, when he invokes 'the skin of the planet' for instance, doesn't he? The great upsurge of faith in the United States came after the Civil War when the blacks, instead of turning on their oppressors, magnanimously adopted the White Man's God, the God of their enemy, and went far beyond the whites—who were then making a mockery of Christ's teachings by completing their butchery of the Indians—by going back in their spirituals to the core of Christianity.

"I'm constantly running into this idea that Carole shares, this idea that I'm not sure which world I'm in, that I don't know who I am. I know very precisely. You can only dissect and understand the spiritual instability of the West Indian if your hands are calm. There's no conflict between the color of my skin and the language I use. My great desire is to make the scene I write about as *true* as possible regardless of the consequences. But perhaps to an American living in such an atmosphere as black-is-black and white-is-white and never-the-twain-shall-meet, a mixed person like myself has to be seen as a mixed-up person. Take a Chinese Trinidadian. He has plenty of social hangups, but no ethnic anguish. None of us have! When one of us blacks comes up here and sees a 'Whites Only' sign, he thinks it's nonsense, and he adds to himself 'They're doing their thing' and obeys the rules. *But he doesn't feel humiliated.* He does feel anger; but for his fellow black Americans, not for himself."

I reminded him of the racial joking he and Margaret indulged in when I was with them in 1966. "I loved it," I said. "It made me feel instantly at ease, and only when I'd written the banter down did I wonder whether it was an obsession."

"It's a West Indian thing," Derek said. "There's an affection in that kind of joking. As you say, it put you at ease. And it put us at ease with you. It was our way of saying, 'We recognize you as our kind of people.' If we'd felt any prejudice in you, we couldn't and wouldn't have made racial jokes at our expense. But now that kind of West Indian ease is being threatened—by the uptightness of the United States with its explosive tensions—so that our government in its official statements and editorials is asking us not to use words like 'nigger' and 'coolie,' even among ourselves! To which I say: Shit! When we say 'lazy nigger' we're recognizing an historical *fact* at a given time, and vis-à-vis the industrious Indian. When we say 'Listen, white man' among close friends, we're saying, 'Stop demonstrating the standard historical associations of what a white man says.' When we say 'Listen, nigger' we're making the same point about standard black hypocrisies. And this is the best thing about normal life in the West Indies—up to now!"

I asked him what he thought about Senator Muskie's recent *gaffe* in stating that the Democratic party candidate couldn't win in 1972 if a Negro should be chosen as his running mate for the Vice-Presidency. And of Charles Evers for being one of the few (if not the only) black leader to applaud Muskie for "telling the truth." I told him that I respected both statements, and that Evers had been one of my heroes for years, the only political leader in the country to whose campaign funds I contributed.

"I agree with them," he said, "but as a Trinidadian I have to believe that Muskie should have been more honest and said, 'I couldn't win with a nigger as running mate,' in which case seventy percent of the blacks would have applauded and voted for him!"

I laughed. "Maybe seventy percent of Trinidadians, but not of American blacks, Derek! If you're serious, you're a little mad. 'Nigger' is still a fighting word up here—to blacks and white liberals alike—and Muskie would have lost ninety-nine percent of both . . . But let's get back to poetry—or forward to it."

"Right on! I'm trying to clarify my thoughts in a paper I'm going to read on this lecture tour, beginning in Manchester tomorrow. It goes a step beyond *Monkey Mountain*. May I try out a sentence or two, on you?

. . . 'The truth of poetry is not a matter of morality, but of revelation—

'In the conventional kind of history, everything depends on whether we read its *fiction*—rewritten, reinterpreted at least every generation—through the eyes of hero or victim. Our servitude to this Muse has produced a philosophy of bitterness, recrimination, mimicry, despair. A great amount of the Third World literature is a literature of revenge written by the descendants of slaves bent on exorcising this demon through the word. Or a literature of remorse written by the descendants of masters obsessed by guilt. And because the literature serves historical truth, it yellows into polemic or evaporates into pathos. The *truly* classic—written by those who practice the tough aesthetic of the New World—neither explains nor forgives history because it refuses to recognize it as a creative force. . . . The old style Revolutionary Writer sees Caliban as an enraged pupil. He can't separate the rage of Caliban from the beauty of his speech. For the speeches of Caliban are equal, in their elemental serenity, in their wonder at the island, to those of its discoverer, Prospero. The language of the torturer has been mastered by the victim. Yet this is viewed as servitude, not as irony or victory!' "

I looked at him in astonishment. "Derek, you won't believe it! Listen to this—" and I read him out of my journal Ginsberg's peroration on *The Tempest* delivered in Paterson just the week before.

"Beautiful, beautiful," he said. "I wouldn't have believed it of him, man! So now let me read you a few sentences more before this lecture of mine is published somewhere and you accuse me of plagiarizing Ginsberg!"

"Read on, Macduff!"

" '. . . The shipwrecks of Crusoe and of the crew of *The Tempest* are the end of an Old World. It should matter as much to the New World if the Old is determined to blow itself up; for an obsession with Progress, which is the same as the fear of failure, is not within the psyche of the recently enslaved. . . . This may sound like Existentialism. But Adamic, elemental man cannot be existential, for his first impulse is not self-indulgence but awe. Existentialism is just another efflorescence of the Myth of the Noble Savage. . . .' "

"If it weren't 2 A.M. and you didn't have to leave for your lecture early tomorrow," I said, "I'd read you my talk with that great Existentialist Mailer."

"That's it! Now I see it!" Derek said. "They're opposites and identical! Existential Man is the Ignoble Savage. The irrational can be used to illuminate, but not to the point of passivity. Isn't that what you were trying to get Ginsberg to say? If you're in a state of pure being, you won't write poetry because you'll feel no need to criticize the world, or even weigh it."

"Ginsberg is turning back to Blake," I said. "His Act Five at the reading last week was the *Songs of Experience*. He's been in India so long, he feels the need to criticize the world again, or at least weigh it."

"There's a danger in detaching Blake from his lyrical genius and falling back on his philosophy as an instant answer to everything," Derek said. "It all hinges on whether you consider him a greater poet than Dante—"

"Dante?"

"Blake can't be superior to Dante because Blake's God is too eccentric. His cosmogony is too private. It appeals to poets so strongly because it's a literary world of symbols, but the symbols are all aspects of Blake's subconscious. That last book of the Paradiso, which Ginsberg pays tribute to, makes the whole *world* cohere . . . You're shaking your head?"

"Maybe we prefer Blake, Derek—I have to admit that I feel

258

much more at home in his world than in Dante's—because we've lost faith in such an orderly world as Dante's with its logical punishments and rewards. We don't *want* it to be that tidy, and cohere. We don't yearn for unity—not at the cost of being stuck with a closed system. We want to get back to the individual, to the eccentric, to Blake with his minute particulars, Blake the nonconformist and revolutionary—even at the cost of incoherence and facing a meaningless death!"

He didn't answer. Or rather, I didn't give him a chance to answer, because I pointed out that he'd miss his bus in the morning if we didn't get some sleep. But he had the last word on the way in to the terminal after breakfast. I was returning to Haiti in a week. Why didn't he join me there— since he'd never been? "We could continue our *Poetics* on the prow of Christophe's Citadelle!" I said.

"I'd love nothing more," Derek said, "but I'm stuck with this lecture tour. Next year . . . But is the Citadelle the right place? I mean, in terms of black destiny the Citadelle, original, awesome, and defiant as it must be, was a dead end. For islanders like myself, or the black man of the New World, to base poetry or philosophy on such ruins of the islands—or on "Africa"—is morbid. As morbid as if the Jew were to cornerstone his future on Auschwitz, or you yours on Hiroshima. All any of us would come up with would be a poetry of revenge.

"The turning point," he added, "was not when Dessalines invoked the serpent-god of Africa at Bois Caïman, but when the tribes were converted to Christianity. *No race is converted against its will.* The slave masters encountered massive pliability. The slave converted himself, changed weapons, adapted the masters' language, purified the soiled cult.

"So here," he concluded, "the poetic tradition begins: the new naming of things . . ."

EPILOGUE

The art of the academy and the *avant-garde* have one thing in common: they are self-conscious. "Only the familiar transformed by greatness is truly great," Pasternak says, and he goes on to cite Pushkin, "whose works are one great hymn to honest labor, duty, everyday life" and who had written: "Now my ideal is the housewife, my greatest wish a quiet life and a big bowl of cabbage soup." In great art, Pasternak and Pushkin are saying, there is too much at stake for grownups' games, too much of a need for humility in pursuing the meaning of life itself to permit the distraction of either autoanalysis-in-public or competition for the tastemakers' laurels.

Isn't that what Frost is talking about when he says, "They hate me for singing misunderstandings. They call me reactionary for settling for the writing of a few things the world can't deny"? Or Hemingway and Mailer, when the first says that happiness is in inventing from knowledge "though rougher than a corncob," and the second that there's a "tonic for the psyche" in "this primitive need to recognize our physical resources"? The problem of all three, as presented here, was to escape or by-pass the monstrous masks their wounded egos had fashioned in self-defense, masks before which their biographers and press agents had bowed down gloatingly. And mine was to disclose what was gentle and childlike enough in each of them to have kept the imprisoned artist there still alive.

What was it that Borges and Neruda, for all their vaunted differences and antipathies, had in common? Wasn't it the capacity to keep the Nick Adams in them—submerged under those façades of metaphysical fantasy and political rhetoric—

subject to instant recall? "Beauty is very common actually. In the future maybe everyone will be a poet"—can those be the words of the blind intellectual in his library? "The great writer is not very conscious of what he is saying. He just has to say it in that particular way"—is that the rational Marxist, the loyal Party member, speaking? What a pity they didn't meet that day in Buenos Aires! Di Giovanni and I might have driven them through those dilapidated slums toward which Borges, for all his air of witty detachment, yearns passionately; as passionately as Neruda for those shacks across the Andes "that sing like guitars when the wind blows through them." And who could possibly claim that García Márquez, the defiant exile in his Barcelona apartment, is more alienated from Colombia than all those patriot-poets whose eyes never stray from Bogotá's mile-high bastion or the rotting wharves of Barranquilla?

Exiles all, wanderers over the face of the earth, internationalists deeply committed to their roots by the necessity of being poets.

For Stanley Kunitz the exile is prenatal. Unlike Frost, who had to block out the California of his upbringing and live in London to find his New England voice, Kunitz's Jewish-immigrant childhood has been his Testing Tree. What else could have kept him young, tuned more compassionately to the promises and betrayals of "America" than any Puritan's great-grandson, ". . . open to the cosmos, to something bigger than oneself"?

Did Allen Ginsberg and Octavio Paz need India to find themselves? Only to be more quintessentially citizens of Paterson, N.J. and Mixcoacá, D.F. Where would Paz be if his mysticism—"My poems are only fragments of the great poem being composed by all poets"—were all? Without Mexico in his blood, a professor of aesthetics? "The 'god' that Ginsberg feared William Carlos Williams had overlooked turned out to be Emerson's Oversoul, Wordsworth's Nature, Prospero's despair at the thought of rejoining a world without magic. But how prescient was Derek Walcott's fear that Ginsberg might step off this precipice into Nothingness, and that Mailer's Existential Man might turn out to be the Ignoble Savage! "If you're in a state of pure being, you won't write poetry, because you'll feel no need to criticize the world or even weigh it."

If art, then, is not in either holding a fixed position or entirely letting go, but in having the capacity to take advantage of the happy accidents of one's situation, how fortunate I was, finally, to stumble in Brazil on two poets who so exemplified creation's poles! . . . Vinícius, the worldly night club singer, confessing that his "innocence" and "self-confidence" returned to him only when his Black Mother exorcized his demons; João Cabral, minister plenipotentiary of the intellect, admitting that poetry begins "with finding names for nameless things" and that "motivation" can be a denial of what is most basic in man and art. And how fitting —could it happen anywhere but in Brazil?—that these great antithetical spirits should feel nothing but love and respect for each other.

INDEX

New Directions Paperbooks

Walter Abish, *Alphabetical Africa.* NDP375.
Ilangô Adigal, *Shilappadikaram.* NDP162.
Brother Antoninus, *The Residual Years.* NDP263.
Guillaume Apollinaire, *Selected Writings.*†
  NDP310.
Djuna Barnes, *Nightwood.* NDP98.
Charles Baudelaire, *Flowers of Evil.*† NDP71.
  Paris Spleen. NDP294.
Gottfried Benn, *Primal Vision.* NDP322.
Eric Bentley, *Bernard Shaw.* NDP59.
Wolfgang Borchert, *The Man Outside.* NDP319.
Jorge Luis Borges, *Labyrinths.* NDP186.
Jean-François Bory, *Once Again.* NDP256.
Kay Boyle, *Thirty Stories.* NDP62.
E. Brock, *Invisibility Is The Art of Survival.*
  NDP342.
  The Portraits & The Poses. NDP360.
W. Bronk, *The World, the Worldless.* NDP157.
Buddha, *The Dhammapada.* NDP188.
Hayden Carruth, *For You.* NDP298.
  From Snow and Rock, from Chaos. NDP349.
Louis-Ferdinand Céline,
  Death on the Installment Plan. NDP330.
  Guignol's Band. NDP278.
  Journey to the End of the Night. NDP84.
Blaise Cendrars, *Selected Writings.*† NDP203.
B-c. Chatterjee, *Krishnakanta's Will.* NDP120.
Jean Cocteau, *The Holy Terrors.* NDP212.
  The Infernal Machine. NDP235.
M. Cohen, *Monday Rhetoric.* NDP352.
Cid Corman, *Livingdying.* NDP289.
  Sun Rock Man. NDP318.
Gregory Corso, *Elegiac Feelings American.*
  NDP299.
  Long Live Man. NDP127.
  Happy Birthday of Death. NDP86.
Edward Dahlberg, *Reader.* NDP246.
  Because I Was Flesh. NDP227.
David Daiches, *Virginia Woolf.*
  (Revised) NDP96.
Osamu Dazai, *The Setting Sun.* NDP258.
  No Longer Human. NDP357.
Coleman Dowell, *Mrs. October Was Here.*
  NDP368.
Robert Duncan, *Roots and Branches.* NDP275.
  Bending the Bow. NDP255.
  The Opening of the Field. NDP356.
Richard Eberhart, *Selected Poems.* NDP198.
Russell Edson, *The Very Thing That Happens.*
  NDP137.
Wm. Empson, *7 Types of Ambiguity.* NDP204.
  Some Versions of Pastoral. NDP92.
Wm. Everson, *The Residual Years.* NDP263.
  Man-Fate. NDP369.
Lawrence Ferlinghetti, *Her.* NDP88.
  Back Roads to Far Places. NDP312.
  A Coney Island of the Mind. NDP74.
  The Mexican Night. NDP300.
  Open Eye, Open Heart. NDP361.
  Routines. NDP187.
  The Secret Meaning of Things. NDP268.
  Starting from San Francisco. NDP 220.
  Tyrannus Nix?. NDP288.
Ronald Firbank, *Two Novels.* NDP128.
Dudley Fitts,
  Poems from the Greek Anthology. NDP60.
F. Scott Fitzgerald, *The Crack-up.* NDP54.
Robert Fitzgerald, *Spring Shade: Poems
  1931-1970.* NDP311.
Gustave Flaubert,
  Bouvard and Pécuchet. NDP328.
  The Dictionary of Accepted Ideas. NDP230.
M. K. Gandhi, *Gandhi on Non-Violence.*
  (ed. Thomas Merton) NDP197.
André Gide, *Dostoevsky.* NDP100.
Goethe, *Faust,* Part I.
  (MacIntyre translation) NDP70.

Albert J. Guerard, *Thomas Hardy.* NDP185.
Guillevic, *Selected Poems.* NDP279.
Henry Hatfield, *Goethe.* NDP136.
  Thomas Mann. (Revised Edition) NDP101.
John Hawkes, *The Cannibal.* NDP123.
  The Lime Twig. NDP95.
  Second Skin. NDP146.
  The Beetle Leg. NDP239.
  The Blood Oranges. NDP338.
  The Innocent Party. NDP238.
  Lunar Landscapes. NDP274.
A. Hayes, *A Wreath of Christmas Poems.*
  NDP347.
H.D., *Hermetic Definition.* NDP343.
  Trilogy. NDP362.
Hermann Hesse, *Siddhartha.* NDP65.
Christopher Isherwood, *The Berlin Stories.*
  NDP134.
Gustav Janouch,
  Conversations With Kafka. NDP313.
Alfred Jarry, *Ubu Roi.* NDP105.
Robinson Jeffers, *Cawdor and Medea.* NDP293.
James Joyce, *Stephen Hero.* NDP133.
  James Joyce/Finnegans Wake. NDP331.
Franz Kafka, *Amerika.* NDP117.
Bob Kaufman,
  Solitudes Crowded with Loneliness. NDP199.
Hugh Kenner, *Wyndham Lewis.* NDP167.
Kenyon Critics, *Gerard Manley Hopkins.*
  NDP355.
P. Lal, translator, *Great Sanskrit Plays.*
  NDP142.
Tommaso Landolfi,
  Gogol's Wife and Other Stories. NDP155.
Lautréamont, *Maldoror.* NDP207.
Denise Levertov, *Footprints.* NDP344.
  The Jacob's Ladder. NDP112.
  The Poet in the World. NDP363.
  O Taste and See. NDP149.
  Relearning the Alphabet. NDP290.
  The Sorrow Dance. NDP222.
  To Stay Alive. NDP325.
  With Eyes at the Back of Our Heads.
  NDP229.
Harry Levin, *James Joyce.* NDP87.
García Lorca, *Selected Poems.*† NDP114.
  Three Tragedies. NDP52.
  Five Plays. NDP232.
Michael McClure, *September Blackberries.*
  NDP370.
Carson McCullers, *The Member of the
  Wedding.* (Playscript) NDP153.
Thomas Merton, *Cables to the Ace.* NDP252.
  Emblems of a Season of Fury. NDP140.
  Gandhi on Non-Violence. NDP197.
  The Geography of Lograire. NDP283.
  New Seeds of Contemplation. NDP337.
  Raids on the Unspeakable. NDP213.
  Selected Poems. NDP85.
  The Way of Chuang Tzu. NDP276.
  The Wisdom of the Desert. NDP295.
  Zen and the Birds of Appetite. NDP261.
Henri Michaux, *Selected Writings.*† NDP264.
Henry Miller, *The Air-Conditioned Nightmare.*
  NDP302.
  *Big Sur & The Oranges of Hieronymus
  Bosch.* NDP161.
  The Books in My Life. NDP280.
  The Colossus of Maroussi. NDP75.
  The Cosmological Eye. NDP109.
  Henry Miller on Writing. NDP151.
  The Henry Miller Reader. NDP269.
  Remember to Remember. NDP111.
  Stand Still Like the Hummingbird. NDP236.
  The Time of the Assassins. NDP115.
  The Wisdom of the Heart. NDP94.
Y. Mishima, *Death in Midsummer.* NDP215.
  Confessions of a Mask. NDP253.
Eugenio Montale, *Selected Poems.*† NDP193.

Complete descriptive catalog available free on request from
New Directions, 333 Sixth Avenue, New York 10014.   † Bilingual.